PREHISTORIC
ROCK ART IN CUMBRIA

Landscapes and monuments

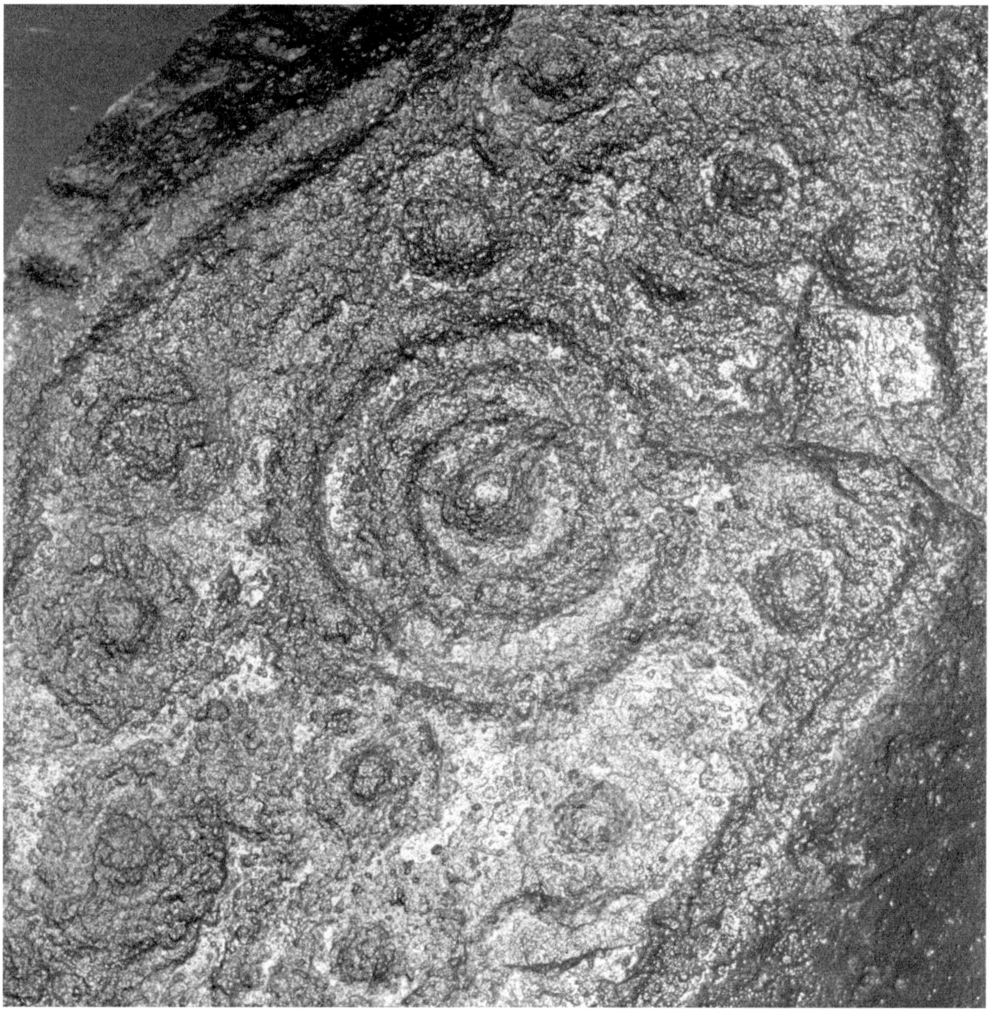

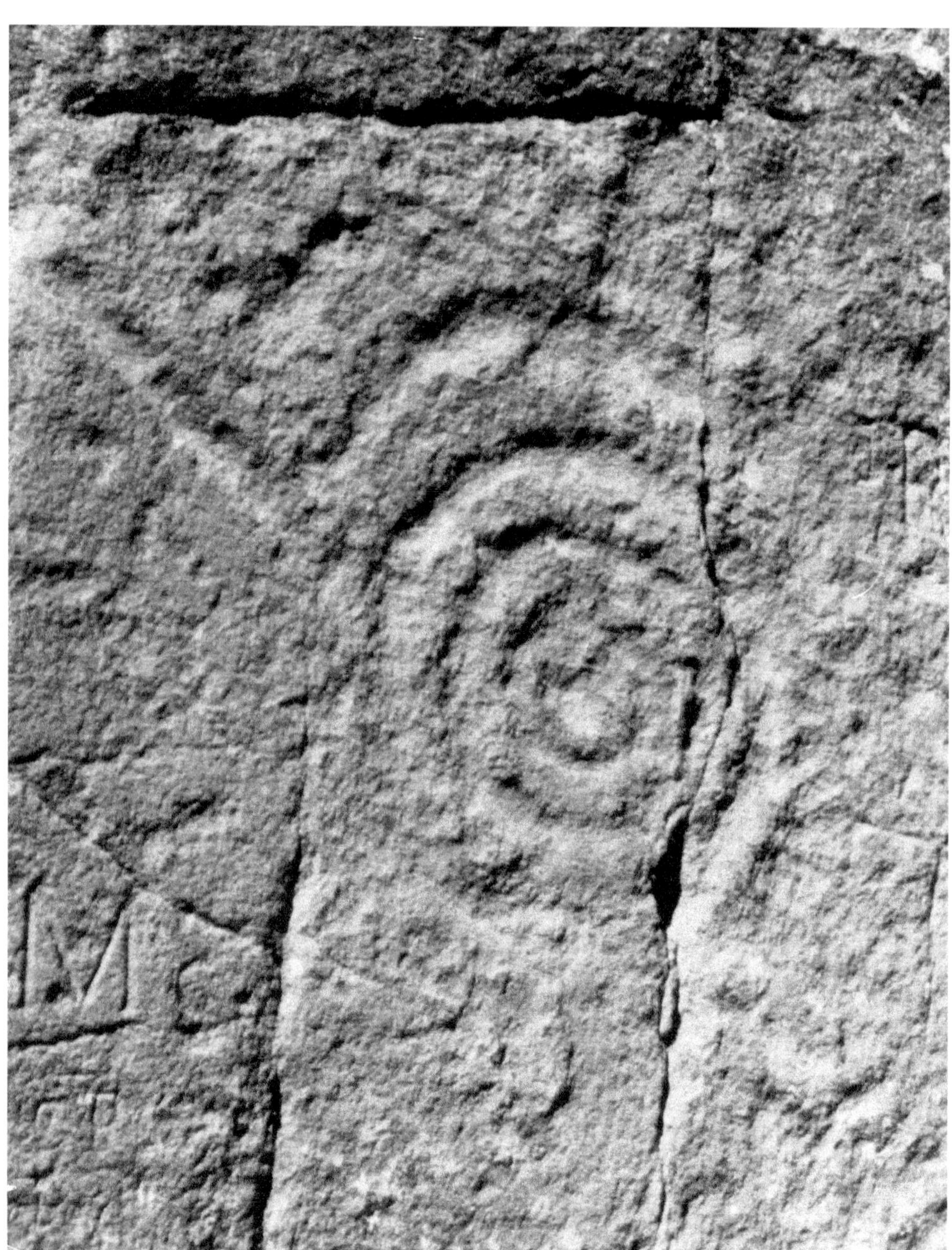

PREHISTORIC ROCK ART IN CUMBRIA

Landscapes and monuments

Stan Beckensall

Maps by Paul Brown

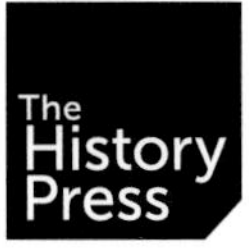

First published 2002

Reprinted 2017 by

The History Press
The Mill, Brimscombe Port,
Stroud, Gloucestershire, GL5 2QG
www.thehistorypress.co.uk

British Library Cataloguing in Publication Data.
A catalogue record for this book is available from the British Library.

ISBN 978 0 7524 2526 9

Typesetting and origination by Tempus Publishing Limited.
Printed in Great Britain by TJ International Ltd, Padstow, Cornwall

Contents

Foreword

Between 1985 and 1987 I carried out research on the Neolithic axe quarries at Great Langdale, and every day as we travelled to the site we noticed an enormous rock in the enclosed land beside the road. I never went to look at it for the simple reason that I had yet to become aware of the archaeology of rock art. That is why I never saw the carved designs at Chapel Stile.

Ironically, it was on a day when the weather was too bad for us to work at Langdale that we decided to take a trip across the Pennines. We visited Ilkley Moor where a group of local archaeologists had been recording a large number of rock carvings. We were intrigued by what we found there, and that first encounter with British rock art set me thinking. Little did I know that 10 years later I would publish a book entitled *Rock Art and the Prehistory of Atlantic Europe*.

That happy accident led me to make many friends and to visit many fascinating sites, but it would be quite wrong to suggest that rock art had not attracted the attention of archaeologists before. It was simply that the best work had been carried out by local people and had not had the impact that it deserved. As I learned more about the subject, I met many of them. It did not take long to discover that Stan Beckensall was one of the leaders in this field. His knowledge, enthusiasm, persistence and energy are famous, and so is his ability to make new discoveries and to encourage other people to do the same.

When I worked at Langdale, it hardly occurred to me that rock art might provide a vital element in the archaeology of north-west England. That is no longer true, and this book tells us why. It captures beautifully Stan's feeling for the countryside and flair for this kind of research. It is the work of a born teacher, who wishes to share his knowledge and enjoyment with other people. What he says is important, and how he says it is important too. Like the carvings he has done so much to publicise, this book is accessible to everyone.

Professor Richard Bradley

My thanks to Richard, who has brought his special talents and perception to the subject and spread his influence among those of us who pursue this quest.

This book completes my study of the rock art of northern England, which now includes Northumberland, County Durham, Swaledale, Wensleydale and Cumbria. It will link up with the work being done in west Yorkshire by the Ilkley Archaeological Group, so that there is now a great range of country and data available to historians. This is by no means the end, as new sites are being discovered all the time, as more enthusiasts take to the field.

Stan Beckensall

1 Introduction: an overview of rock art

Cumbrian Prehistoric Rock Art: Symbols, Monuments and Landscape (1992) was the result of my earliest research into this area. By then I had completed an account of every known piece of rock art in Northumberland, which includes some of the finest in the world. The contrast between the areas then was that almost all of Cumbria's art appeared on monuments and 'portable' examples.

Now the picture has changed as a result of discoveries in October and November 1999, of outcrop sites in the valleys of the Lake District. Discoveries in the Ullswater valley and Langdale were made in two ways: by local people clearing moss from rocks, and by a systematic search conducted in Langdale with the clear guidance of a theory that rock art is found at sites in the landscape significant to prehistoric nomadic hunters and pastoralists.

These discoveries are stunning. In particular there are two massive rock surfaces, one tilted and the other vertical, that exhibit all the symbols that make up known rock art, arranged with an individuality that one has come to expect, but not on such a dramatic scale. Not only that, but two students (as they were then) took a photograph in low-angled light of a spiral on one of the most well-known rocks at Castlerigg stone circle in 1995. Although I could not see the spiral, I was able to take a rubbing of it and draw it. Since then two lozenge shapes, a partial cup and ring and a curved groove have been found on the stones of the circle. At Long Meg, another great stone circle, hikers discovered the beginnings of two spirals on a fallen stone, again confirmed by my rubbing.

All this is a tribute to diligent observation and to a new awareness of where rock art might be and how to go about finding it. Marks pecked onto rocks with a hard stone chisel 4000-5000 years ago have been waiting a long time to be recognised. Some have been quarried away, and some still wait to be revealed, but in the last three decades at the end of the millennium there has been a great triumph of discovery. This book celebrates these discoveries, describes each panel of rock art, and tries to place it in a context.

Cumbria is a superb county, as the constant flow of visitors confirms. Its varied landscape generates a special sense of the power of place in its high mountains with their sharp edges, cloud-capped peaks, great tracts overlooking valleys, the majesty of the valleys themselves, a richness of vegetation that changes colour with the seasons, and the sweep of its coastline. It has attracted visitors and settlers for centuries; despite the overwhelming impact of landforms on our mind, we can still locate traces of even the earliest people here who used this landscape. Rock art is one of the signs of this human intervention. As we look for it, we may also saturate ourselves in the beauty that has inspired so many to visit, to roam the landscape and to write about it.

The region was badly affected, to say the least, in 2001, by the outbreak of foot and mouth disease, which has had a terrible effect on farming and tourism. Visitors have been cut off from this great landscape; now that restrictions have been eased they will return.

Rock art is only one facet of the kind of interest that will attract people to the county; it may be visited for its own sake. For others, it will be an integral part of a wide-ranging interest and pleasure that Cumbria offers.

What is rock art?

Some rocks, mainly in northern Britain and in Ireland, have had marks hammered into them with a hard pointed stone tool. This process is particularly clear when a rock has not suffered much weathering or when it is freshly excavated. You can see the pick marks, varying from a tiny nail-like point to a small chisel end. The tool needs to be harder than the rock surface, and that is one reason why the most common rock surfaces used in Britain are sedimentary rocks such as sandstone.

The pick often excavates a small circular depression known as a *cup*, the most common symbol used. Sometimes grooves are added, leading from the cup as a *duct*, or surrounding the cup in an unbroken or broken ring. Thus the term *cups and rings* has been used from the time they were discovered in the early nineteenth century.

A rock may be zoned by the addition of *grooves* that can be straight, curved, serpentine and zigzag. Many cups can be enclosed by grooves of different shapes.

A less common form is the *spiral*.

From the arrangement of these basic forms and their relationships to one another, *motifs* and *panels* are formed, often taking into account the variations in the rock surface, such as undulations and cracks.

Whether all the shapes produced in this way are *art* is questionable. Some please us, but we have to go further than to look for attractive patterns, for the act of chipping the surface of the rock appears to have had a deep significance to the prehistoric people who made them. We bring different ways of looking at things when we approach primitive art. It may please or move us, or it might leave us cold or bewildered. We must, however, realise that we cannot easily, or even at all, project ourselves into the prehistoric mind.

The illustrations of the main elements of rock art and the way in which these are combined give a clearer idea than words of what it's all about.

Where rock art is found

Cumbrian rock art is part of a much larger distribution that spreads from the Orkneys to the south-west of England, and covers parts of Ireland. It is found in two main contexts: a) on earthfast and outcrop rocks in the landscape, and b) on and in monuments such as standing stones, stone circles, stone avenues and burial cairns.

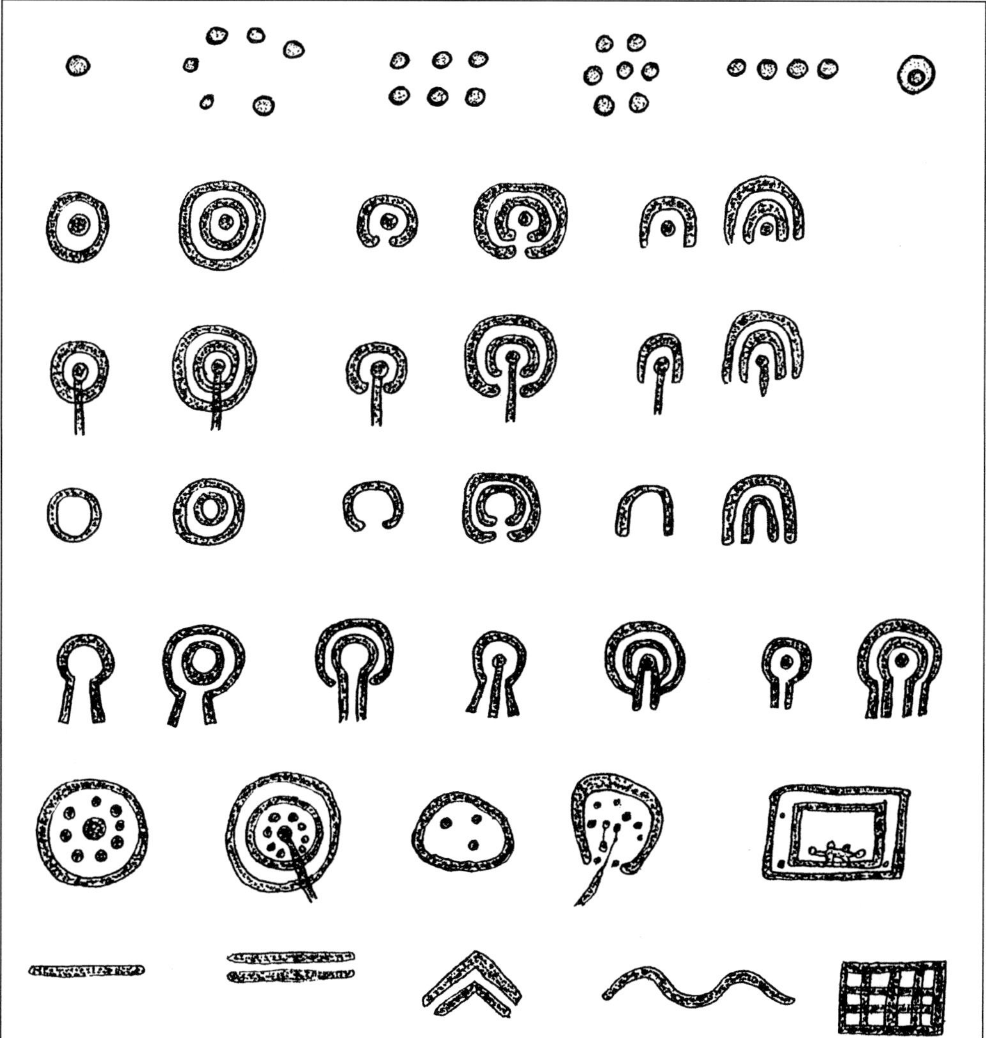

1 *The main elements of rock art: (a) cups; (b) rings, penannulars and arcs around cups; (c) cups with a groove leading out; (d) rings, penannulars and half-ovoids; (e) keyhole designs; (f) cups enclosed by grooves; (g) lines, chevrons, serpentine groove and grid*

Much rarer, it occurs in rock shelters in Northumberland. Sometimes 'portable' rocks such as small cobbles and boulders, some possibly displaced from monuments, are found in walls, on the edges of fields and on clearance heaps. The original context of such rocks is often impossible to locate.

The major rock art areas such as Galloway, Argyll, Northumberland and Yorkshire gave people extensive outcrop rocks to work with, whereas there is little suitable rock in the south. It could be that the motifs elsewhere have been on perishable materials such as cloth, wood or leather, or tattooed on people's skins. If there is no suitable rock, there will be no rock art.

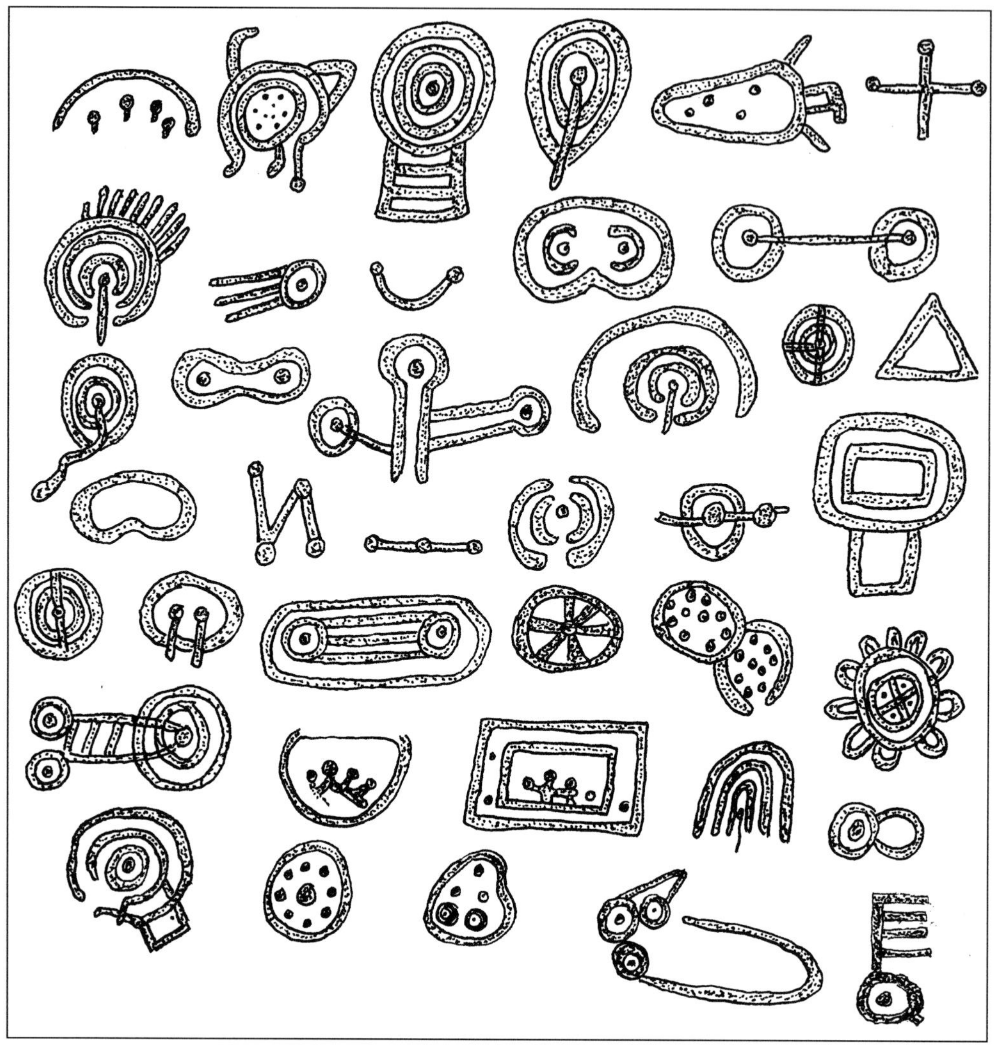

2 *Examples of motifs across Britain to show variations on themes*

One must also be aware that there may be motifs of a different kind that have not yet been widely recognised. For example, at Skara Brae Neolithic village and on stone slabs inside the chambered tomb of Maes How (Orkney) there are thin incised parallel and crossing lines.

The map (**3**) shows the distribution of rock art; it is concentrated in northern Britain, but there are examples in the south, many connected with burials. Rare forms such as axes appear on the sarsens at Stonehenge and on graves in Kilmartin, Argyll. Ireland has widespread rock art, particularly spectacular on the chambered tombs of the Neolithic period.

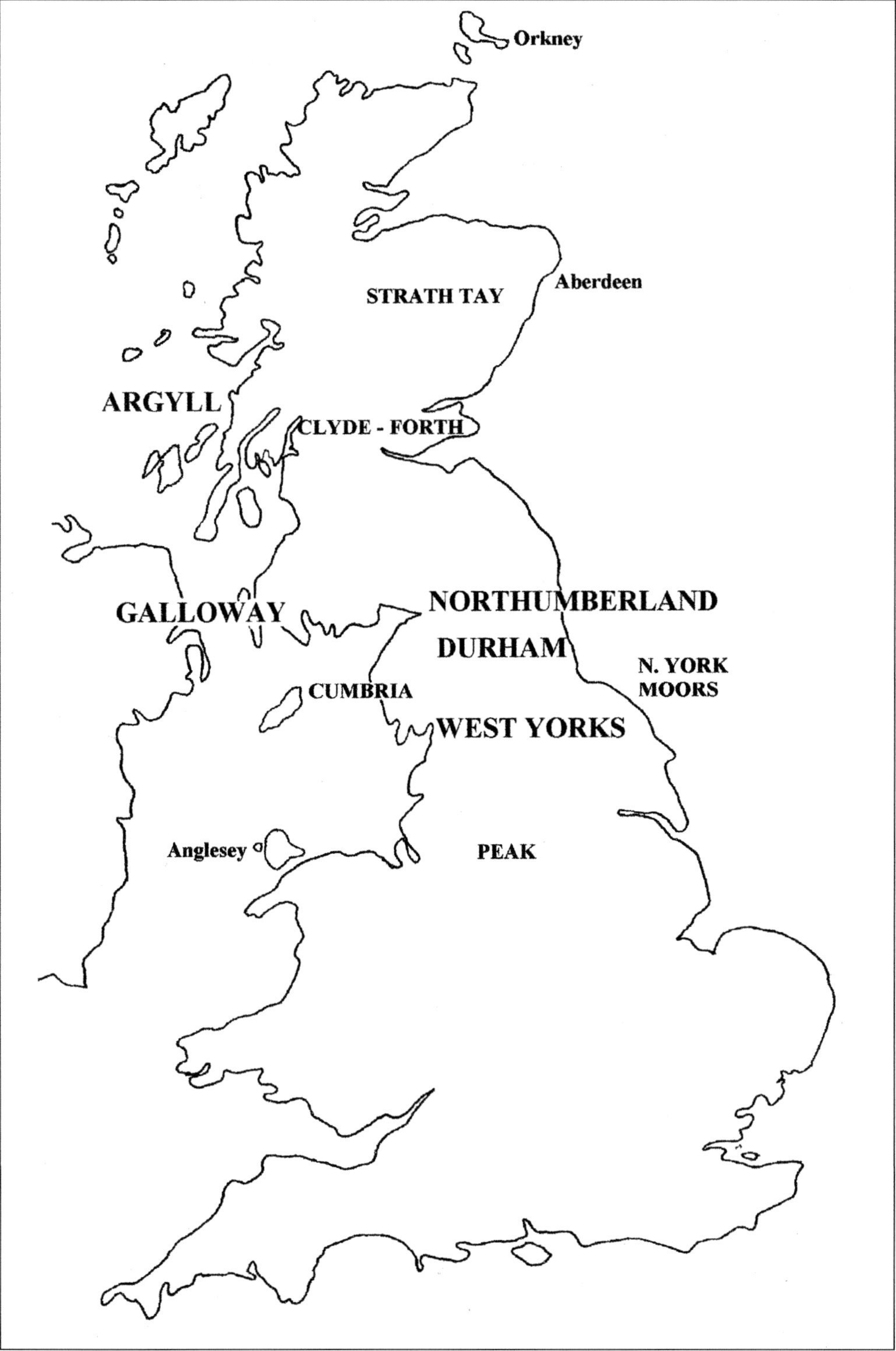

3 *Map of the main rock art areas in Britain, with the larger lettering showing the greatest concentrations of motifs*

When was it made?

Although it is impossible at the moment to date art on the rocks in Britain, it is possible to date it approximately according to where it is found. In the landscape it appears in the type of country that would have been favoured by hunters and pastoralists: the areas that are now moorland above rivers, where the soils are thin and would have supported light forest. The marked rocks are at good viewpoints, where they 'sign the land' and mark or overlook the kinds of routes where seasonal grazing and migration of animals would have taken place. Of course it is not possible to say exactly what kind of vegetation would have been growing, and whether or not the viewpoints of today were not obscured by trees, but there is a logic, a pattern in the way they cluster in high places. Some also mark sources of water such as streams and water holes essential to grazing animals.

A nomadic way of life was most common to hunters and herdsman. With the coming of arable farming, hunting and herding would have remained important to supplement agriculture, but the cultivation of fields tied farmers to one place. We associate the people who made the marks on the rocks with the Neolithic period, extending into the early Bronze Age. If transhumance (moving animals seasonally to different pastures or for slaughter) were practised, a detachment of people could have been responsible for looking after animals in the upland pastures; afterwards they could have returned to a more settled community.

It is the monuments that give us another clue to when the marks were made, for some of them are pecked onto stones that are incorporated into dateable graves. These have only been noticed in a very small proportion of burials; the motifs were taken out of the open air, where they used to look skywards, and were turned face downwards and invisibly into the earth. Some cobbles were deliberately decorated as part of burial cairns, and some slabs that cover graves (cist covers) are marked on the underside and side slabs. This means that the last date for the use of the motifs was

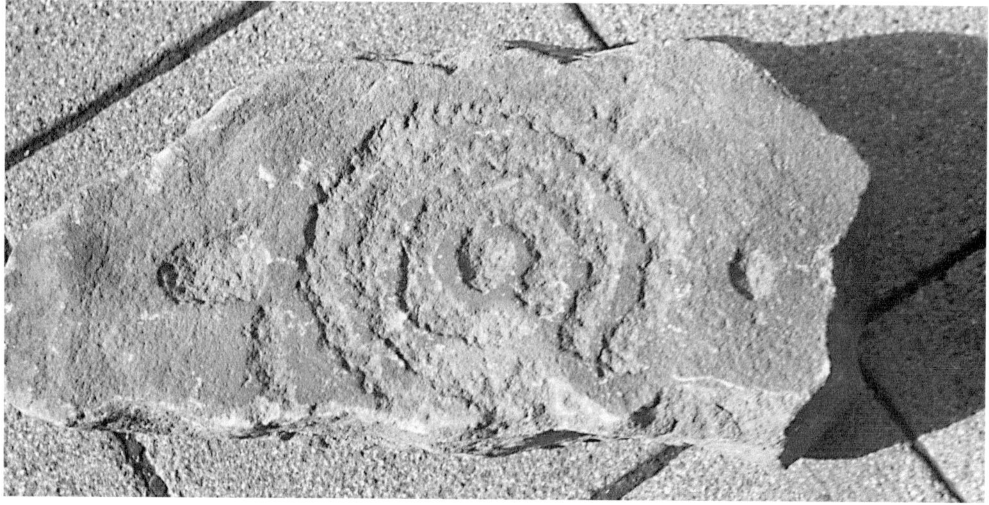

4 *The Stag Stone Farm rock, showing the individual pick marks in the motif*

that of the burial, although the marks may have been made earlier and removed from their original places. This was done in a period that extended into 2000 BC. The motifs were then used in a different way; their meaning had changed.

Marks on standing stones show that there is a ritual significance, but it is difficult to say whether the marks were put on the stones before, during or after their erection. Such problems of use and timing will become clear when we look at the Cumbrian examples. The standing stone circles appear to have had many uses, among which was that of a community centre, a place where all the scattered farming communities and nomads could meet – a fixed point that established their communal identity, a focus of trade, a place of ceremony.

The motifs

An outstanding feature of British rock art is that almost all of it is abstract. If we compare it with motifs in Galicia, we see that the designs have much in common, except that pictures of deer appear on the Spanish rocks.

Because it is abstract, there is a danger that we read into it whatever we like. Fair enough, as our response is going to be to some extent subjective, but this does not mean that the people who made it saw it in this way. Ronald Morris, a Scottish archaeologist and solicitor, listed 104 'meanings' that he had gleaned from many sources, and gave them marks out of 10. In dealing with the past, flights of imagination in the guise of explanation are not confined to rock art, and we must be very careful not to base theories on insufficient evidence. Those of us who have studied rock art most are careful about giving it a specific origin and 'meaning', as we realise the extent of our ignorance.

What is very impressive is that prehistoric people, working with the same common symbols, managed to produce such a variety of designs. This is amply demonstrated by the illustrations in this book.

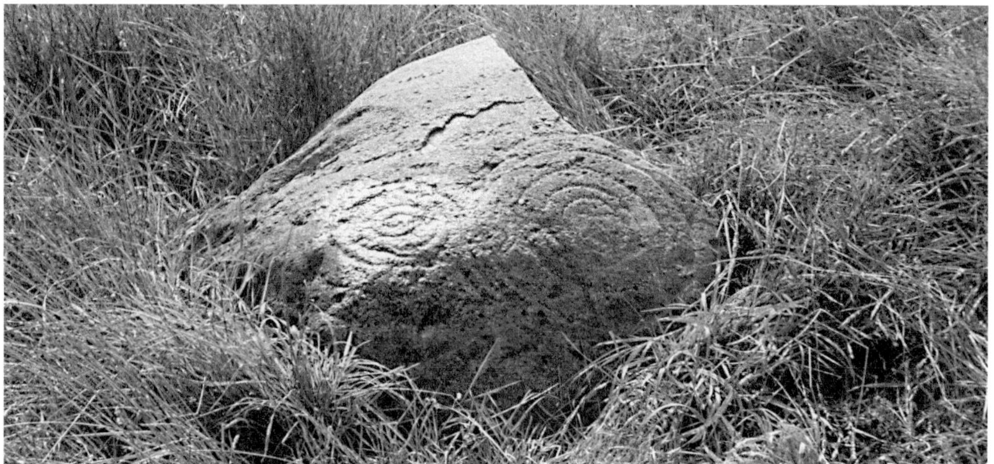

5 *Motifs on Little Meg cairn kerbstone*

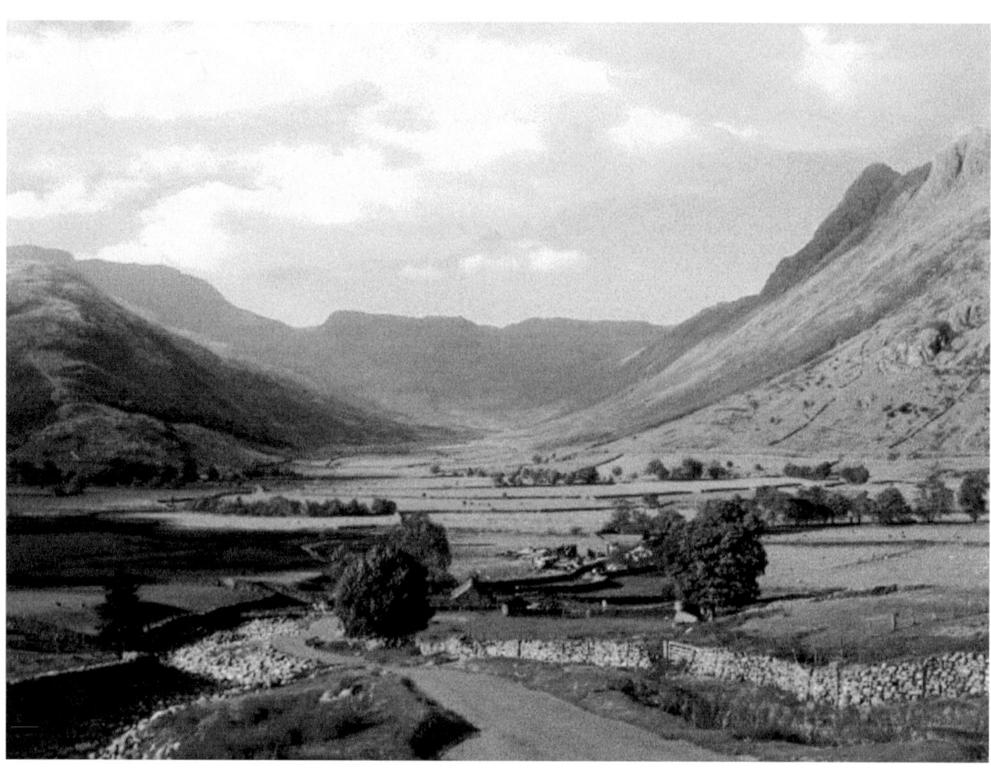

6 *Wall End to Pike o' Stickle, Upper Langdale Valley*

KEY

✪ Henge Monument

☆ Cairn

○ Stone Circle

◉ Cup and Ring Stone

✪ Cairn Circle

☆ Stone removed from site **P** Penrith Museum

T Tullie House Museum **M** Senhouse Collection Maryport

⁘ Settlement ● Cup marks & other motifs

▲ Standing Stone △ Grid North

X Stones present location unknown △ O/S Triangulation Pillar

Roman Signal Station -------- Footpath

Maps based on the Ordnance Survey with the permission of the controller of Her Majesty's Stationery Office NC/01/27 Crown Copyright

The following Ordnance survey maps can be used in conjunction with the published maps Outdoor Leisure The English Lakes 4,5,6,7. Howgill Fells 19 , Explorer series 19.

7 *Key to the map opposite and to all other maps*

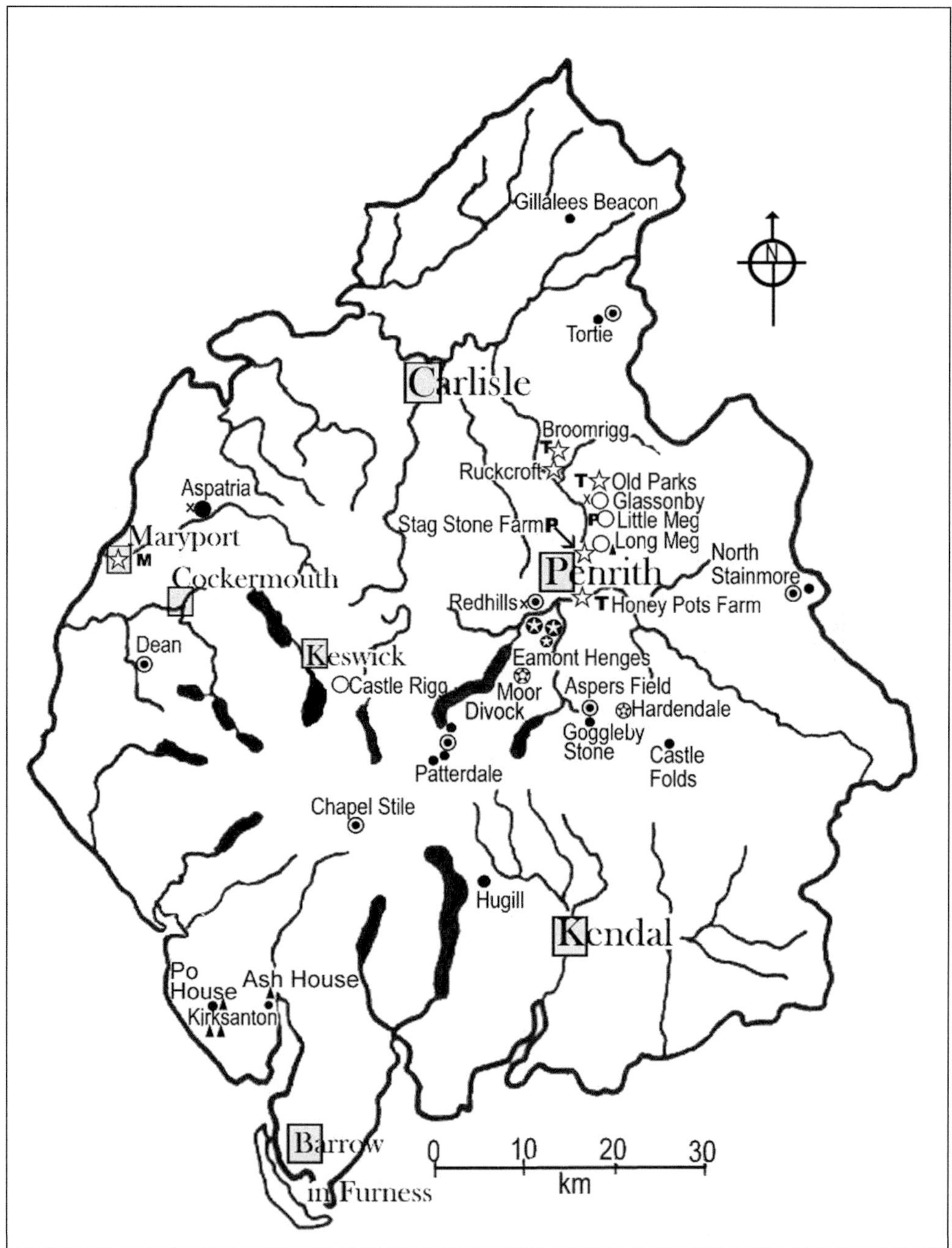

8 *The distribution of Prehistoric rock art sites in Cumbria*

15

Research in many parts of the world attributes great importance to these motifs, which are some of the earliest forms of communication between prehistoric people. We tend to separate secular from sacred, but this might not have been the case among people whose relationship to the land was so close and interdependent that the land itself was considered sacred.

Dependence on forces outside ourselves and the need to propitiate these forces, and feelings of fear that our crops, animals and friends might die, leads to an urge to mark out places where a link is established between ourselves and the supernatural. This place can be a monumental structure; it can be a special place in the landscape such as an outcrop or cave, rock overhang, a tree or a spring. Some places may become special because of something that happened there, and are commemorated with a symbol.

The use of symbolism to represent this relationship of people with land, with each other and with the gods, is timeless and universal. What symbolism does in words or in visual art forms is to acknowledge that there are things that cannot be expressed simply; we need symbolism to represent the many layers of experience, relationships and aspirations.

Cumbria has cups and rings of the common type: cups, a cup at the centre of one or more penannulars or rings, sometimes with a groove leading out of the cup, ovals, spirals, lines, parallel lines, lozenges and chevrons.

The landscape

Cumbria has a variety of rocks, including sedimentary rock such as Eden Valley sandstone that appears as outcrop near Long Meg and on the monolith itself. Igneous and metamorphic rocks, produced by heat and pressure, make up large tracts of the mountainous regions. They include the Andesite tuff that provided material for a specialised prehistoric axe quarry at Langdale, and the flat surface of a block that had broken away from a mountain and formed a good vertical surface to cover with motifs. Whinstone from Honey Pots Farm was a particularly difficult hard rock to decorate. There are many boulders that have been moved and moulded by ice, some of them providing material for standing stone circles, avenues and stone for the construction of burial mounds.

At the core of Cumbria are the great mountain valleys with their steep sides and lakes. Communications there are determined by landforms, and in the valley floors are limited opportunities for arable farming and extensive hunting and fishing grounds, a vast larder and source of skins and furs.

Away from the volcanic mountains there is a variety of scenery that includes the Pennines, the Solway and the coast. There are rich farmlands, red soils, wide rivers and valleys, and we are looking not just at one way of life in prehistory, but of many systems of survival and surplus. The axe quarries had an extensive export trade, and the rough-outs must have been brought down the mountain to be shaped and polished. Some of these sites have been located, including some on the coast.

Presumably goods were exchanged for these products. Rock art must always be seen in its landscape context, and is part of the story of how people came to grips with their environment in order to survive and be happy.

It is important to know what vegetation covered the land in prehistoric times, to know what kind of landscape the motif-makers lived in and used.

Landscape history A contribution by Deborah Long

If we could know what the landscape surrounding sites with prehistoric art looked like when it was being hammered onto the rocks and used, this could add considerably to our understanding. However, this is not easy. One of our main problems is that we do not know exactly when rock art sites were in use. Given that our best estimates put rock art at some time between the fourth millennium BC and the end of the second millennium BC, changes in the landscape would have occurred over this 1500-year period, some of them significant.

Another problem is that motifs are rarely located in areas where the environmental evidence needed to reconstruct landscape has been preserved and, just as rarely, where this evidence has been studied. In Cumbria, rock art is found today on outcrops and on monuments, both usually located in the central Cumbrian valleys, just above the valley floors. In contrast, environmental evidence is found in peat bogs and small lakes. These are rarely located on valley sides, being restricted to valley tops or floors.

In addition, sites that can tell us something about the environmental history of Cumbria in the period between the fourth and second millennium BC are very few. Although sites in central Cumbria have been studied in the past, these early studies were rarely dated using radiocarbon techniques and we cannot therefore be confident about when changes were happening. These studies provide just outline pictures of vegetation change in prehistory. More recent research includes a raised mire site just north of the Solway Firth, which may give us some idea of the environmental history of northern Cumbria. Its distance from our field area, however, limits its value. A second site is a coastal raised mire on the west coast, just south of the Esk estuary.

In very general terms, the environmental evidence we have tells us that the period during which these motifs were likely to have been made was a time when woodland regeneration was occurring across the uplands and trees were reclaiming clearances made earlier in the fourth millennium BC. Humans were withdrawing from the wooded valley tops and sides. These uplands were covered with oak-, hazel- and birch-dominated woodland with small clearances. It is likely that the valley sides were also wooded, although we do not know whether the motifs and monuments there were located in clearings. Then from about 2300 BC the evidence suggests that clearances were once again being made in upland areas, although these seem to have been small and short-lived, suggesting perhaps intermittent use of the uplands. These were perhaps for seasonal grazing, as clearances would increase the amount of young leaves and plants available to browsing animals. From this time in the lowlands,

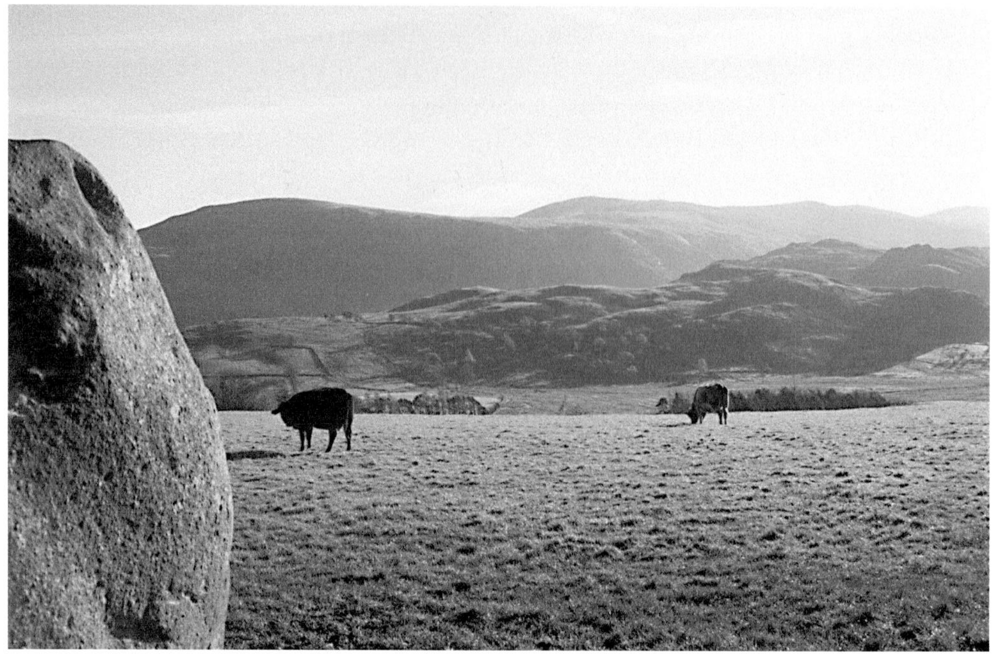

9 *Lake District landscape, from the Castlerigg stone circle*

human activity seems to become more intense with a consistent record for arable farming from about 1800 BC. However, as arable activity became more widespread the practice of motif making appears to have died out.

On the coastal areas of west Cumbria, a slightly different picture emerges from the environmental evidence. Woodland clearance with evidence for pasture and arable farming starts in this region much earlier than elsewhere, from around the third millennium BC. Although this is within the period of rock art, there are few known sites on the west coast. Human activity there seems to have been more intense and more persistent from about 2900 BC. Supporting the environmental evidence for the extensive clearance of woodland, there is archaeological evidence in the form of lithic (worked stone) scatters and heath sites for continuous occupation, although perhaps of temporary use. Given the continuity of occupation, it is interesting that there is again very little rock art in this area, perhaps suggesting that it was not strongly associated with settlement and farming.

What the environmental evidence does confirm is that the period of rock art marks the very start of increasing human exploitation of the landscape when great changes in the appearance of landscape began. As these changes in the landscape and vegetation cover gathered speed, the practice of rock art faded.

With these preliminary observations, some of which can be supported by the Bibliography, we turn to a detailed survey of where the rock art is in Cumbria, its form and possible purpose.

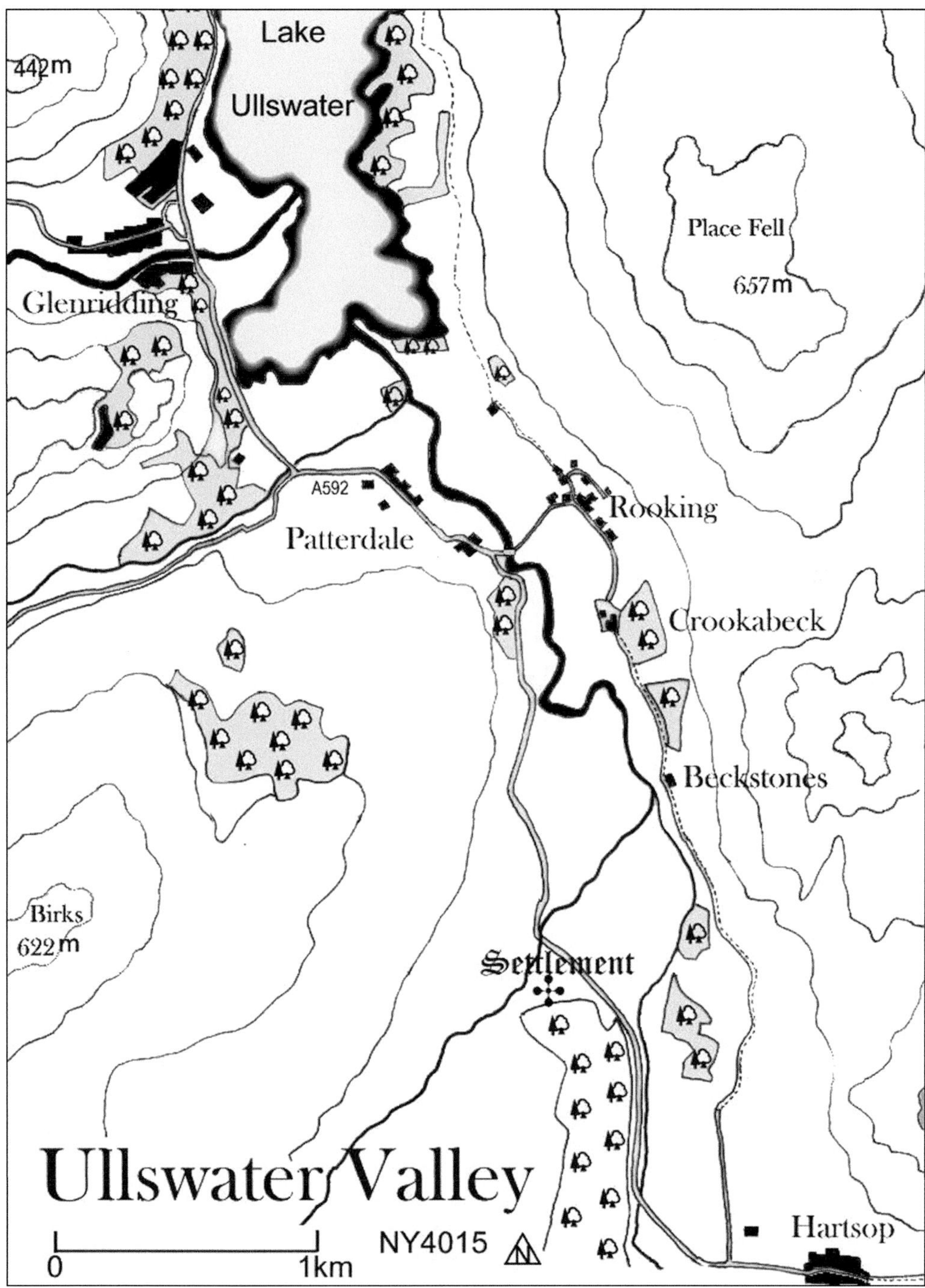

10 *Ullswater*

2 Rock art
in the Cumbrian landscape

The heart of The Lakes

Patterdale lies south of Ullswater in a narrow valley through which the Goldrill Beck, joined by the Deepdale Beck, runs north to empty its water into the lake. The narrow valley floor is flanked on the east and west by steep mountain slopes. The village of Hartsop lies to the east of a bend of the A592 from the Kirkstone Pass north of Brothers Water. The old track from this village runs parallel to the main road to the east as a Bridle Road that goes through Dubhow, Beckstones, Crookabeck and on to Rooking and the eastern shore of Ullswater.

One of the cottages north of Rooking is the home of Tim and Pat Cook. Tim was clearing a long, low outcrop in his garden when he noticed a large number of different-sized cup marks, some linked, some oval in shape. He was to find confirmation in one of my previous books that he had a prehistoric site in his garden.

Tim has described his discoveries at some length in an article, 'Rock Carvings in Patterdale', in *The Year Book 1999* and *Transactions of the Matterdale Historical and Archaeological Society*. Until that article appeared I was reticent about publicising these discoveries at the time, as I wished to respect the privacy of the people on whose land they were found. Such important sites have to be reported to English Heritage so that they can be safeguarded with a preservation order, and this has been done. That does not protect them fully, however.

The story of discovery began when Tim and Pat got to work on their newly-acquired but neglected garden. I leave Tim to say what happened:

> On removing some of the moss and grass I was intrigued to discover a number of circular depressions, mostly about an inch across, but two or three larger and deeper, together with some shallowish grooves and other markings, none of which looked natural.

He referred to a book written by Tim Laurie and me (*Prehistoric Rock Art of County Durham, Swaledale and Wensleydale*) which partly confirmed his suspicions that they were very old and in the 'cup and ring tradition'. He wrote to me, and invited me to come and see them. His splendid photographs were exciting, and meanwhile he had contacted his neighbours who found an even more spectacular marked outcrop. My role was firstly to confirm what they were, to record them by making

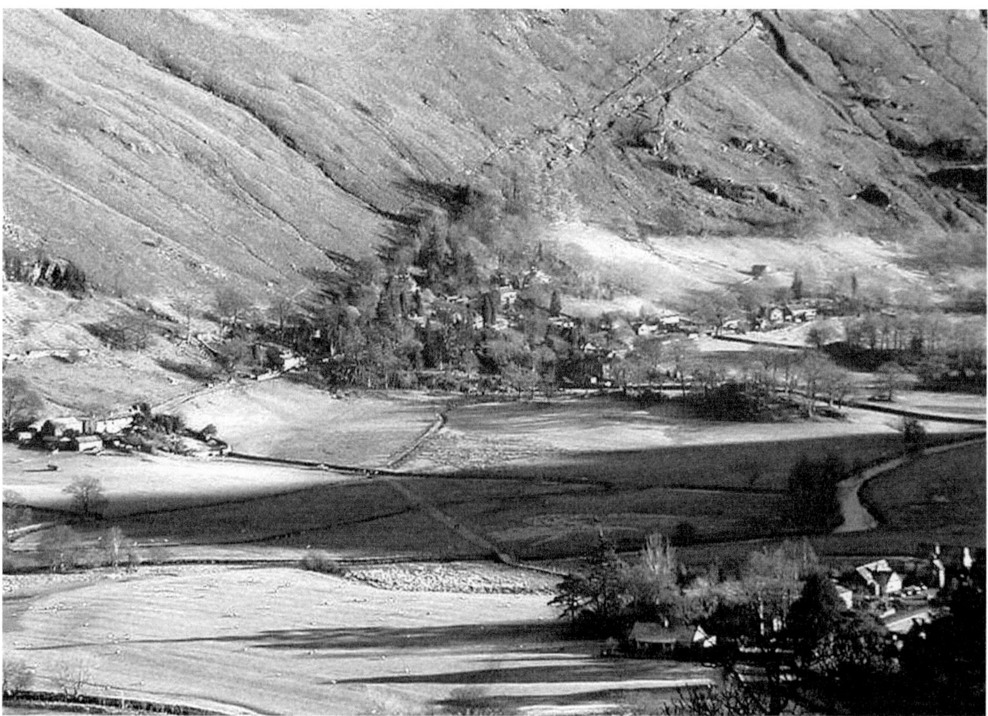

11 *Patterdale: the valley floor from the west*

thorough rubbings on which to base drawings, and to take many photographs in good low light. I then advised on the next step, which was their listing in the National Monuments Record.

The story illustrates admirably the hit-and-miss element in discovering new panels of decorated rock, but does not end there. While I was spending about two full days recording the rocks, many people from the village came to see what was going on; a farmer discovered that she had similar markings on an inverted boat-shaped outcrop in her field of sheep. Once the process of discovery gained momentum, another site was found at Beckstones.

We are often told that history is about people. So is the discovery of the past. Not only did a community become involved in the search, but also the significance of marked rocks to the people of the past in this valley became apparent. In his article Tim Cook has photographically illustrated the rocks with their motifs and used information about rock art to speculate on their meaning. But, like so many others before him, he faces an (as yet) insoluble mystery.

The locations of the groups of markings are referred to in my record as Sites 1–3. The marked rocks are at good viewpoints commanding the routeways to north and south. They lie above the floodplain, and site 3 may have been a small island in marsh. There would have been an abundance of game – good hunting. The valley was protected from extremes of weather by mountains and gave access to the expanse of Ullswater.

The drawings and photographs show that the main symbols are cups, with some ovals. There are also long grooves pecked into the rocks, following the natural downward slopes. The main rock markings at site 2 look as though they may have been influenced by the topography: the trails leading through the valley may have been echoed in the lines pecked out of the rock.

Each site will now be viewed separately.

Site 1

The long narrow outcrop is slightly domed. It is possible that some motifs remain buried. There is a preponderance of cups of varying sizes and depths, some joined, some ovals and some thin rectangles with rounded ends. The outcrop is the highest decorated rock in the valley.

The site is private.

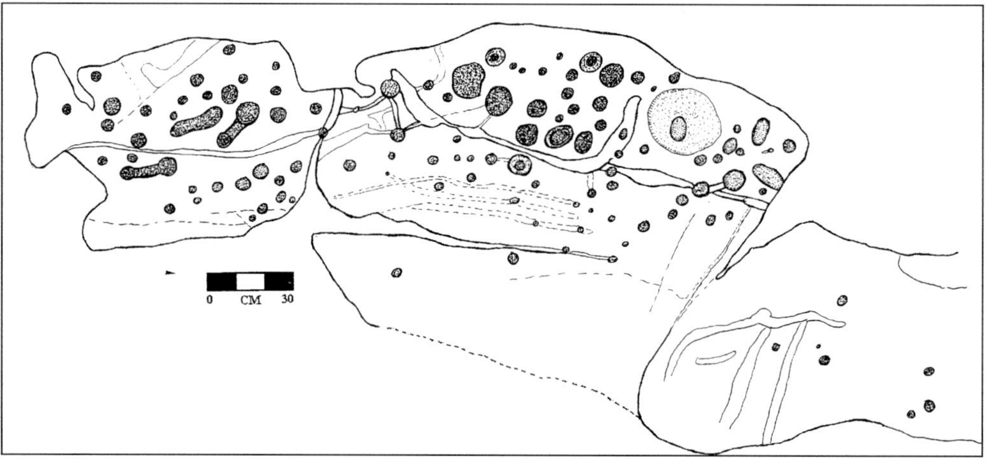

12 *Simple motifs at site 1*

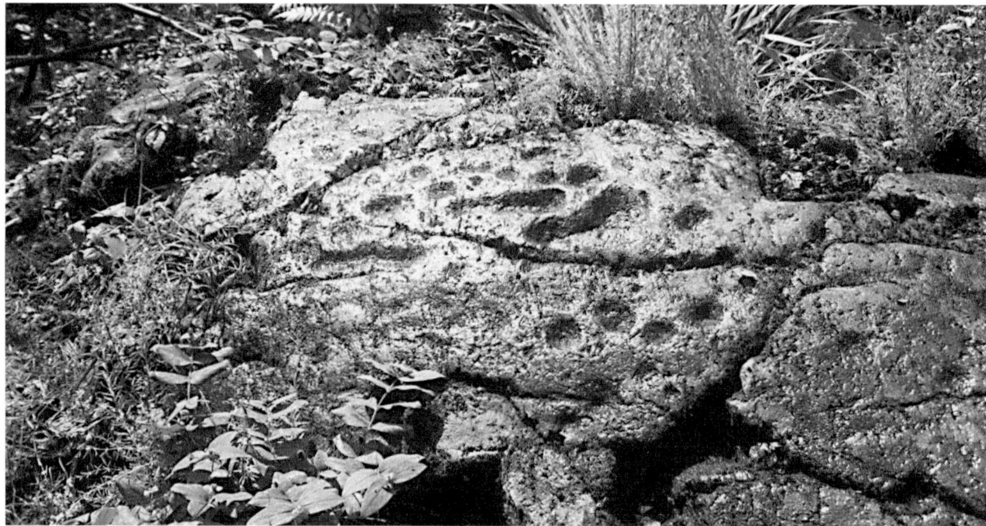

13 *Part of the exposed rock at site 1*

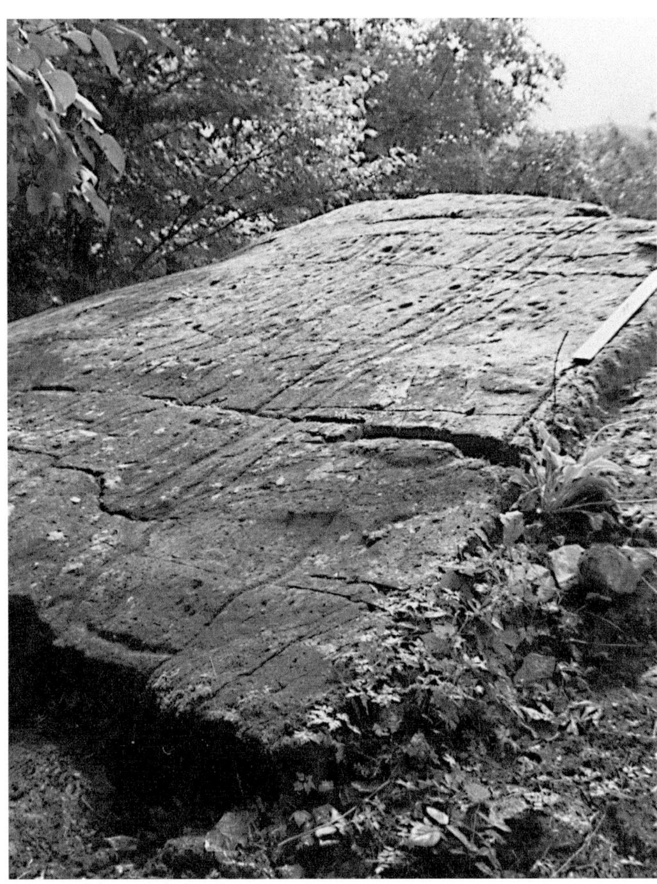

14 *Site 2*

Site 2

The continuation of the rock outcrop from the above site achieves massive proportions. What has been revealed has survived quarrying, for we see alongside it a rock with a quarried face to the west. There are other moss-covered rocks that have cups pecked on them, not all cleared of vegetation (for the past has to take its place in the present). Even allowing for hidden art and quarried rocks, what is left is almost unprecedented in Britain. The motifs are simple: cups, grooves and one angular ring around a cup. What is outstanding is the way the cracks in the fairly smooth surface, pocked in places by small vesicles (gas bubbles), divide the rock from east to west into natural zones. The lesser cracks that run down the rock from south to north have been enlarged and new grooves pecked out to run parallel. Some of these diverge towards the bottom, and one loops to link up with another, enclosing a cup. Some cups are symmetrical, others irregular, apparently taking their places at random, but there is a row between lines like buttons on a coat. At the highest point, where the rock drops away to the south, there is a high concentration of cups. Above, the mountaintops loom on the horizon. At a lower level are other, scattered cups. In places the rock slope is quite steep, which must have caused some problems for those making the cups.

The site is, like the other, strictly private.

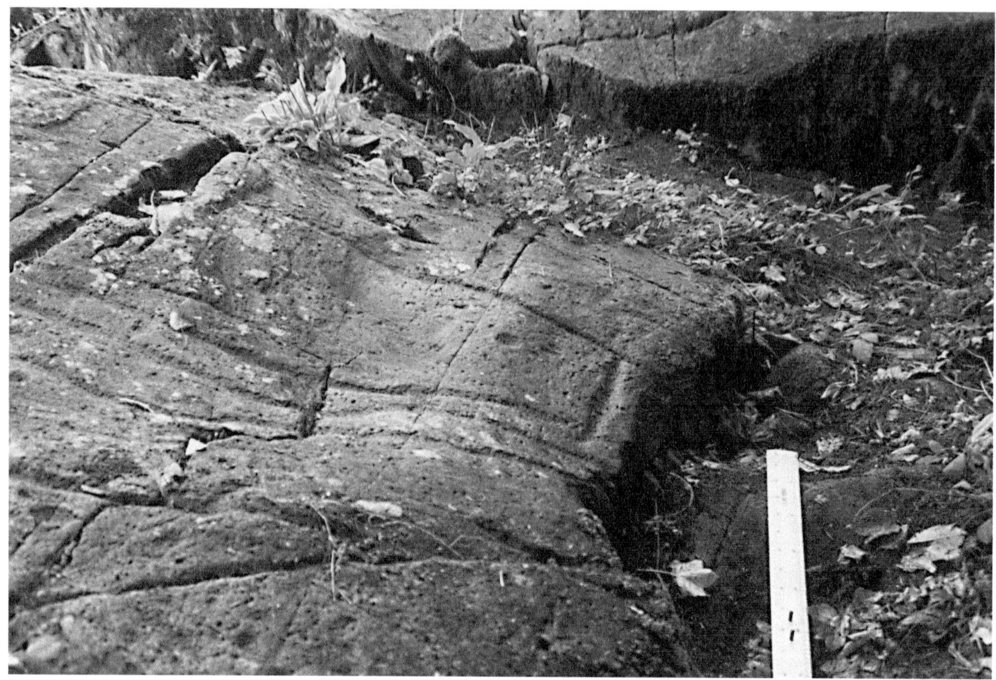

15 *Site 2. Two of the long grooves are joined*

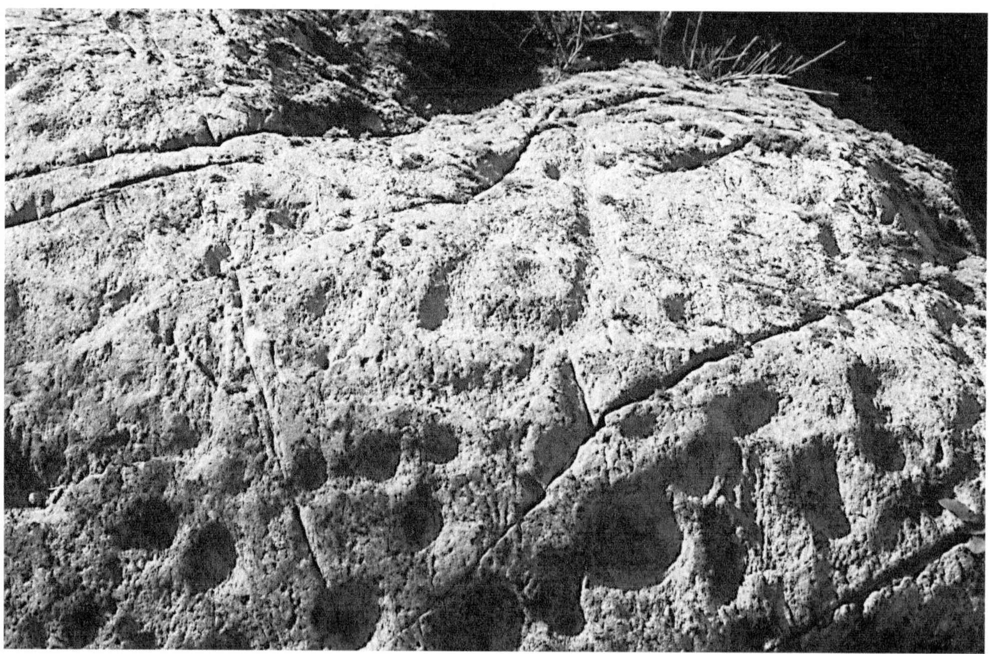

16 *Site 2. Clusters of cup marks to the south at the highest part*

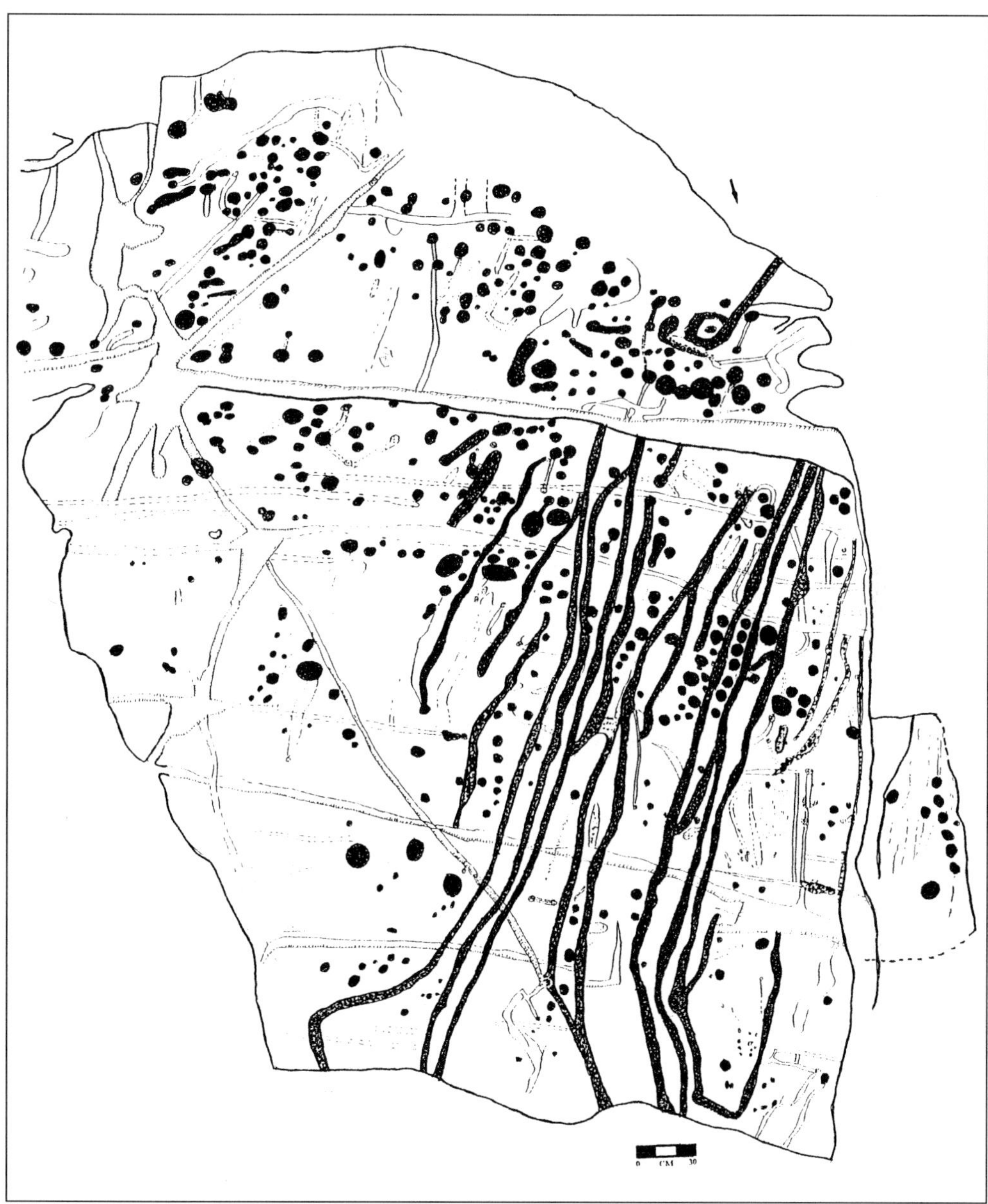

17 *Site 2: the main part of the decorated rock*

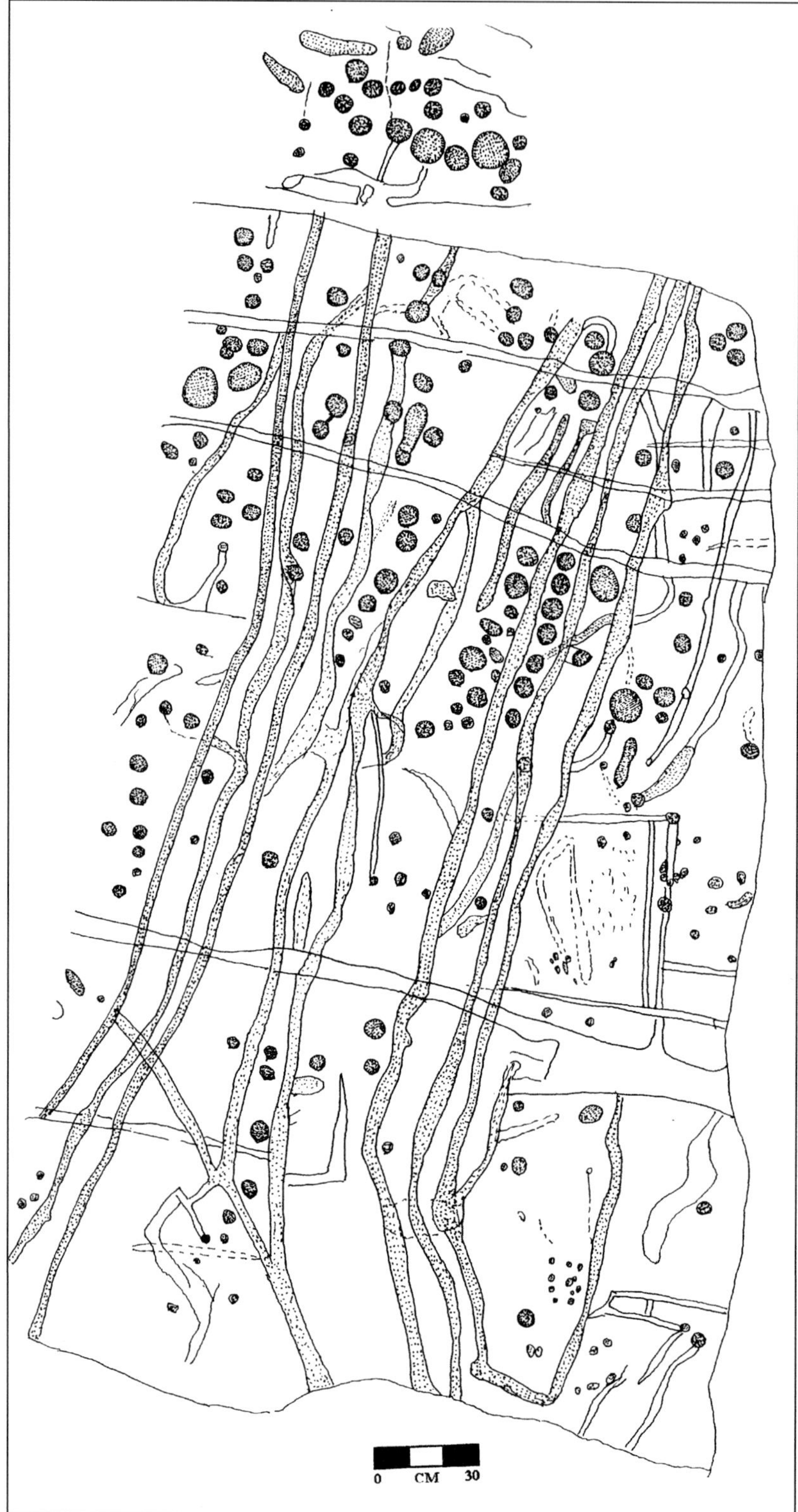

18 *Site 2: detail of part of the large rock. A row of cups is hemmed in by long grooves running down the rock*

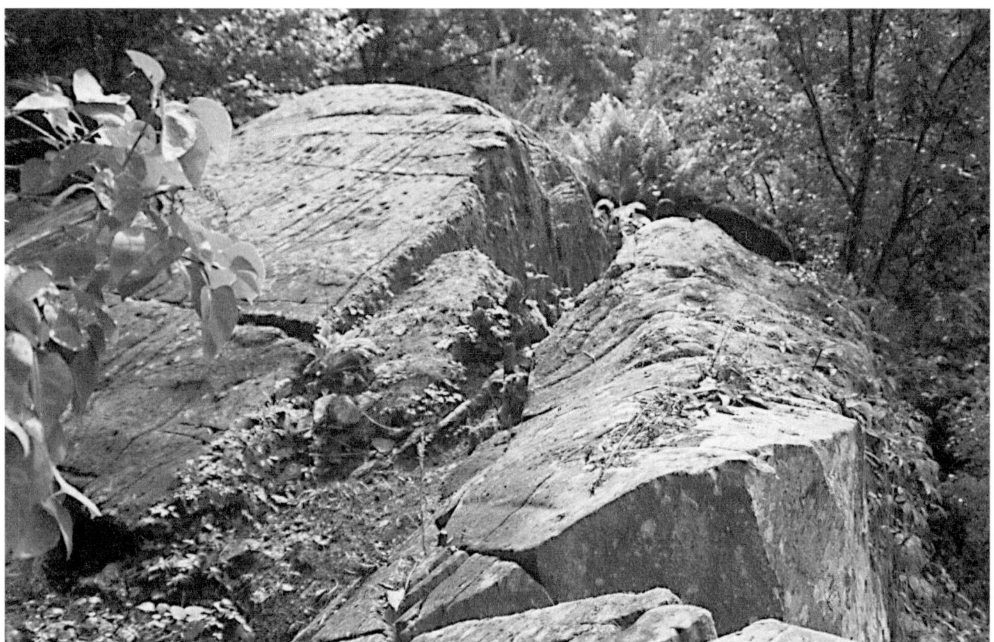

19 *Site 2: most of the outcrop*

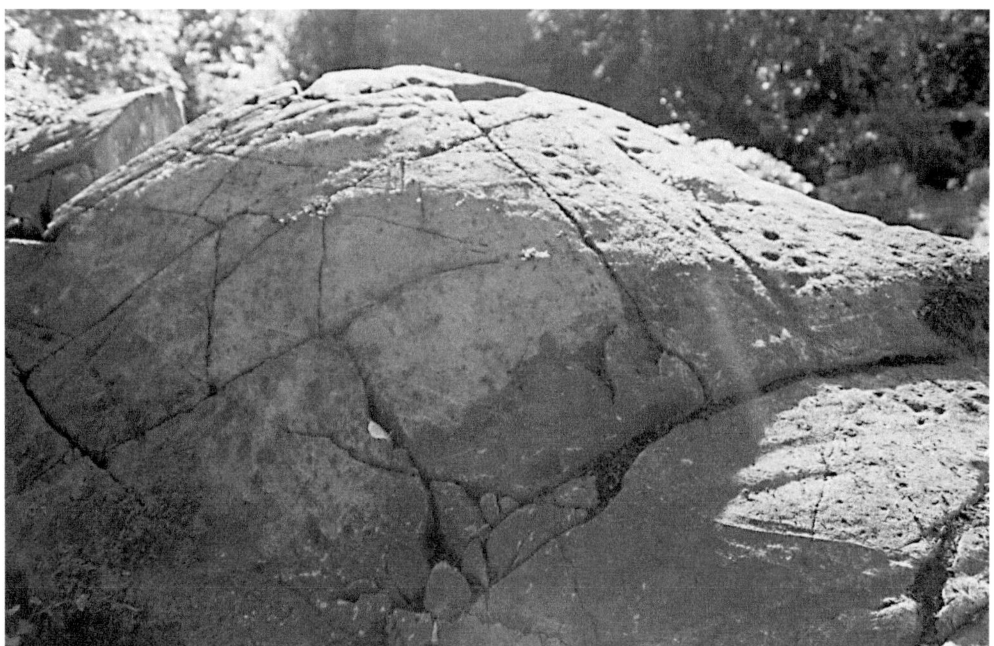

20 *Site 2; north-west*

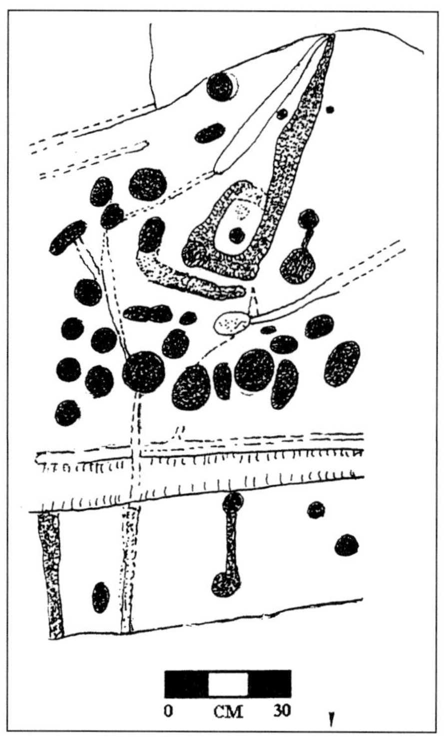

21 *Site 2: south*

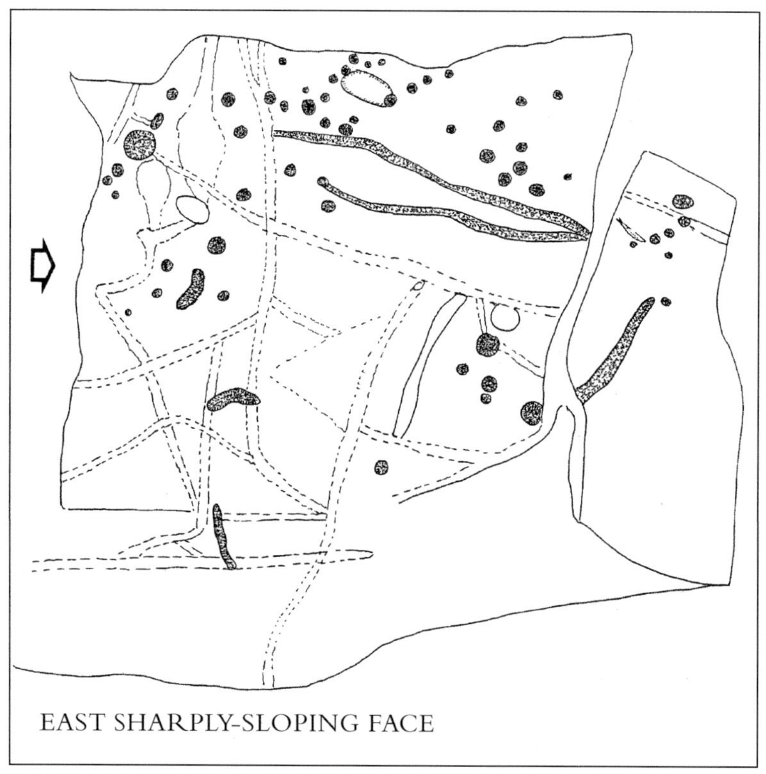

22 *The western edge*

Site 3

On the bend of a stream, the land falls away from a public path to the west, then rises gently again on an outcrop that is a small crag to the north, but smooth where the decoration is found.

The site is strange, for a deposit of small boulders and gravel lies on top in the centre. Badgers have used this for their sets and have burrowed into it. The decorated outcrop lies at the edges of the mound and on top of it, and there is a suggestion that people made use of the natural shape to raise it into a mound that looks like an upturned boat or a long barrow.

Some of the motifs already encountered are there: cups, ovals, lines and thin rectangles with rounded corners, but there are also single rings around cups on a panel at the top of the mound.

The outcrop stands just above the flood plain to the east, and may have been surrounded by marsh for much of the time. In that case it would have been a small island, and as such may have gained an extra significance, perhaps as a refuge. The site has not been excavated; the illustrations show only what has been cleared of superficial vegetation such as leaves and thin grass.

The site is visible from the path, but private.

There are so many similarities in the motifs on these three sites that it is likely that they were all contemporary.

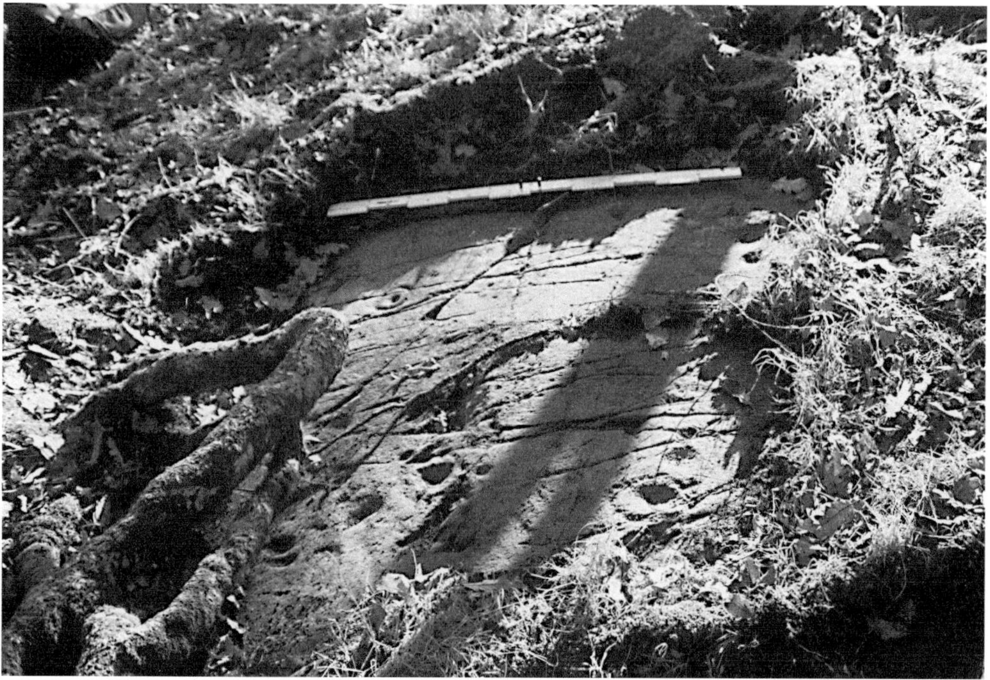

23 *Site 3: ringed cups on partly exposed outcrop rock*

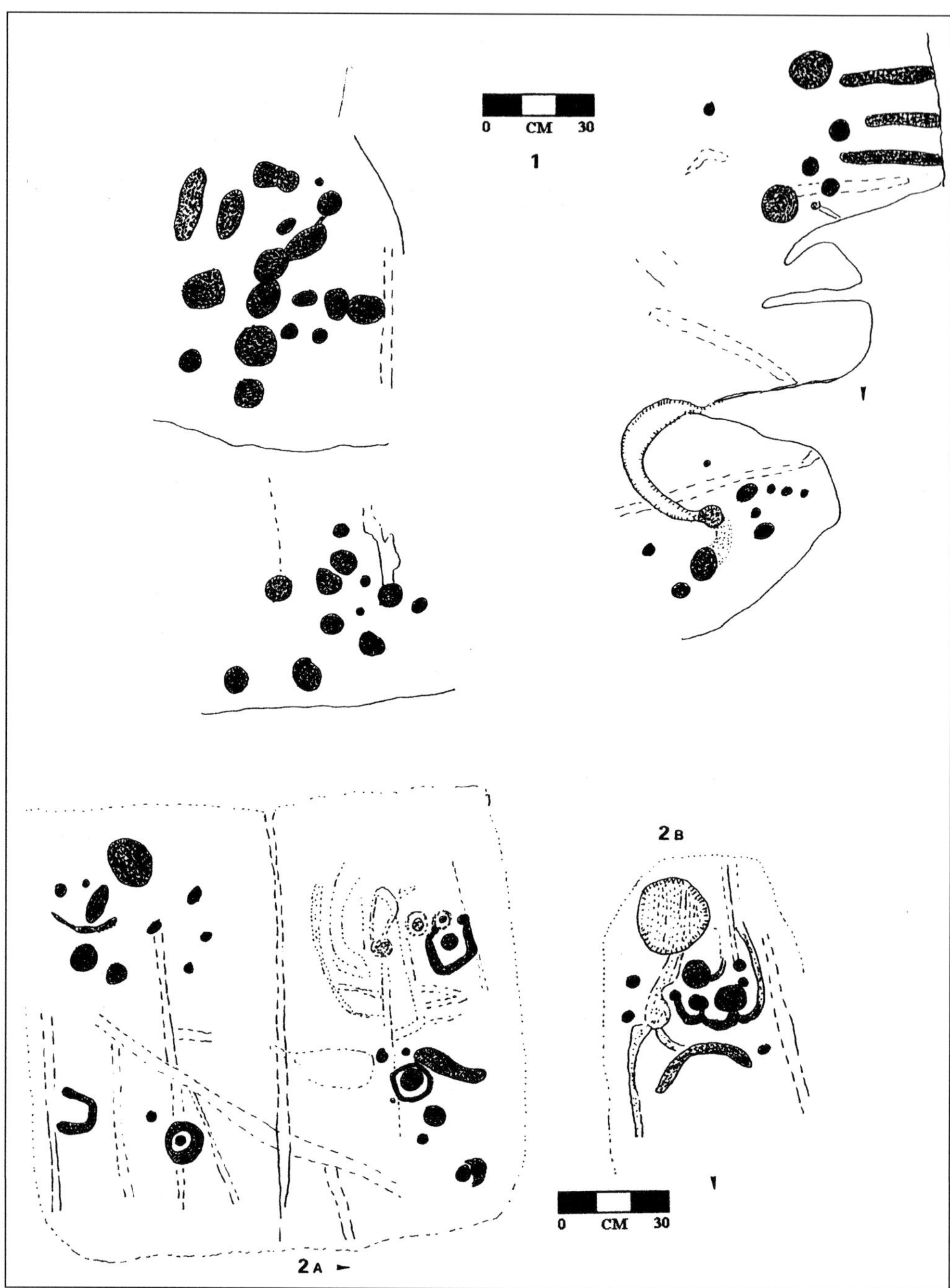

24 *Site 3(a)*

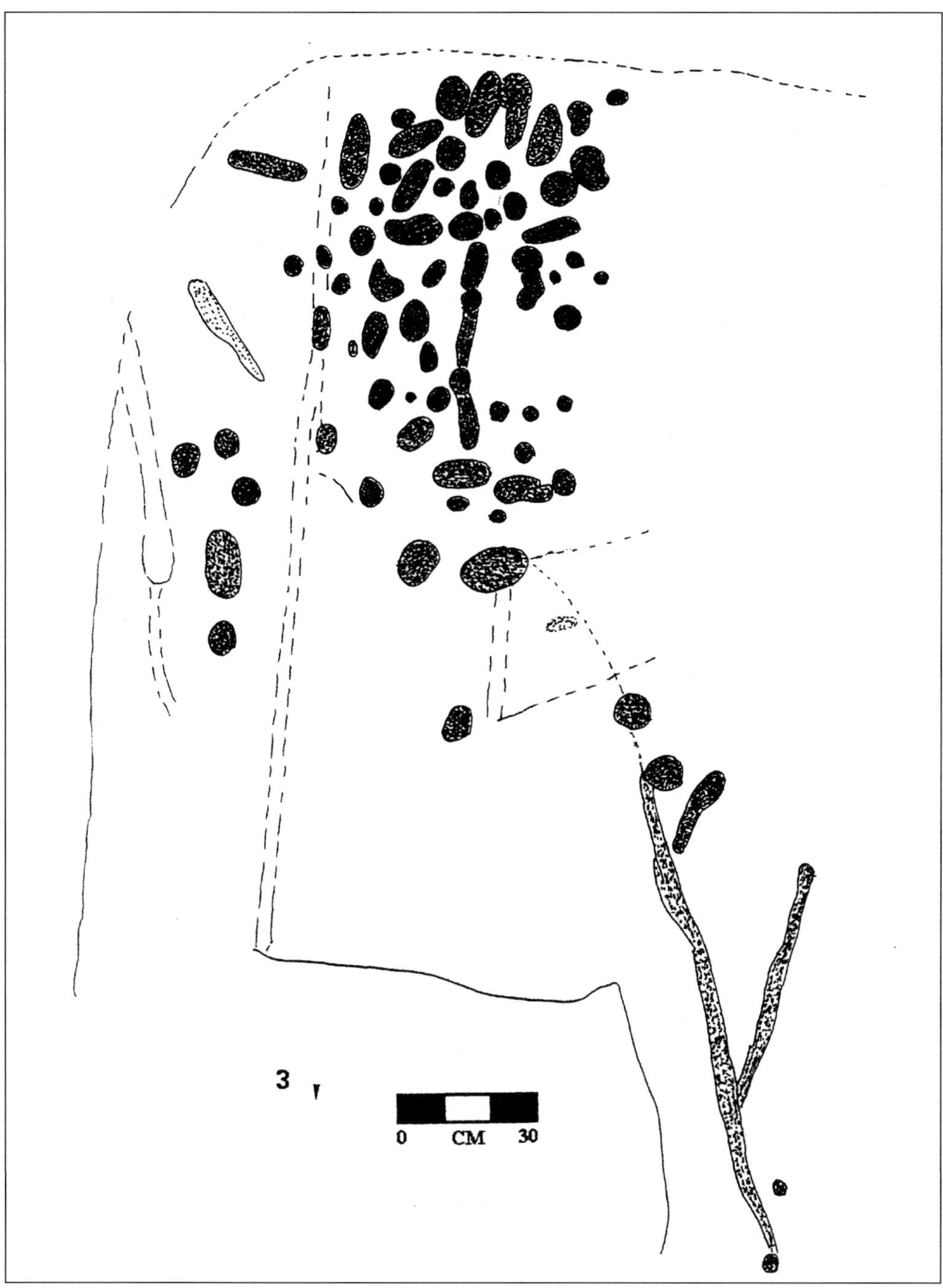

25 *Site 3, west*

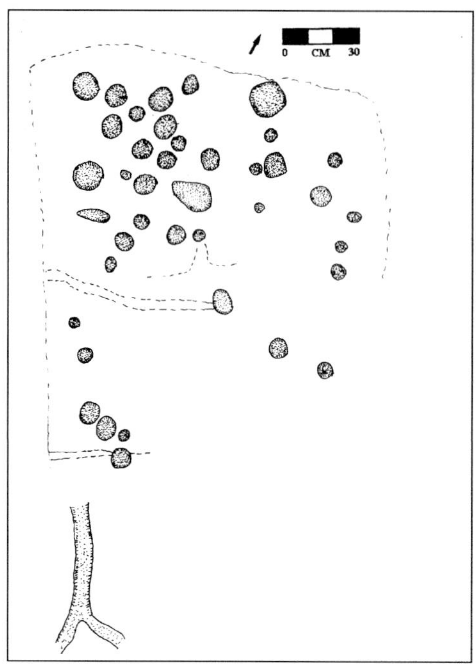

26 *Beckstones*

Beckstones (NY403150)

Once these sites had been found, there was a kind of inevitability that more would emerge. The half-quarried rock that lies beside the track by the houses, marked with cups on top, confirmed the theory that marked rocks follow a routeway that also provides a good viewpoint up and down the valley.

The valley runs between mountain ranges to the east and west, providing a complete contrast in vegetation and topography, with rectangular fields used as pasture and some woodland. There is a strong sense here of the landscape opening up from the Kirkstone Pass to Ullswater, making it a most obvious natural routeway. Beckstones is the most southerly panel of rock art; whether it represents the beginning or the end of the markings we do not know. What we do know is that there is the strongest possible link between these markings and the natural route that skirts the marshy ground to the west, making use of the lower ridges that flank it. The narrow valley, shut in, yet opening out at a long lake, must surely have been the most obvious path through the mountains and a link with the rich fishing and hunting grounds. One can imagine travellers coming down the Kirkstone pass north and seeing this valley open up at their feet. The rock art leads them along the best route north to the lake.

The position of the marked rocks in this landscape differs from others in Britain in that they are almost on the floor of the valley, shut in by mountains. The markings are of a simple kind, but their importance in the chain is obvious. The prominent outcrop on the valley floor has been partly quarried away, and as the cups reach the quarried edge we can assume that there were more.

The land is private, and belongs to the National Trust; the rock is easily visible from the path.

32

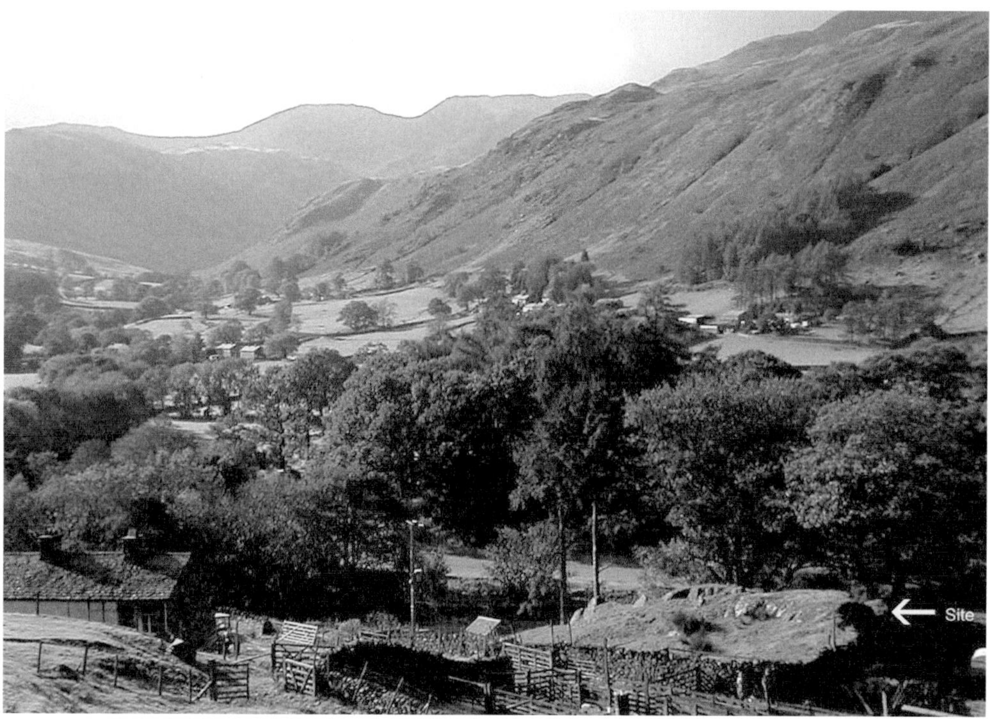

27 *Beckstones farm and rock outcrop, south-west*

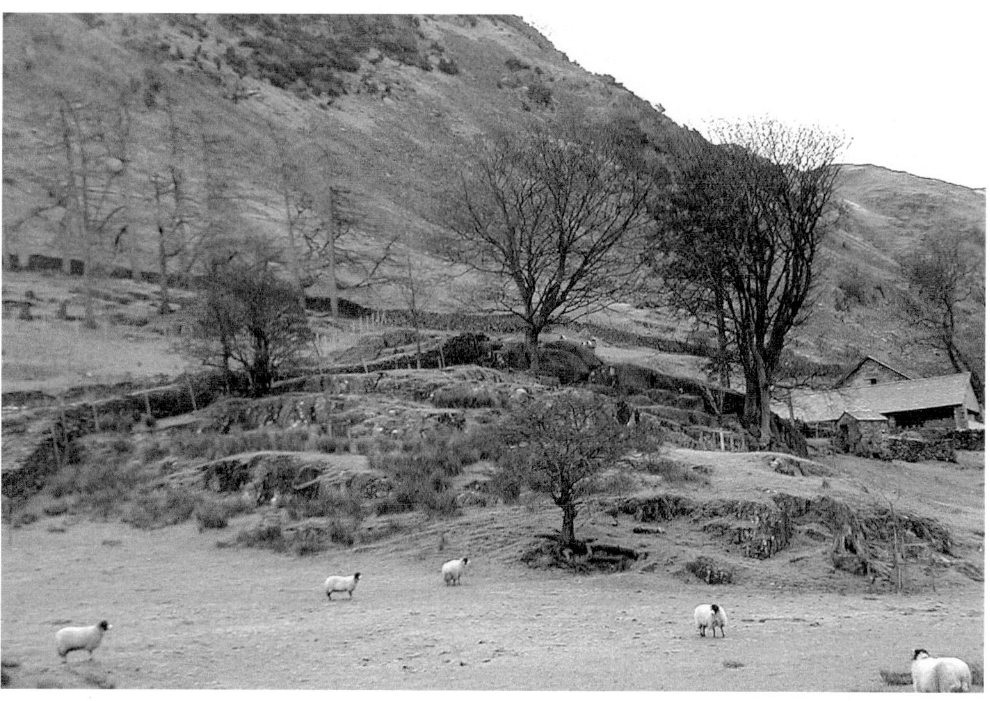

28 *The rock art site is at the centre of the picture*

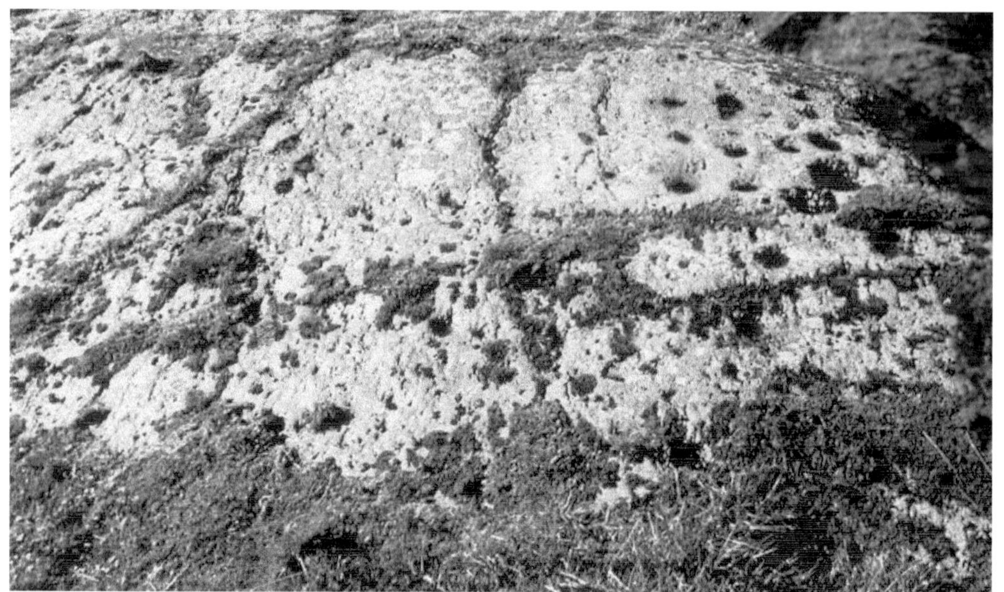

29 *Beckstones: cup marked surface*

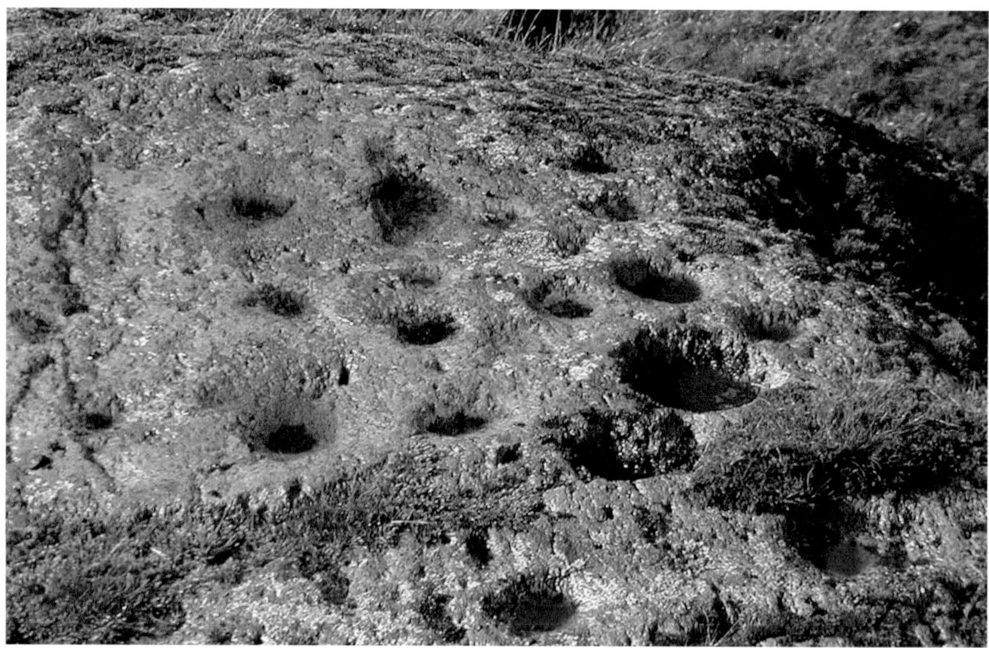

30 *Beckstones: detail*

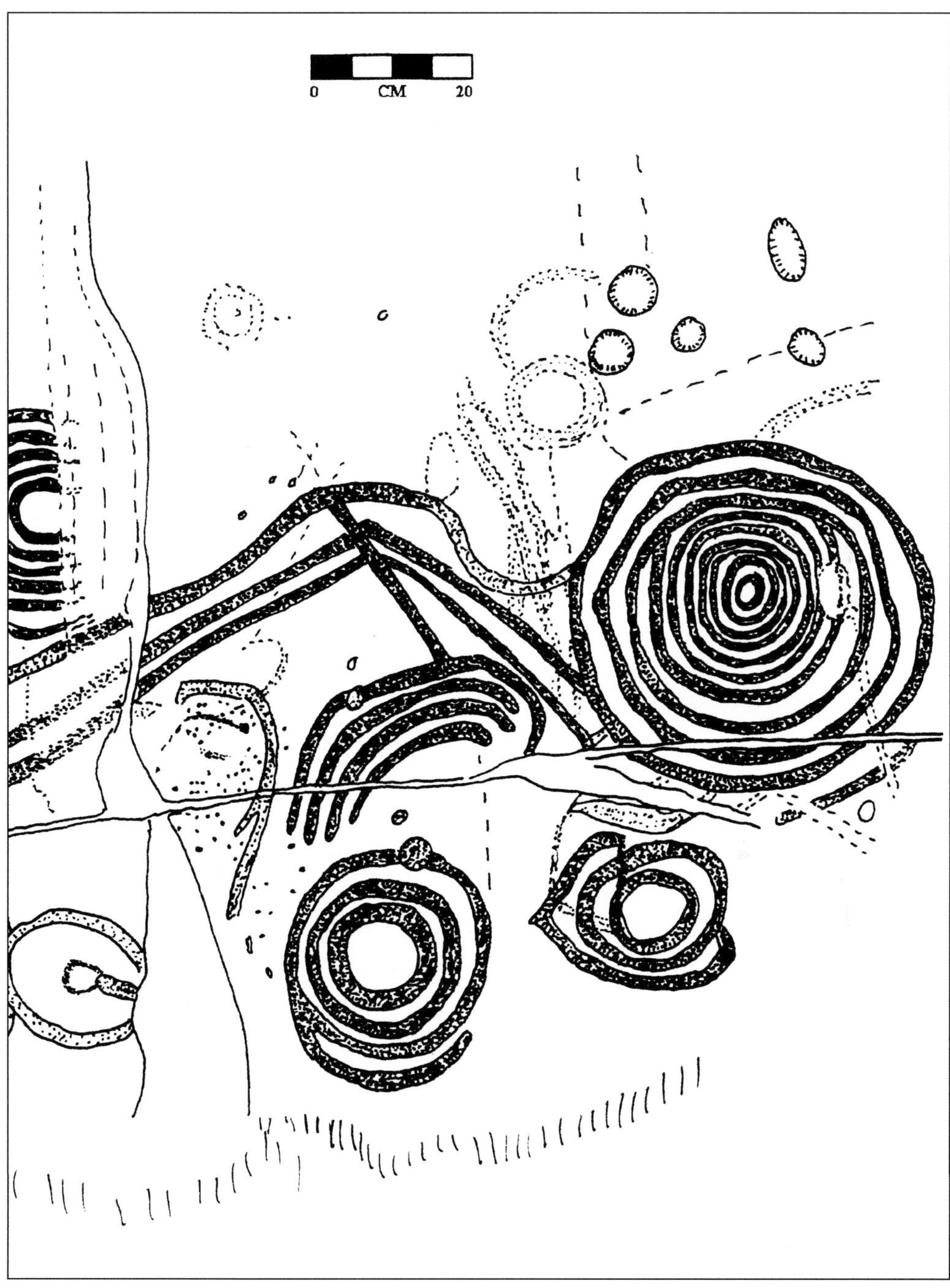

31 *The dramatic motifs at Chapel Stile*

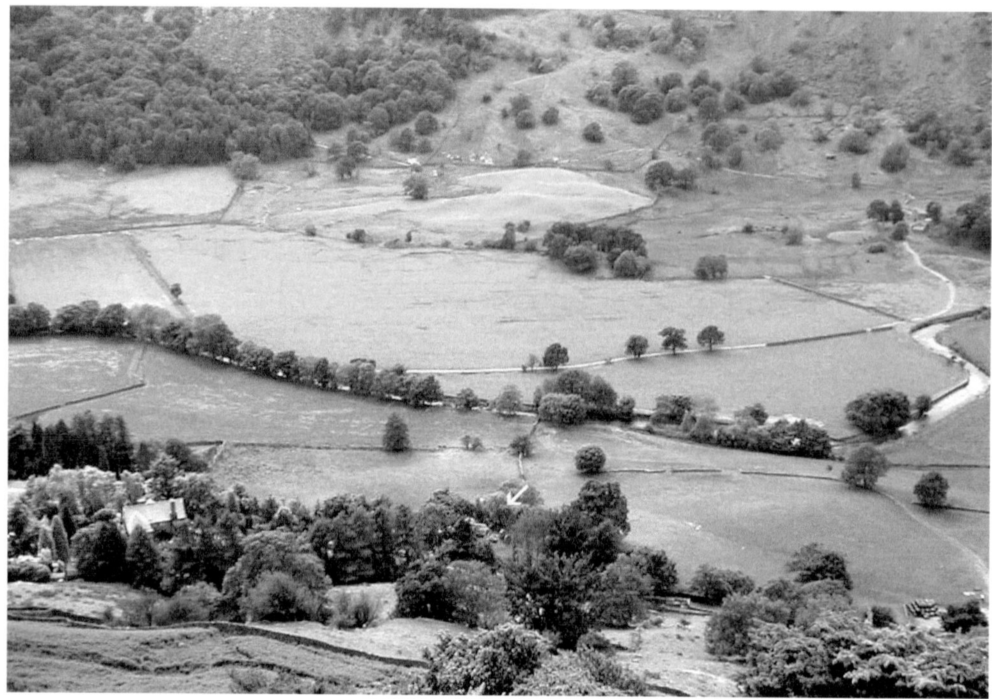

32 *The floor of the Langdale valley with the rock art site arrowed*

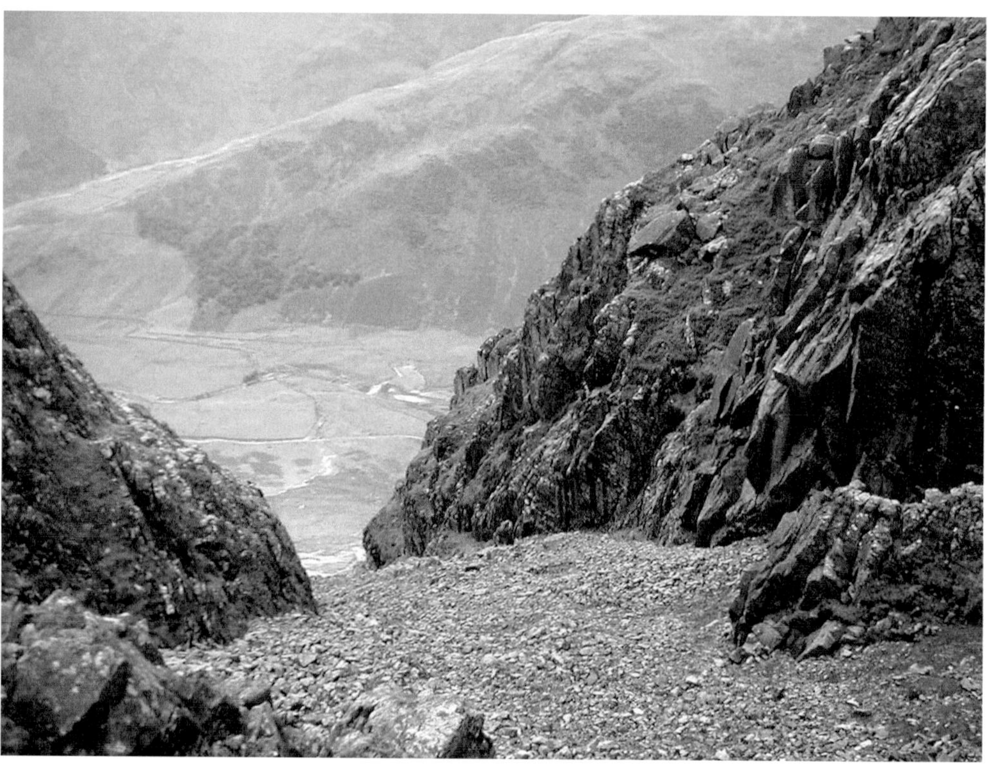

33 *The Langdale valley from the axe quarries of the Pike o' Stickle*

The Langdale valley: Chapel Stile (NY31400582)

It is difficult not to feel great excitement at the discovery of something entirely new when one is introduced to a panel of art like this one. What a joy it is to realise that there is so much more to be found. Its site name is Chapel Stile.

The markings were not discovered until November 1999, yet this is in one of the most visited places in Britain. Had the valley of the Langdale Beck been surveyed thoroughly, it would surely have been found before. The rock is one of a cluster that has broken away from a larger mass in geological times. Its split vertical surface faces east, and the whole has signs of glacial smoothing. It dominates the valley; the decoration is to be viewed from the east. As there are some carved modern letters on the same surface, and as it has been used by rock climbers, the faint patterns may well have been seen, but ignored or not understood.

Paul and Barbara Brown first recorded the decoration as a result of a systematic search during a week's holiday, following the premise that much rock art is found at significant viewpoints, not necessarily at the highest places. Here we have a routeway above the flood level of the valley, as we find at Patterdale. From the rock one looks north to the Langdale Pikes and prehistoric axe quarries, south to the beginnings of Lake Windermere, and west to the other side of the valley. Behind it is a modern road and more mountains. Finds of prehistoric axes from High Close and other places to the head of Lake Windermere and beyond show that the industry extended beyond the outcrops themselves. The 'rough outs' were at the beginning of the process of manufacture; the axes had to be painstakingly polished to become cherished possessions. This valley may have been a vital route for the export of stone axes, and an access to the axe quarries themselves.

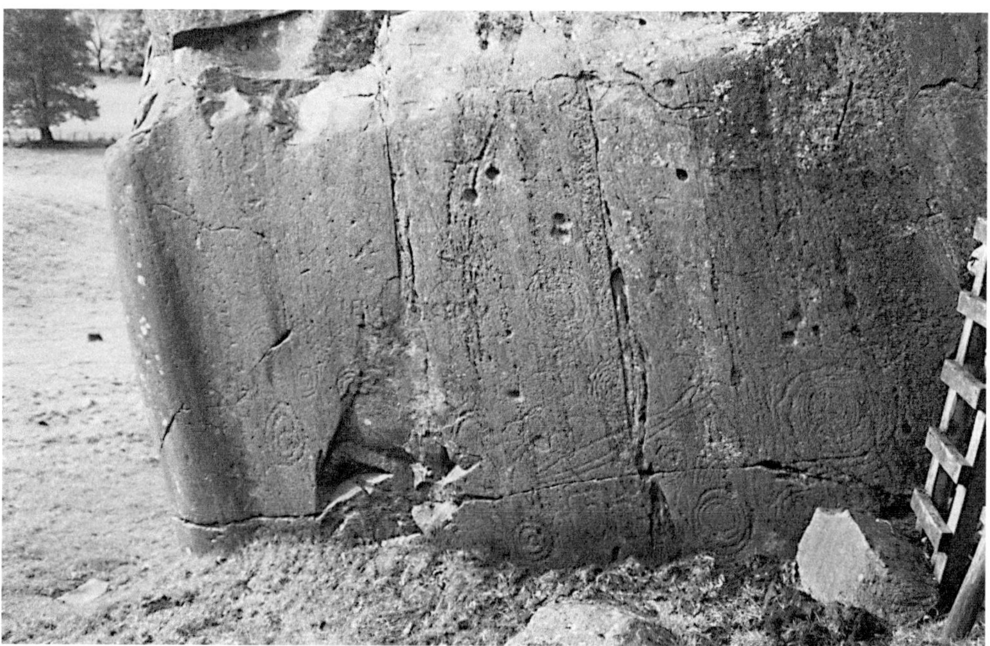

34 *The east face of the marked rock*

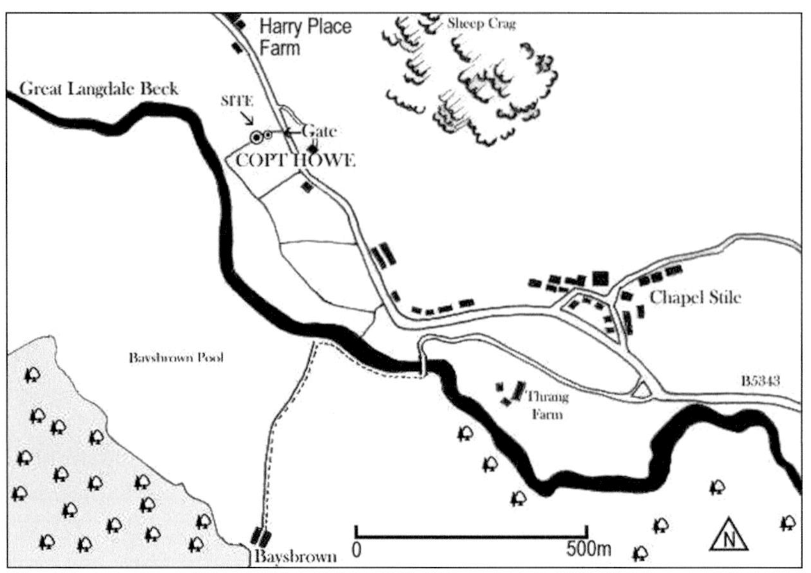

35 *The rock art site in the valley*

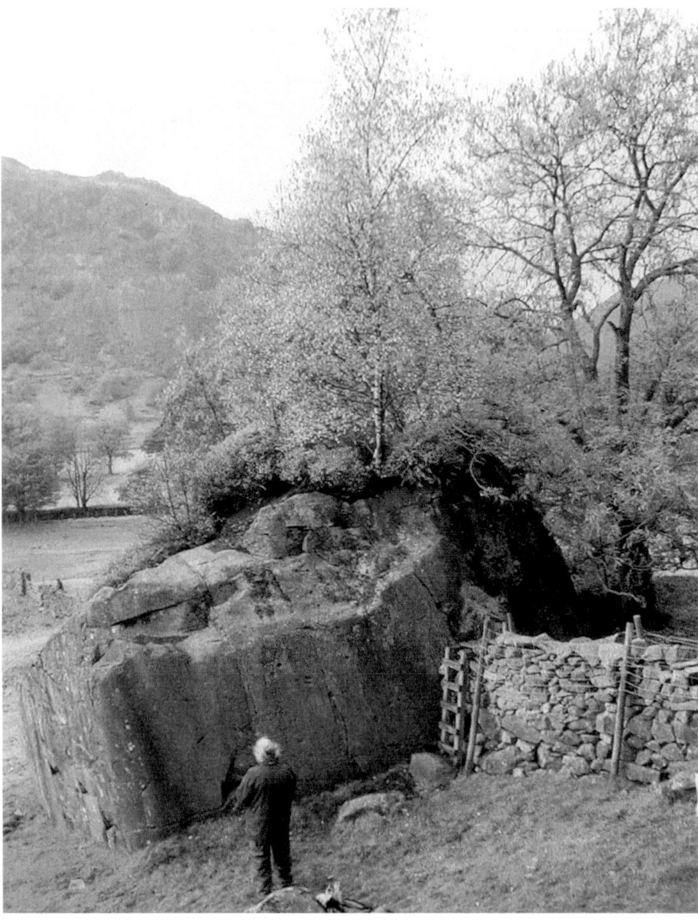

36 *The marked rock in its setting*

The rock is Andesite tuff, a volcanic solidified ash. There are some vertical cracks on the 'working' surface and a long continuous crack at the base parallel to the ground. The surface is pitted in places where there are vesicles, and there are deep cups that may be caused by minerals within the tuff that have fallen out and the resulting hole scoured out; alternatively, they could be artificial.

The Langdale Pikes provide a localised source of material for making high quality axes. Although not all examples of 'exported' axes have been examined in detail ('petrologically identified') by taking samples from them and putting them under a microscope to find their mineral composition, and hence their source, they are visually recognisable. We have a great deal of information about where they were made and to which regions they were exported, for axes are strongly characteristic of the Neolithic period. Those that were polished were the most efficient cutting tools.

The source of the stone was a number of chipping floors where the 'rough outs' were made; they were then taken to the lowlands to be polished (within a 40-mile radius of Langdale) and redistributed from these sites. As the use of these axes extends over hundreds of years the production would have been similarly long-lived. About 2000 Langdale axes are known in Britain; we can assume that there were thousands more. The axes had a quality that made them very desirable as a status symbol; few show signs of being used in the work-a-day world. It would depend upon how easily they were available. The people near the chipping and polishing sites would have more uses for them if they were more easily available. It is highly likely that some of the places to which they were sent had many more people living there than in Cumbria (Humberside, for example). What the Cumbrians received in exchange we do not know. Although some sort of division of labour is implied in axe production, it does not mean that that is all the local population did with their time.

Cumbria dominated axe production in the fourth and third millennium BC. This would surely have brought some prosperity to the people who made them and marketed them.

The large mass of decorated rock in the valley marks one of the natural routeways from Lake Windermere to the flaking floors high in the mountains, where the choice of such a difficult and precious mining area suggests that the rock being mined was not just attractive for use, but had a ritual significance.

In trying to understand the significance of what other archaeologists have discovered I have been forced to speculate. Only 2000 polished axes have been found; but even assuming that many more have not been discovered, if the axe quarries were operating for over 1000 years there would have been masses of the things. However, working on top of a high, cold, dangerous mountain was not possible all the time. Mining must have been seasonal. Perhaps in a warm summer a group of people would have been excused from their other duties of herding, hunting and producing other food to go up the mountain and make more rough outs. Perhaps they were the most skilled men, women and children. There must have been an arrangement for a 'price' or exchange of goods with the grinders and polishers. The finished products were then ready for export. Who collected them? Did people come from other regions? Some needed boats (these polished axes reached Ireland). Were the axes strapped to the sides of beasts or pulled in carts? Did the transporter take them all the way, adding transport costs to the cost of manufacture? Was there a kind of chain of trade in which they went from person to person, or through a middleman? How did the exchange rates work? Was there any rock art on the route from producer to buyer? In an area of low population, did the Lakeland industries bring them a great deal of wealth? If so, is there any sign of it?

The Ullswater and Langdale valley sites are similar, but different: both mark the easiest and most important routeways through the mountains and through sources of food along the valley floors. They differ in that one site is linked geographically to axe production. If we look for a moment at Kilmartin, Argyll, there we have a low-lying 'Mhor' that spans the routes from the sea to the mountains, which in prehistoric time became a great focus of monuments that displayed power and wealth. The rock art of Kilmartin overlooks this vital area, although some of it is incorporated in the burials and on standing stones. The importance of the area is reflected in these symbols of power; its wealth owes much to its geographical position.

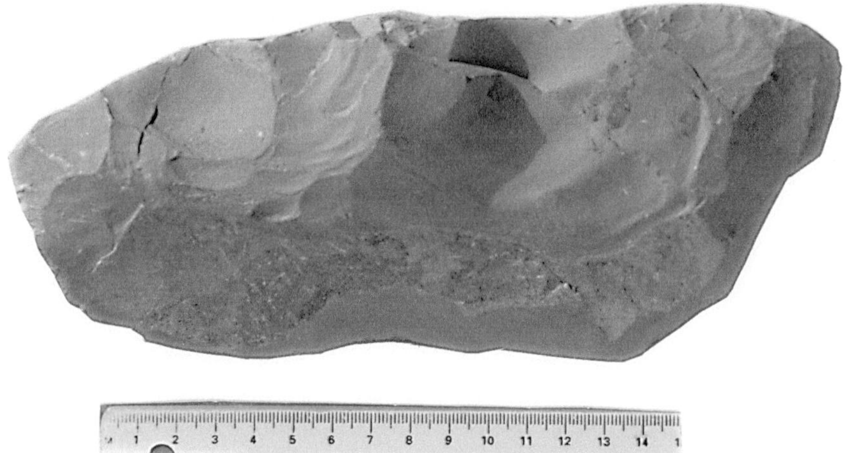

37 *A Langdale axe 'rough out', quarried from the mountain to the north of the site*

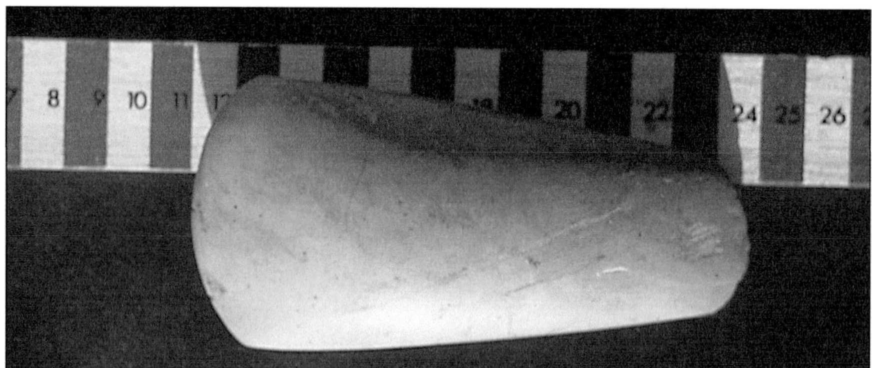

38 *A polished Langdale axe exported into Northumberland*

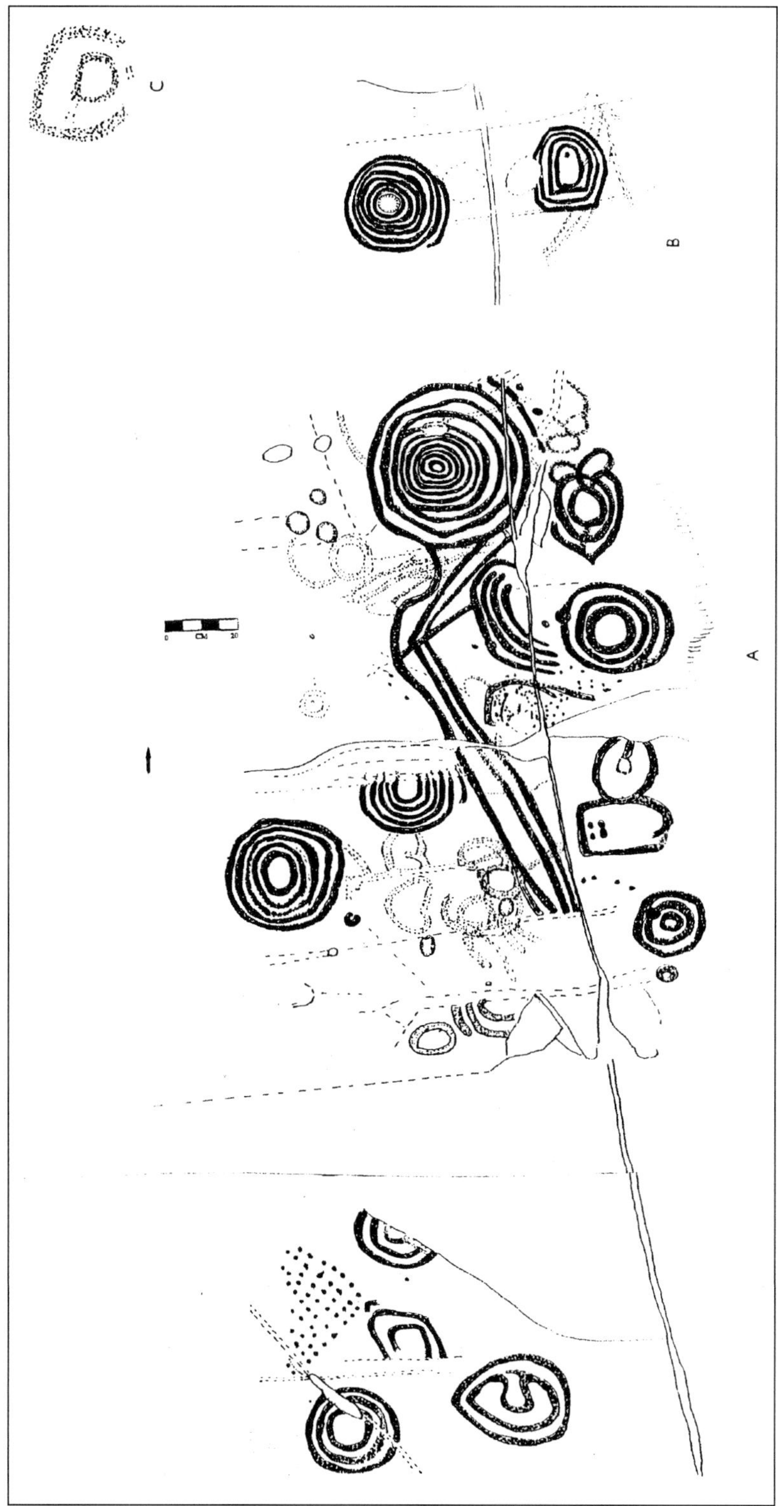

39 *Chapel Stile: the whole rock*

The motifs

A striking feature of the design is the number of concentric rings. The rings have an unworked centre, a boss. At the north end of the rock, isolated from other motifs, a large natural cup has been used as a centre for concentric rings. The rings are not perfect circles, but are formed by pecking from point to point in line sections; sometimes the use of a natural crack in the rock emphasises this angularity. It is a common characteristic of British rock art. The rings are generally close together, and in the figure with the greatest number of rings they are very tightly packed close to the centre, then the gap widens towards the outer ring. The angular arrangement of the grooves is clearly seen in the drawing. Not all the rings are complete. There are four concentric arcs.

A figure to the south on the panel is made up of two pear-shaped concentric grooves, but the inner groove has been formed into a loop in the centre. The natural cracks have some motifs focused on them, such as concentric rings or ovoids, and whether subsequent erosion and flaking have interfered with the fullness of the designs or whether the natural faults did not allow the design to continue is not clear.

Not all the designs are complete, and motifs may have been made at different times. One of the most unusual motifs is a cluster of pecked midget/micro cups that form a triangle. The lines of cups within the triangle are slightly curved, and one wonders whether it was intended to join these cups to form curved lines.

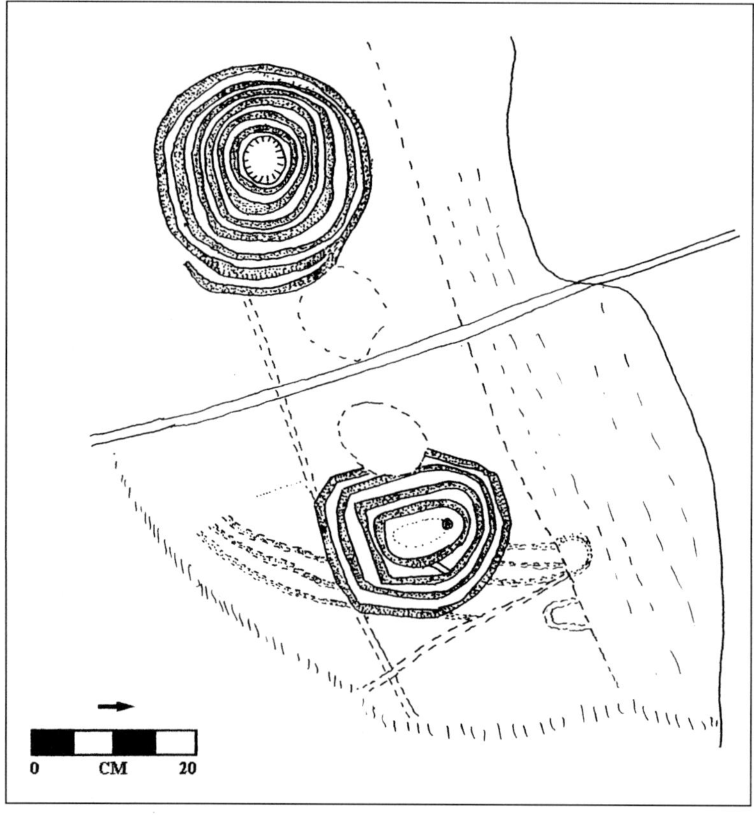

40 *Close detail of the motifs at the north end. More may be covered with moss*

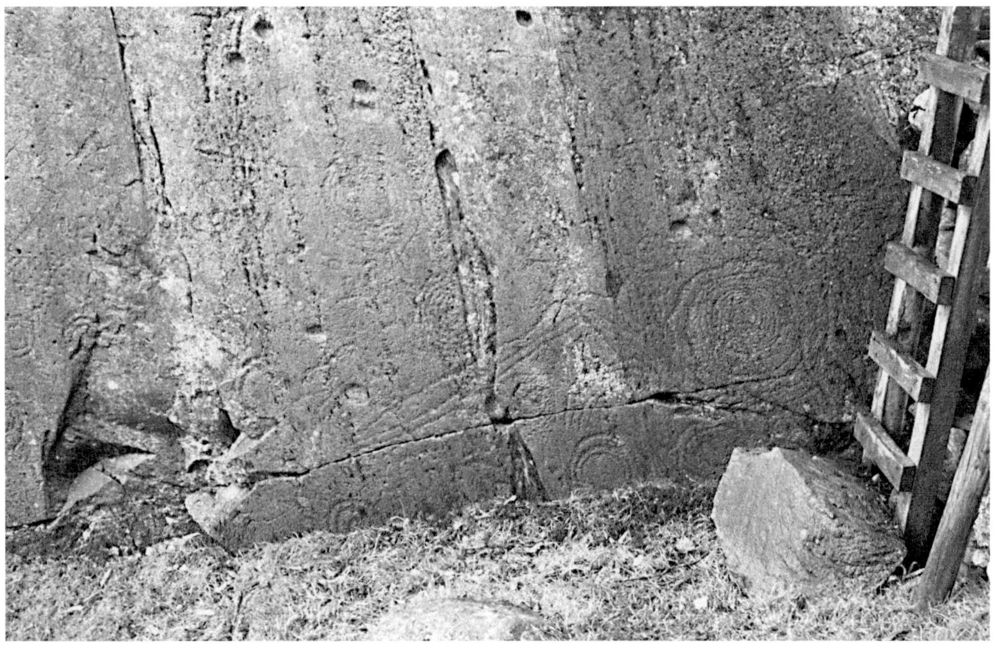

41 *The lower part of the rock face*

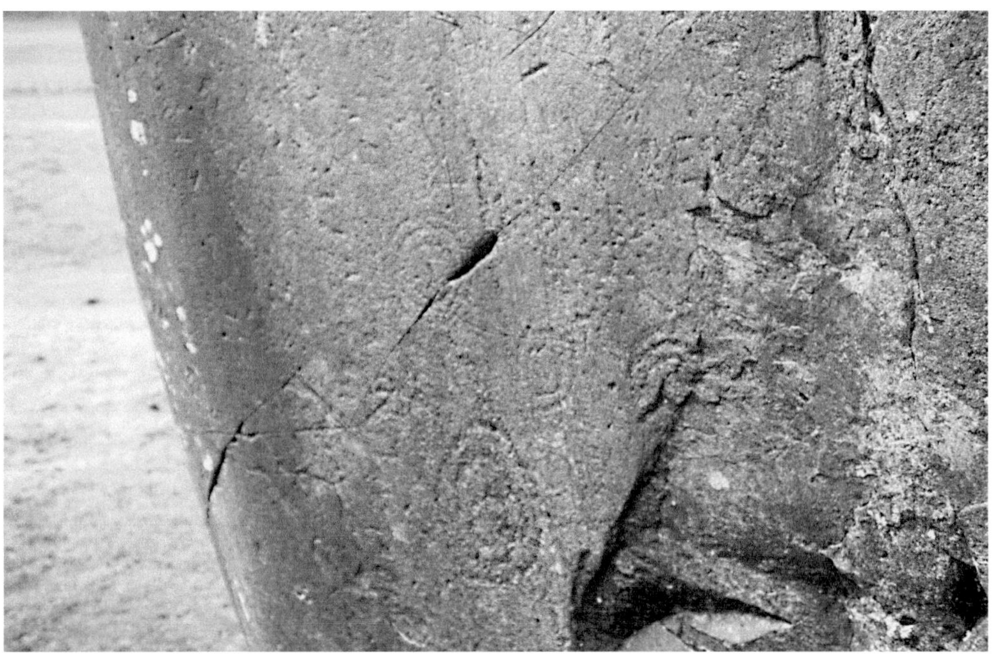

42 *The south part of the rock*

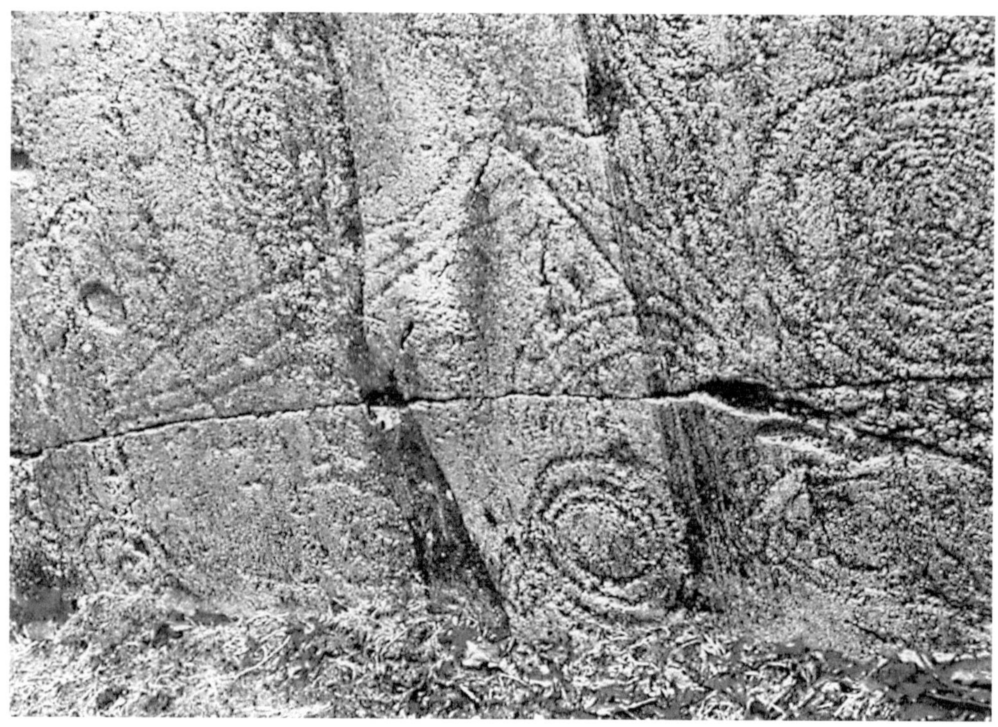

43 *Details of the lower motifs*

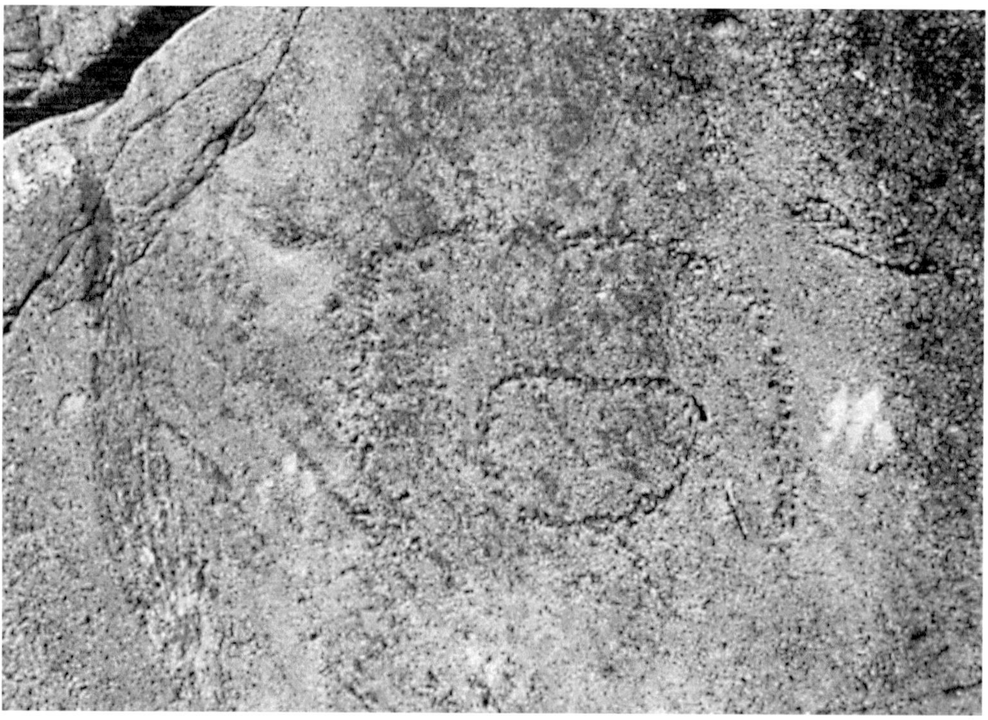

44 *A detached motif on a block to the east of the main one*

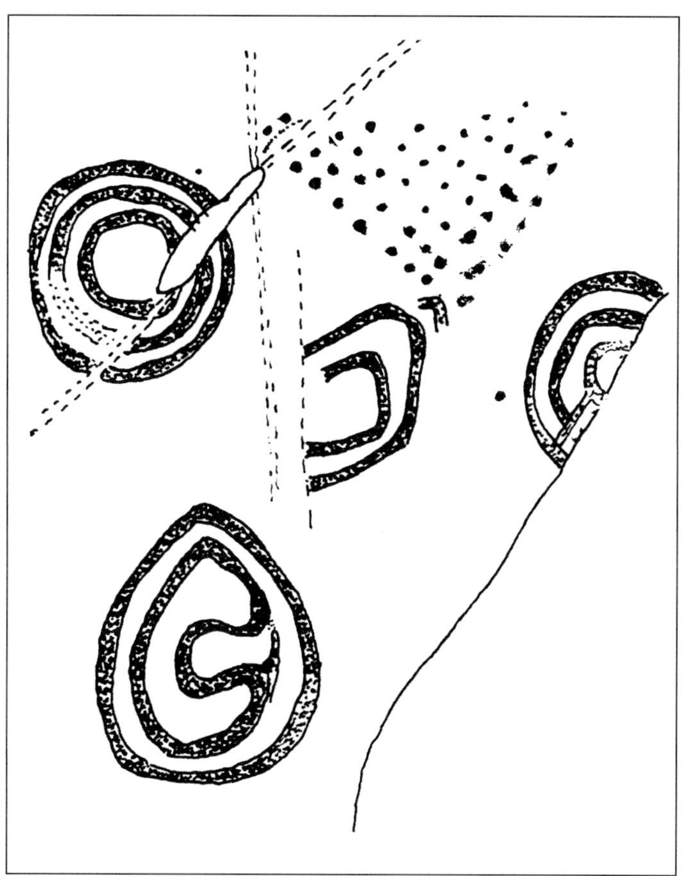

45 *The southern motifs*

46 *The far north end*

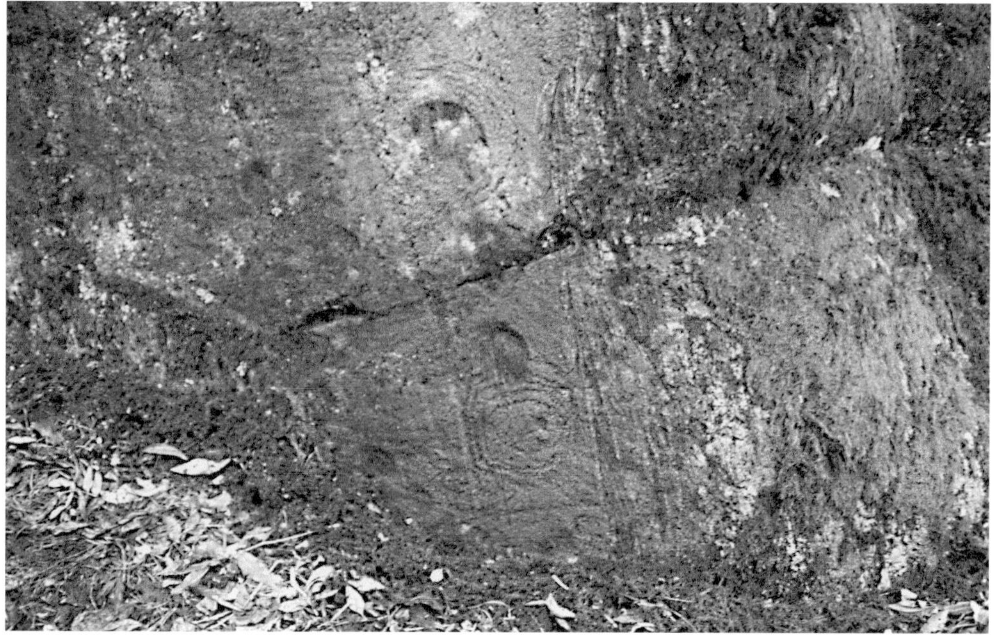

Some markings are much fainter than others, and may have preceded later motifs. There are many 'tentative' arcs on the rock. The more one examines the rock surface, the more possibilities there are of faint and unfinished motifs. There is the beginning of a small spiral in the centre section, and below that a heart-shaped groove and a faint occulus (eye shape). Further below is a cluster of oval motifs and lines radiating from them.

The most prominent motifs are the three parallel lines that run from south to north and form a chevron before breaking away: two remain together, and the top one links up via a curved groove to the outer ring of a large multiple-ringed figure centred on a small unworked circle. The chevrons are linked by an extra single groove to four concentric arcs. Above the loop that connects the top parallel groove to the multiple rings are several faintly pecked lines and a circle with an attached arc.

Below the horizontal crack at the base of the rock are varied grooved figures. One with three concentric rings has a cup in the second ring. There is a rectilinear grooved enclosure with four small cups inside, and an oval that intersects it. A figure with three concentric rings, one of which has a cup in it, has an attached arc. Two concentric rings have a curvilinear groove touching the outer ring in two places.

To the north there are two figures, one above the other. The top one is centred on a cup-shaped hollow; it has six angular concentric rings and an extra arc from the outer one. Natural cracks form a frame into which the lower figure fits: four very irregular roughly concentric grooves. There appear to be three peck-marked parallel lines running in from the south, echoing the larger motif in the centre section, and traces of these lines running north away from the figure.

There may be more motifs under the moss to the north. There may be more pristine motifs below the present level of the grass. There may also be microscopic chippings of stone from the time when the motifs were made, and signs even of a tool. There is another motif on the rock face a few metres to the east, which appears tentative, and there may be more. There is a case for an excavation of the highest order here, and until that happens the site must not be touched.

There is evidence on the rock of the size of the tool used to make the marks. In the middle section above and below the horizontal crack are many small pick marks inside an angular arc. The triangle of slightly larger pick marks in the south section was made possibly with a likewise larger tool.

That all this visible evidence should have survived for at least 4000 years may be because the face is literally quite tough, vertical, and reasonably well sheltered. The modern 'writing' between the south and central section is luckily only limited vandalism.

The significance of this remarkable rock is not yet fully understood, and a wider archaeological search may give us more information. The motifs as a group are unparalleled in Britain. There are parallels between *individual* motifs and some in the Irish Boyne Valley Passage graves; they do not fit the 'cup and ring' tradition of neighbouring Northumberland. Assuming they are connected with the production of axes, these objects, that may have as much to do with status as practicality, are produced in the Neolithic and early Bronze Age, with an extensive market.

The motifs were most likely hammered into the rock at the same time as the axes were being made.

Meanwhile the rock is there, it is large, and it controls, visually, the comings and goings in one of the most important prehistoric valleys in the world. It is also a work of art in its own right, for the variety and combination of motifs is sensitive and skilled.

Connections and speculations

The Patterdale and Langdale sites incorporate the use of long grooves; at Patterdale the linear grooves echo some at Lordenshaw in Northumberland on a sloping surface, but their arrangement with so many cups is unprecedented. The Chapel Stile rock has concentric rings and ovoids with unmarked centres, like the concentric rings on Little Meg, Maryport and Glassonby. The chevrons are like those on the Glassonby kerbstone, but as a total composition Chapel Stile remains unique.

Paul and Barbara Brown have produced their own interesting scenario for the location in Langdale; here timber was felled in prehistoric times to make rafts for transporting goods on water, including the prized axes, to Lake Windermere. There would have been abundant birds and animals for food, fur, feathers and skins. Perhaps the community that specialised in axe production would have had a service community on its doorstep. Perhaps some of the rough outs of axes could have been polished here.

Today the land belongs to the National Trust and has a tenant farmer. Although it is private, there is a gate in the wall opposite a small lay-by on the only road, and one can see the decorated surface from this spot.

Similarities between this kind of rock art with curvilinear designs in Ireland suggest a link across the Irish Sea, but it is not clear from which direction the link was made.

To find further examples of 'art in the landscape' (i.e. not on monuments), we move to the far north east of Cumbria, where discoveries are fairly recent.

Tortie Cottage, Hallbankgates (HO111-2 NY589578)

In an area of rough, upland pasture, scarred by extensive mining, a boulder on the side of a rounded, quarried hill and a large block of stone face each other across a small stream.

'Tortie', the name of the cottage, probably means 'shaped like a tortoise', and it is so unusual that it is worth noting some other Cumbrian examples: Tortie (1387 Midgeholme); Torty, 1859; Tartais, 1603; the Tartoyse and Tartaisrigge, 1603 (Spadeadam). The name may have been transferred to this site, but the hill here fits the description. Another strong contender for meaning is that Tortie is a diminutive of a tortoiseshell cat.

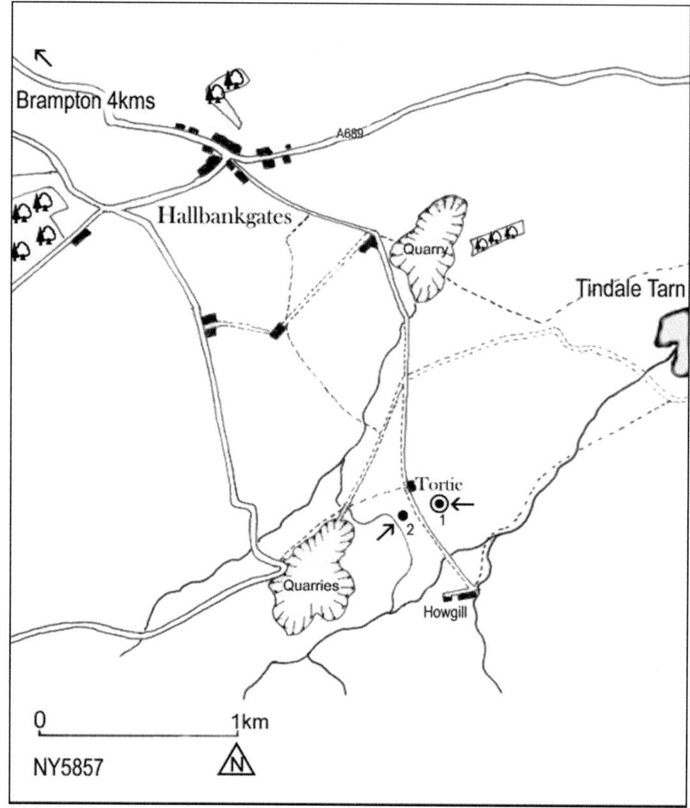

47 *The Tortie sites*

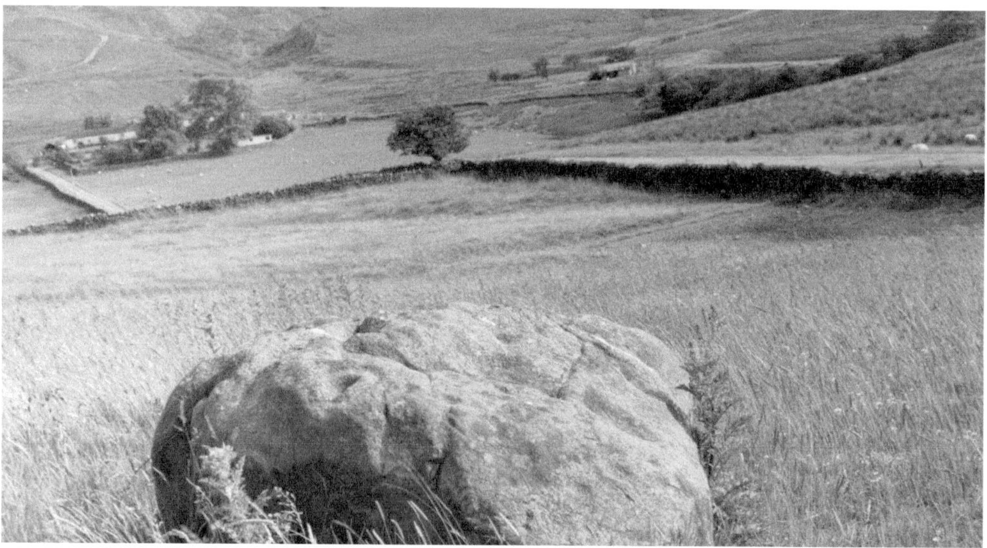

48 *Tortie 1*

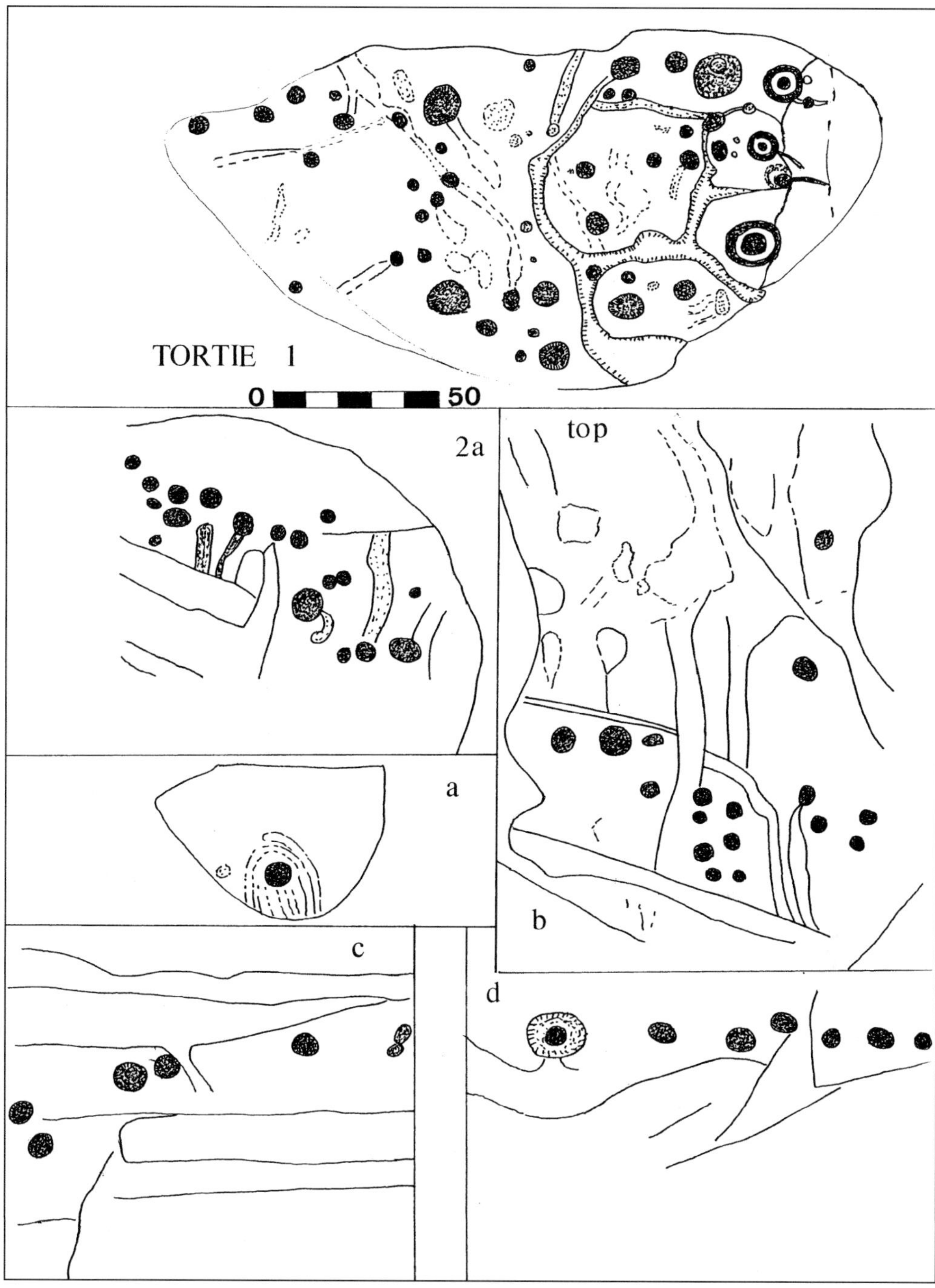

49 *Tortie: all the markings on the two rocks*

Tortie 1 (NY598578)

Colin Richardson excavated the site of stone 1, discovered by Jennifer Waldron in 1987, in 1988. It lies on a slope that faces south west.

Before excavation, the large earthfast sandstone boulder appeared to be embedded in a mound, but the discovery of a socket hole suggests that one of its original functions was as a standing stone, later to fall and to accumulate material around it, perhaps as field clearance. The present north end would have slotted into the socket with the ringed cups at the base. Other stones in the field, of limestone, sandstone with some glacial erratics, some almost completely buried, suggest possible settings and alignments that can only be understood by further excavation. An earth and stone wall that runs east of the stone towards the hill in the north-east becomes a double line at one place. This 'extra' linear mound has a small standing stone with a cup mark to the east, and could be the remains of a track or avenue, or it could be connected with quarrying activity.

The stone could be part of a more complex arrangement, but whatever the case it is clear that its position, although not the highest point in the immediate landscape, commands extensive views and can be seen from the hills.

Low-light observations and wax rubbing have revealed cup marks over the whole surface of the boulder, three complete rings around three of the cups and a partial ring around another. The grooves that form the rectilinear feature are largely natural, but enlarged in part, with a cup pecked into the groove.

Tortie 2 (NY588587)

This table-like block of sandstone has distinct cups made on its vertical sides, but nothing artificial on top. It has been a favourite local picnic site for years. It was probably dropped into position by ice.

2 (a) east has a ledge with a cup, but the half-ovoids picked out by the rubbing and included in the drawing are probably natural as part of the strike of the rock. The vertical surface above this ledge has clear cups, some related to grooves.

2 (b) faces north, with cups mainly close to the base.

2 (c) faces south, and *2 (d)* faces west.

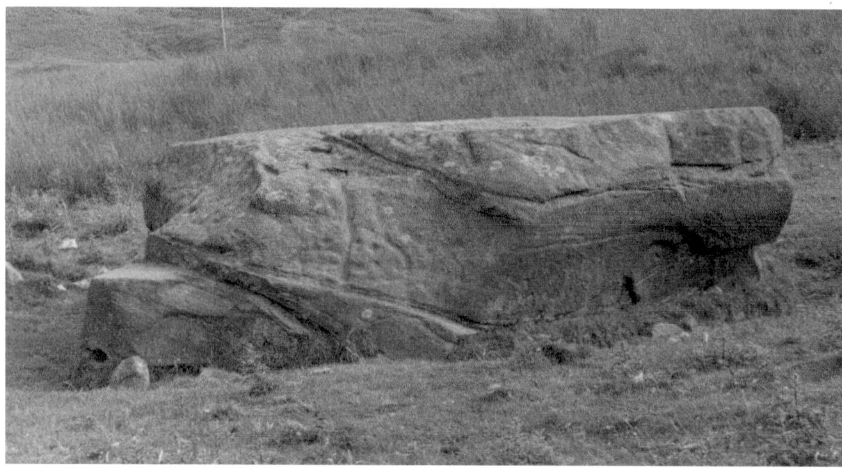

50 *Tortie 2*

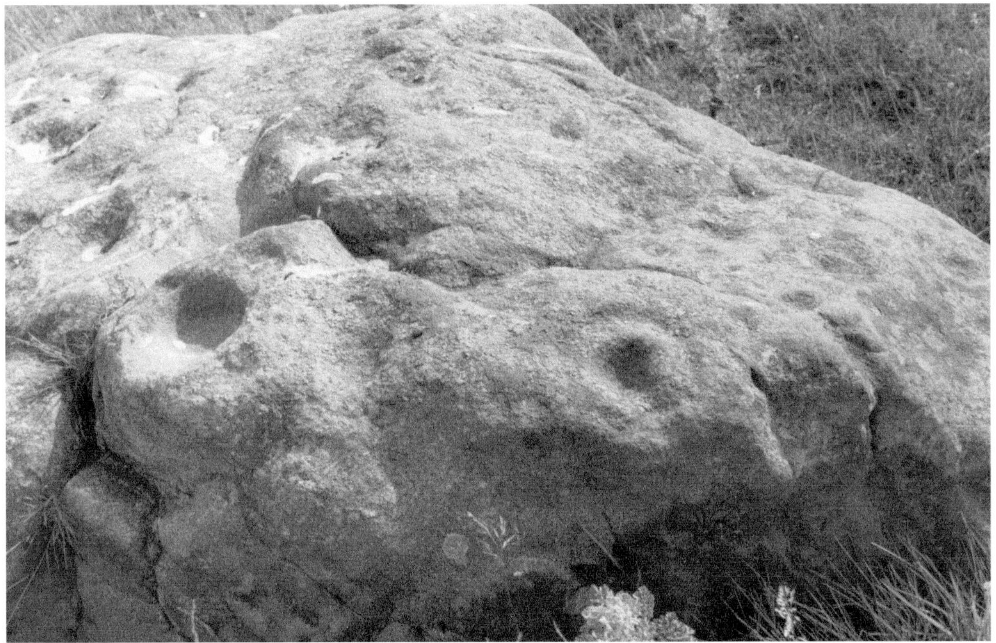

51 *Tortie 1*

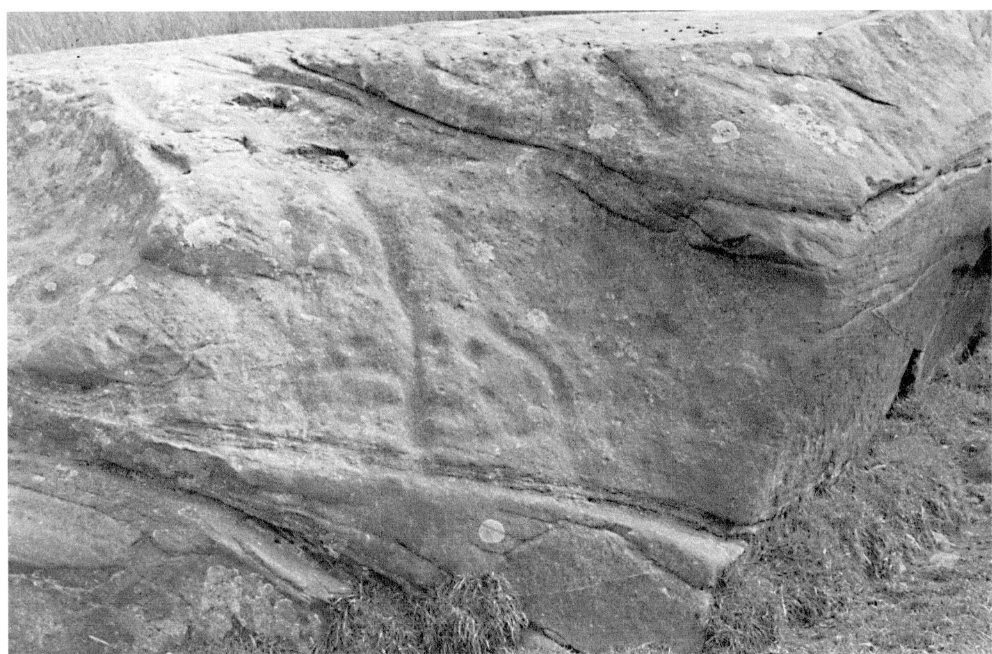

52 *Tortie 2*

Tabular blocks like this (e.g. Fontburn in Northumberland) are usually marked on the top surface; not so here. The rock at Old Bewick (Northumberland) has its most elaborate decoration on top, but there is also a horizontal line of cup marks on its vertical surface. Why the top surface of the Tortie rock is not decorated is unknown.

The next site is described here because it lies in the same region of Cumbria. The marked boulders described may be part of monuments rather than 'landscape' art.

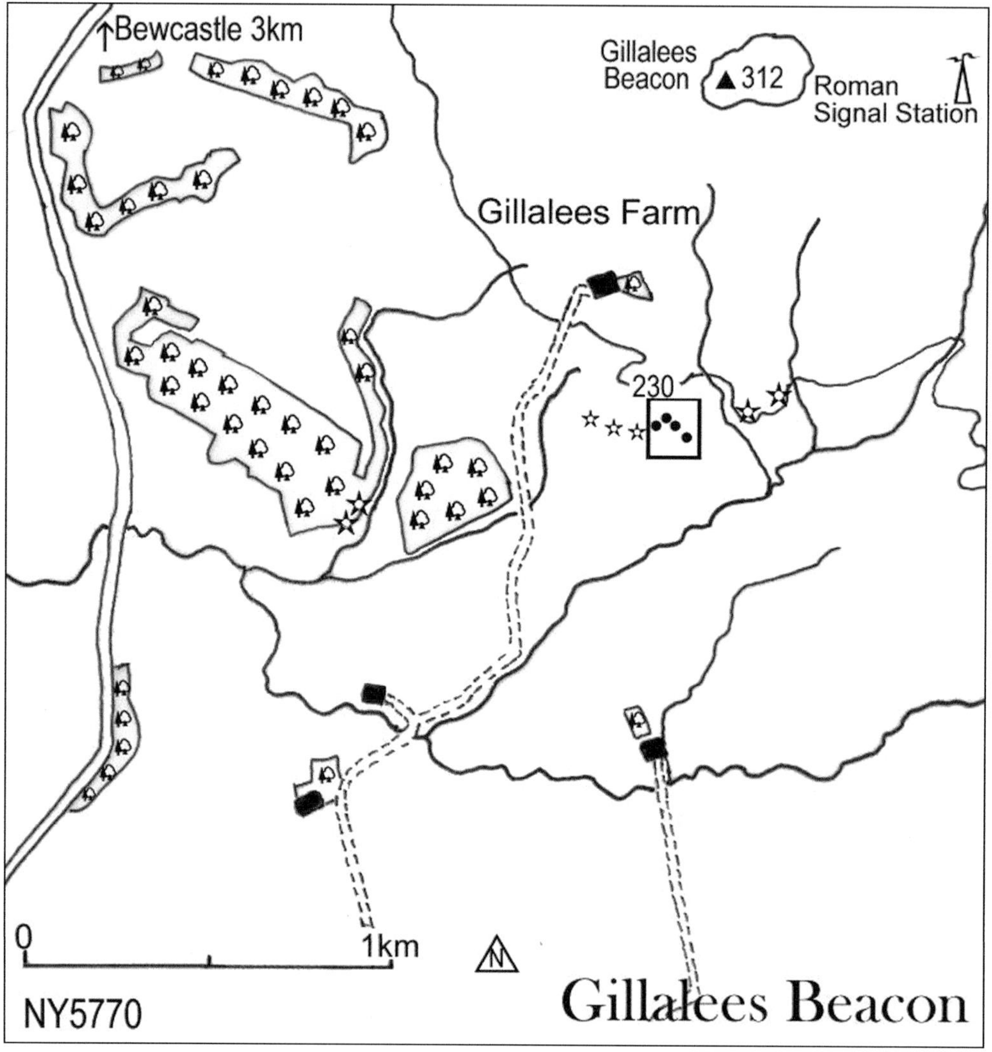

53 *Gillalees site location*

Gillalees (H001121 NY57127088)

The name may mean Gille's Fields. The site is reached by a private narrow metalled road from the B6385 Greenhead road via West Hall and Rinnion Hills. It borders a military Danger Area.

Just before you reach the farm field gate there is a partly quarried low sandstone ridge. The continuation of this ridge east towards two massive mounds has smaller mounds on it, and to the north, roughly parallel, are earthfast boulders in the rig and furrow, four that are marked. Only one had been previously reported, and I discovered the others in 1992. The link between burials, trackways and motifs is important, and more fieldwork is needed in this area.

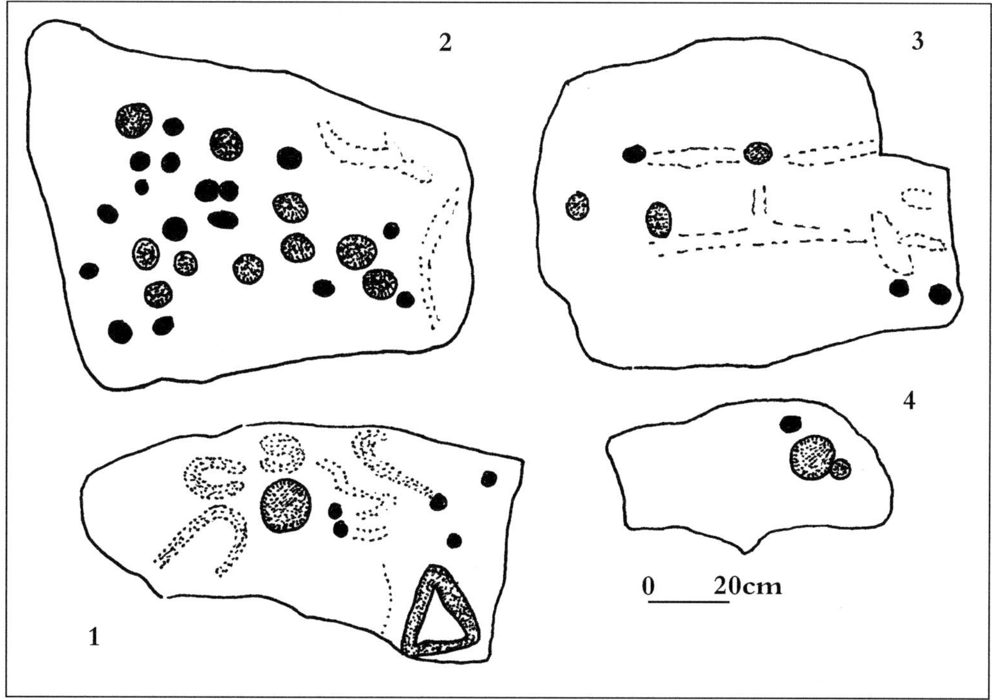

54 The drawings show cup marks of various sizes and depths, some oval. The triangle and large cup on No.1 are deep, but there are shallow curved grooves too, some very faint. The triangle is a rare motif

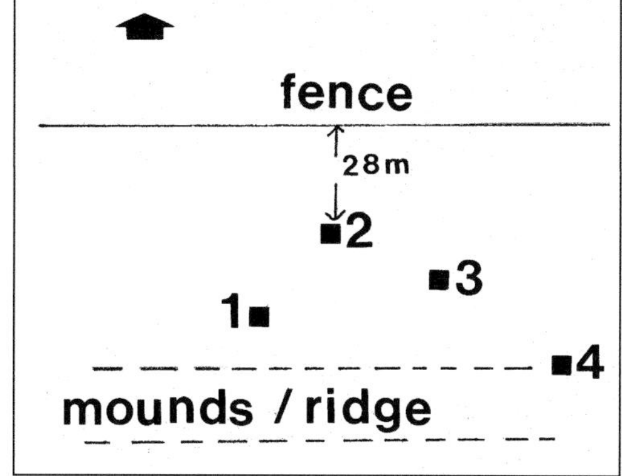

55 Sketch map of the locations of the above

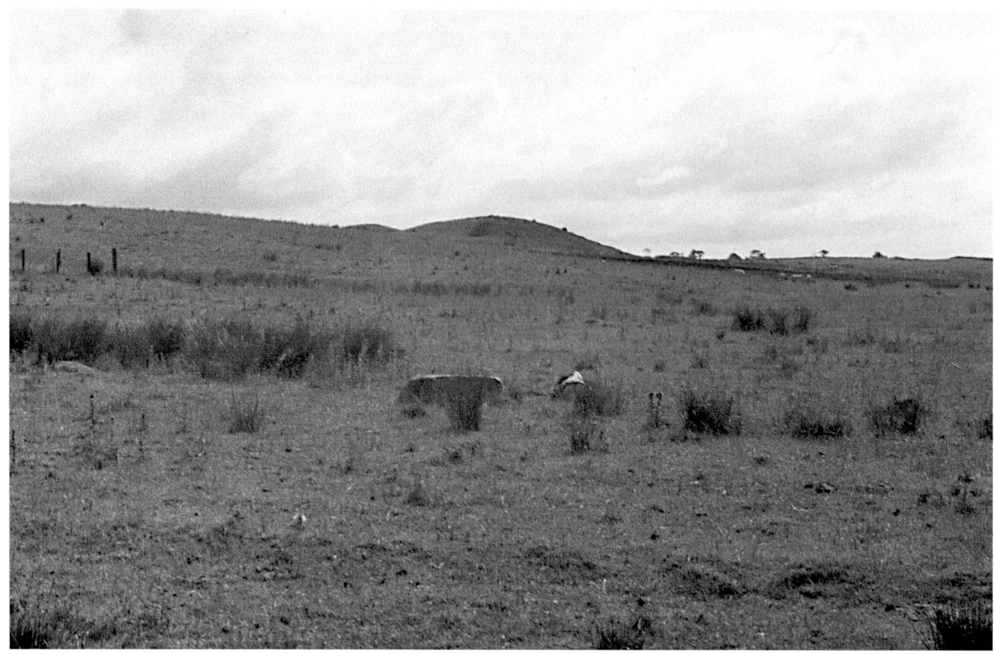

56 *Gillalees locations*

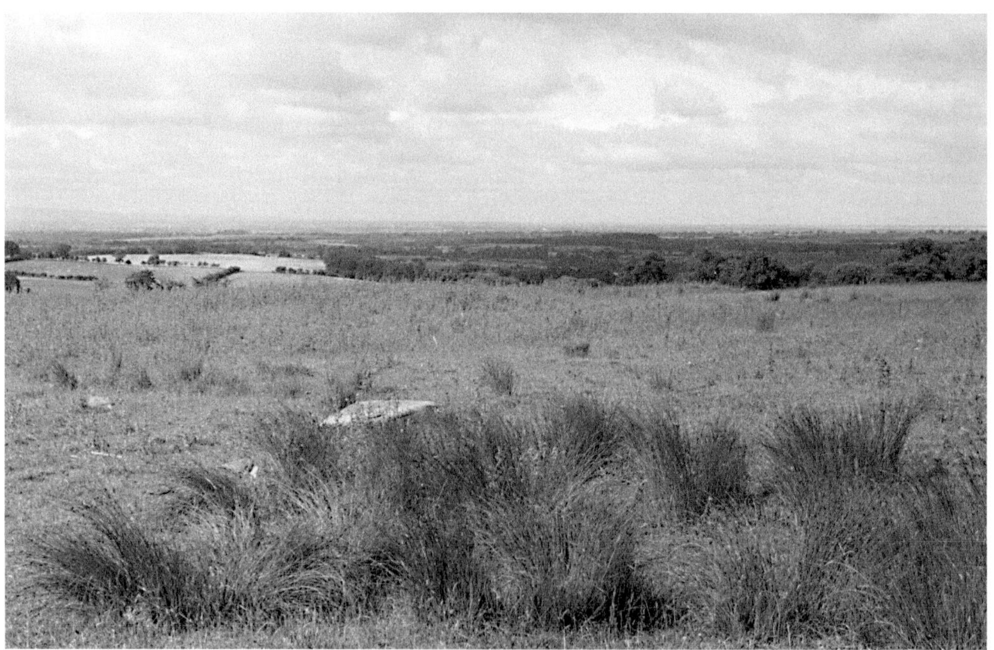

57 *Gillalees locations*

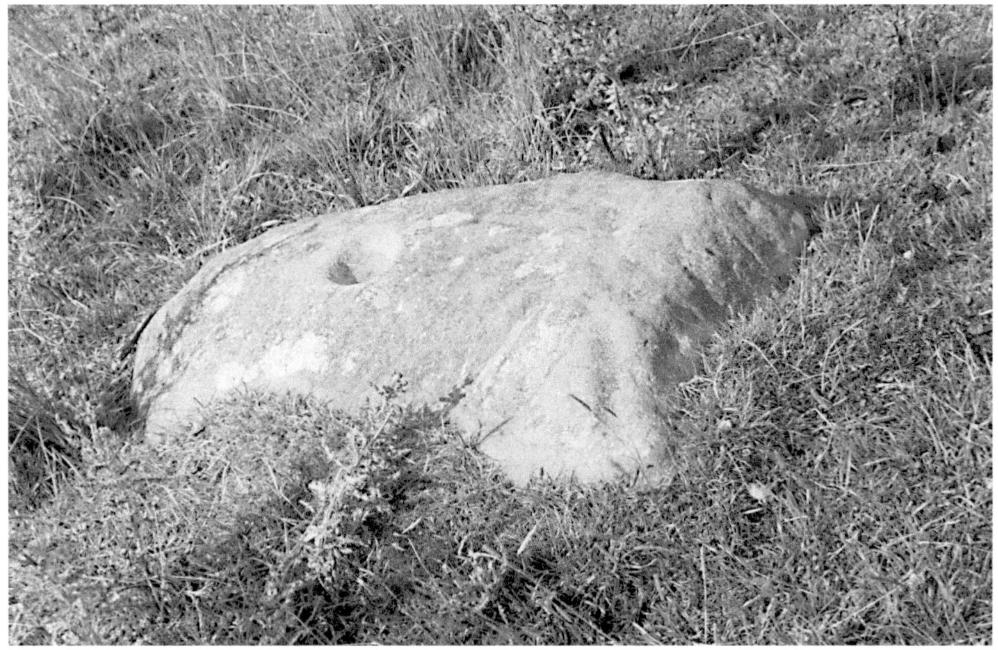

58 *Gillalees: cup-marked earthfast boulder*

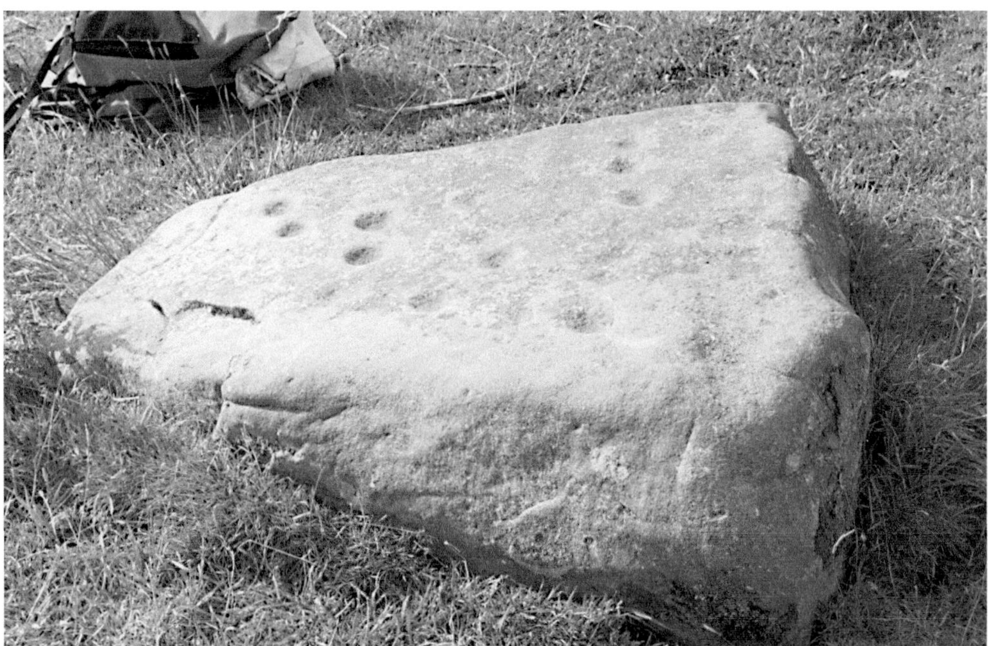

59 *Gillalees: cup-marked slab*

3 Circular monuments and rock art

Henges and stone circles

Cumbria is a land of dramatic stone circles and henges. It is thought that the earliest stone circles, dated to around 3500 BC, may have been constructed in Ireland, but the start of circle building in Cumbria 300 years later establishes the major tradition in Britain.

Monuments such as these capture and store meaning, and are meant to be enduring. We have records of over 1000 stone circles in Britain, but there are also circular ditched enclosures, embanked enclosures, circles of wooden posts, and thousands of round burial mounds.

There is something intrinsically satisfying about a circle, and when people are arranged for a discussion in a circle instead of sitting as though in a bus, there is more sense of equality, of participation. The circle can exclude some people, although they may look in from the outside if there is no big barrier. Those inside can be in a privileged position, and look outwards.

Only a few stone circles are directly associated with rock art, but many see in the circular motifs of cups and rings a common impulse and symbolism. As the Cumbrian henge sites and stone circles form clusters in some areas, especially around Penrith, we shall now look at two of the most significant henges, bearing in mind that some stones circles began their lives as henges and show clear signs of enclosing ditches and circles of stone. This will also provide some additional sites of interest for the reader to visit within the same areas as the rock art, although no motifs have yet been found there.

Mayburgh Henge (NY519285) lies between the village of Eamont and the M6. The henge is a gapped ring made as a huge wall of boulders and cobble stones enclosing a circular area 87m (287ft) in diameter. Although there is only one stone standing inside this enclosure, the others having been blown up, it is one of only 13 British henges out of 78 that have stone circles inside them. There used to be an additional four stones flanking the entrance gap.

King Arthur's Round Table (NY523284) is visible close by. It is different in style, having a circular ditch interrupted by two causewayed entrances (i.e. the ground has been left undug there to form a bridge). The upcast from the ditch forms a surrounding bank. The site had another small henge that was destroyed when a new approach to Lowther Park lodge gates was made in 1878. Much archaeology has been destroyed at the two still-visible sites.

56

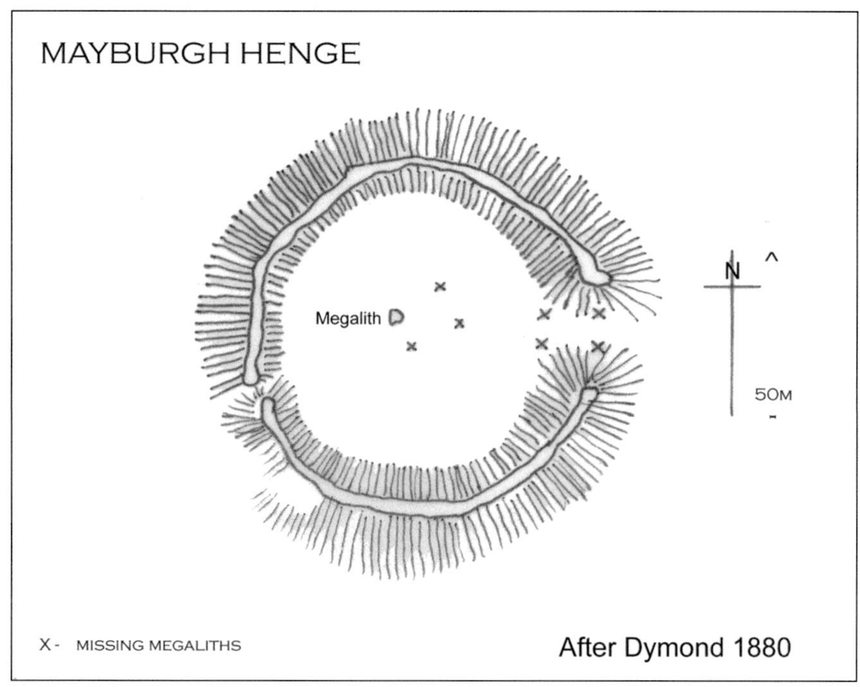

60 *Mayburgh henge*

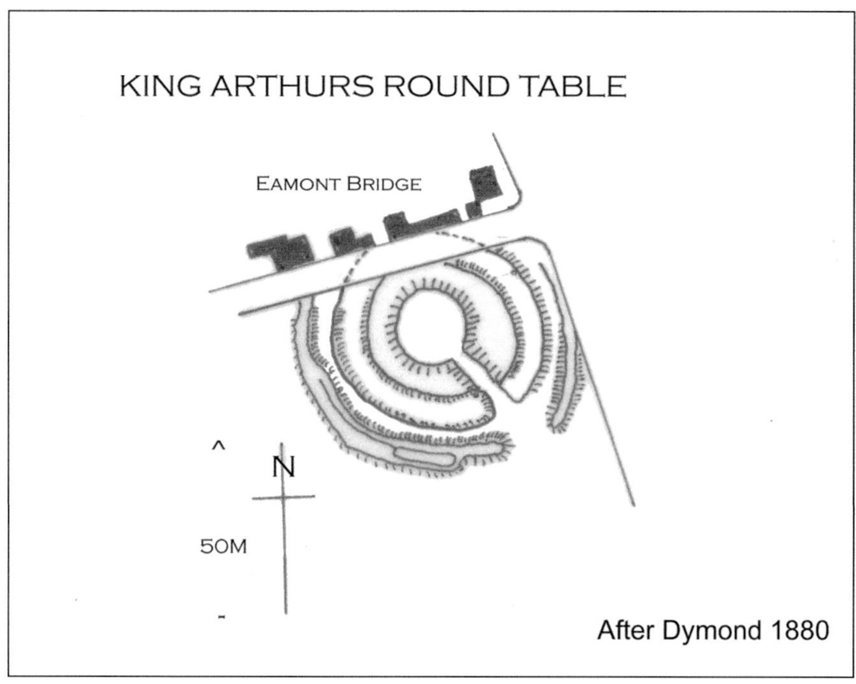

61 *King Arthur's Round Table*

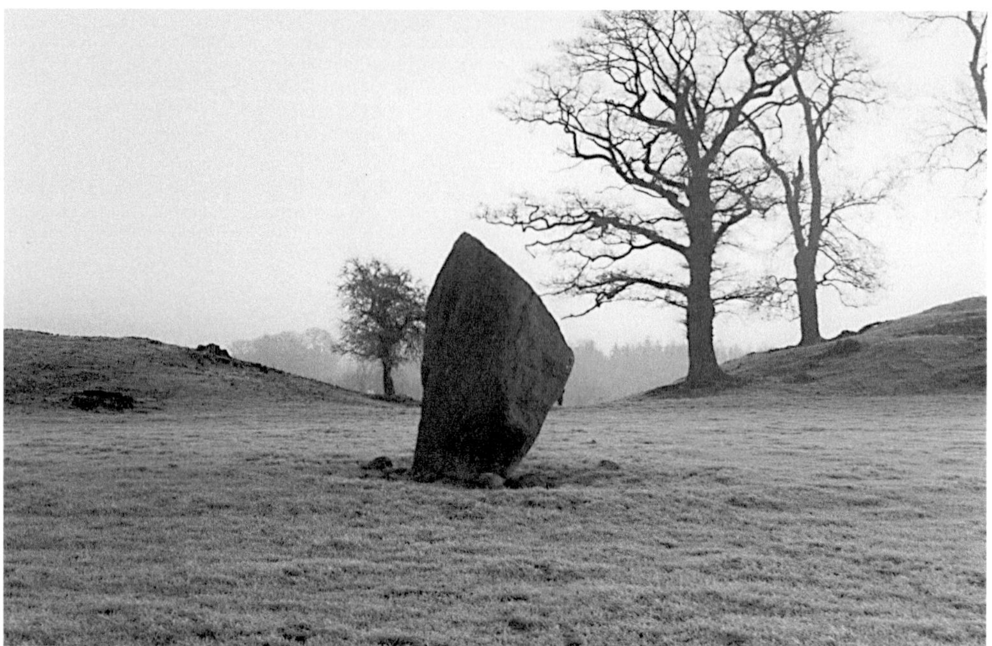

62 *Mayburgh henge: a solitary stone at its centre is all that remains of a setting of several others. The entrance frames the stone at the top of the picture. No rock art has been found at this site or the next, in contrast to Long Meg where there are similar circular monumental structures*

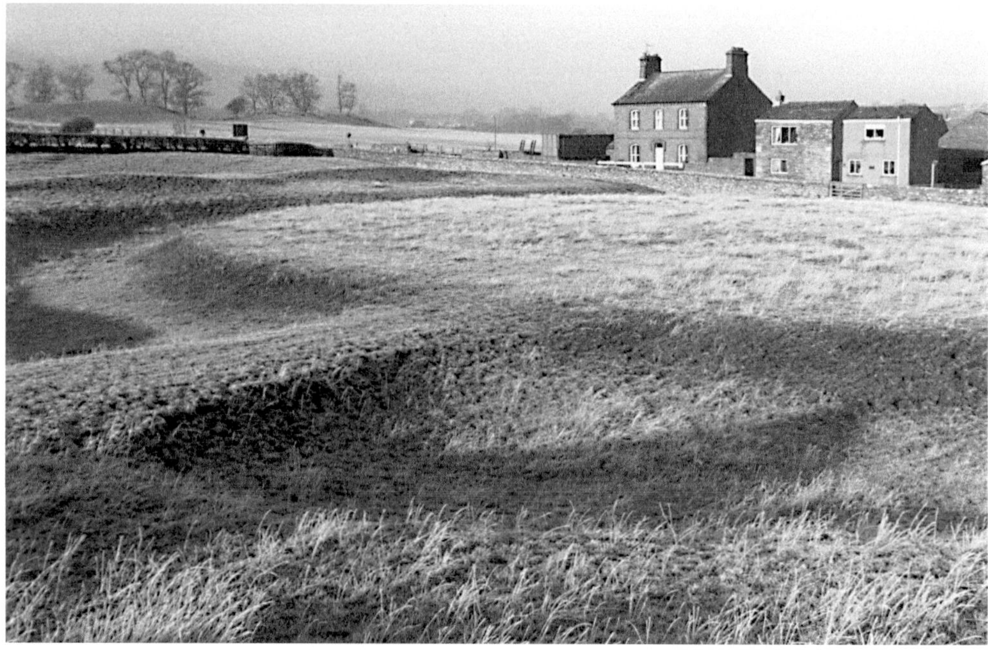

63 *King Arthur's Round Table became a tea garden and had its outer ditch cut off for the construction of a road*

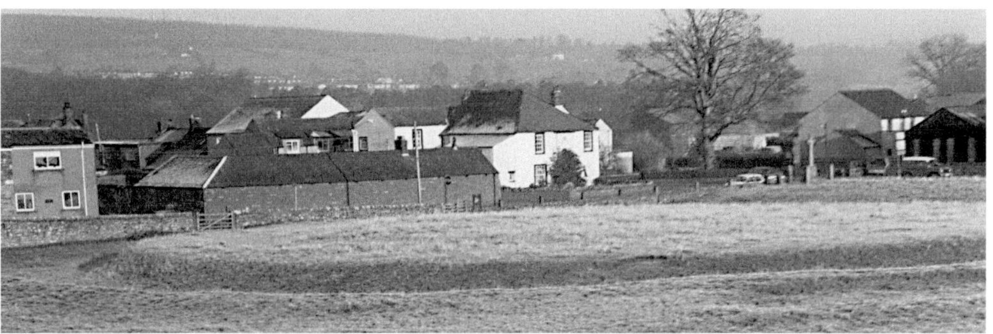

64 *Eamont village beyond the henge*

The importance of this clustering of monuments becomes particularly relevant when we move east of Penrith to look at stone circles that include rock art.

Long Meg and her Daughters (HO1101 NY571372)

This site is protected by law, has free access, and is easily reached by road, $5\frac{1}{2}$ miles from Penrith and 2 miles north of Langwathby. The name Penrith is of Welsh origin, and means 'the main ford'. This watery connection continues with Langwathby (settlement at the long ford) and Salkeld (a wood where the sallows grew).

If Long Meg is approached from the south, the tall pillar of red sandstone is visible before the other stones. The site is high above water, and built on a slope. Its name belongs to obscure legend of the type that attributed many stone circles to the work of devils and witches, or warned the wicked of retribution, for here are 70 or so petrified witches who have transgressed and been punished. There is confusion in the historical record about the number of stones, and there are legends about such stones being uncountable!

Long Meg was a witch, and her daughters may have been turned to stone for dancing on the Sabbath. The site is a huge ceremonial enclosure, but instead of having walls and a ditch like a henge, stones were used to make a circle, flattened to the north. The value of air photography is nowhere better demonstrated, for crop and parch marks taken with infrared film show that Long Meg is not alone. There are other enclosures on the terrace of land, the most impressive being a huge interrupted ditch that surrounds the present farm and runs against the flattened north part of the circle. There is nothing to be seen of this on the ground, and further details can only be revealed by excavation. It looks as though the flattened part of the stone circle deliberately takes this ditched enclosure into account, suggesting that it was visible at the time the stone circle was constructed, and in use at the same time. This alters considerably our view of Long Meg.

We also know from Stukeley in 1725 that there was a smaller stone circle near by, although there is no trace of it now, and the aerial photograph shows an egg-shaped enclosure east of the large circle, and an enclosure south of Brustop Wood. Today the centre appears empty, but in the seventeenth century John Aubrey quotes from Sir William Dugdale: 'In the middle are two Tumuli, or barrowes of cobble-stones, nine or ten feet high.' There is also a legend about a 'Giant's bone and Body found there.'

It is probable that later burials were placed inside the circle, covered with cobbles from the surrounding area, and any interference with such mounds could have led to the discovery of bones. As animal deposits might also have been made, the discovery of giants may be accounted for by an inability to distinguish between some animal and human bone. Stone circles are not cemeteries, even though they may have included human burial during their building and use. Fire, charcoal, cremation and burial all play a part in stone circle ritual. The place chosen for this centre of a scattered community can have 'power' without our having to discover mysterious lines of force or other emanations. Its position in the landscape, the views that it commands, can explain its choice as a meeting place and ritual centre. The building of a monument like Long Meg can be a more impressive testimony to the 'sanctity' of a site that may have been used for hundreds of years, and the choice of this place can be complex beyond our understanding.

Wordsworth wrote of it:

> Though it will not bear a comparison with Stonehenge, I must say, I have not seen any other relique of those dark ages which can pretend to rival it in singularity and dignity of appearance.

What he did not know was that the whole terrace, extending to Little Meg, Glassonby and Old Parks has major sites of ritual activity that range from the

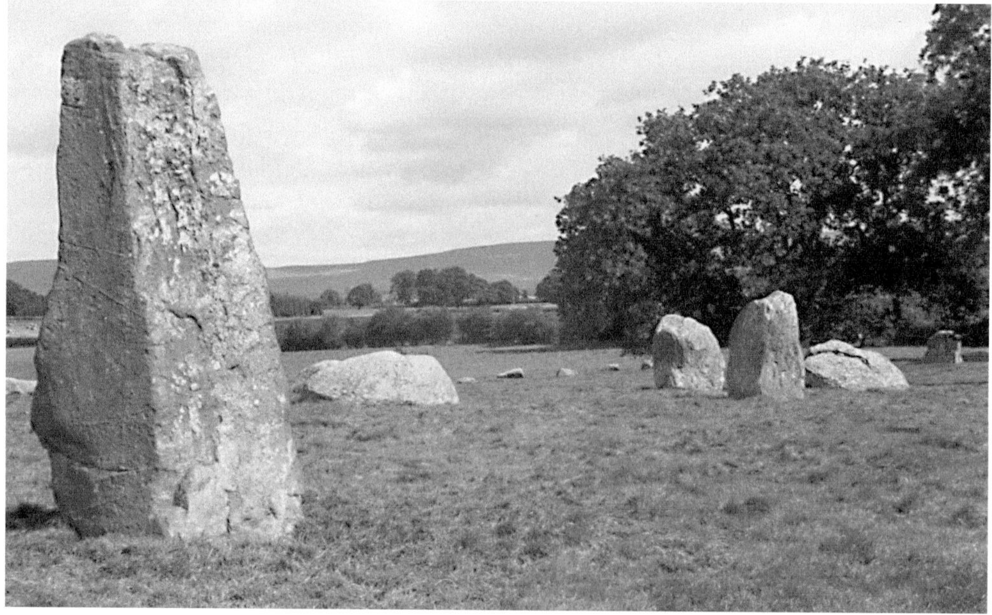

65 *Long Meg, with the portal stones to the right*

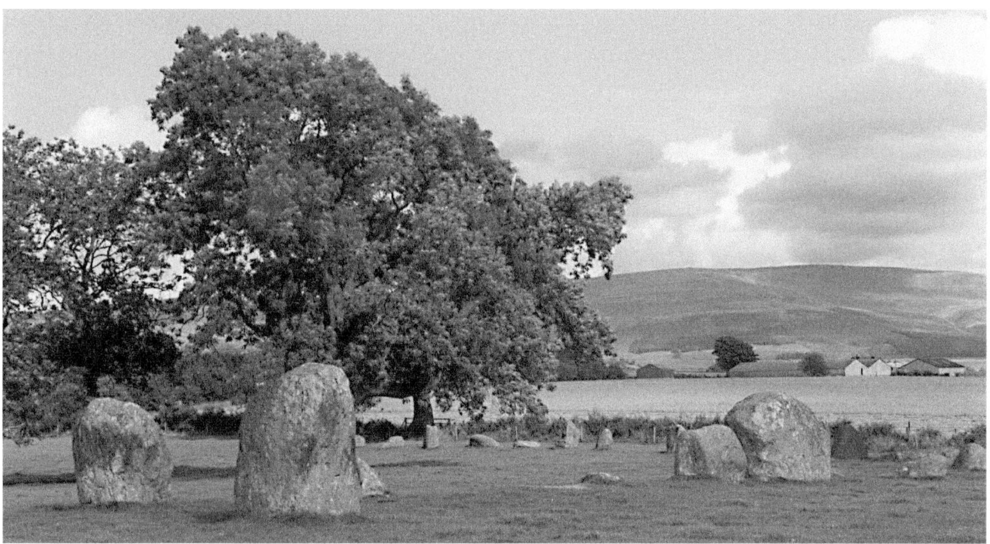

66 *The Long Meg stone circle, with the Pennines in the background*

Neolithic to the early Bronze Age, and that the motifs pecked into the stone were part of this ritual.

The stones of the circle are glacial igneous and metamorphic erratics that were probably lifted from the nearby land surface. The average block weighs nine tonnes. Two of the largest blocks are placed singly to the east and west and weigh about 30 tonnes. The south-west entrance has two extra stones outside the circumference, and this forms a 'portal', a doorway into the circle. It is outside this portal that Long Meg is found, aligned from the centre of the circle on the point of the midwinter sunset.

Long Meg dwarfs the other stones, and the choice of red sandstone further emphasises the difference. Unlike the glacial erratics, this is sedimentary, and may have come from cliffs flanking the River Eden $1\frac{1}{2}$ miles away, or from Lazonby Fells. It is 3.8m high and weighs about 9 tonnes. However, it is the choice of this rock for a display of symbols and motifs that gives it a very special role at the site.

The 'witch' idea could have come from the 'nose' shape and the long head or hat. The broad side that looks towards the circle is covered with motifs; the rest is unmarked. Aubrey Burl (Burl, 1999) says this:

> From the middle of the ring it is not central to the entrance but is in line with the western circle-stone and portal. Almost rectangular in section its surfaces are roughly weathered except the east side, which is smoother and angled 64 degrees from True North. This is a full 20 degrees from the bearing between the middle of the circle and Long Meg and is a good reason for believing that the pillar was there long before the ring. If not, from the evidence of other sites, the flattest and best edge should have faced the circle.

Burl sees its positioning as an example of 'solar precision'.

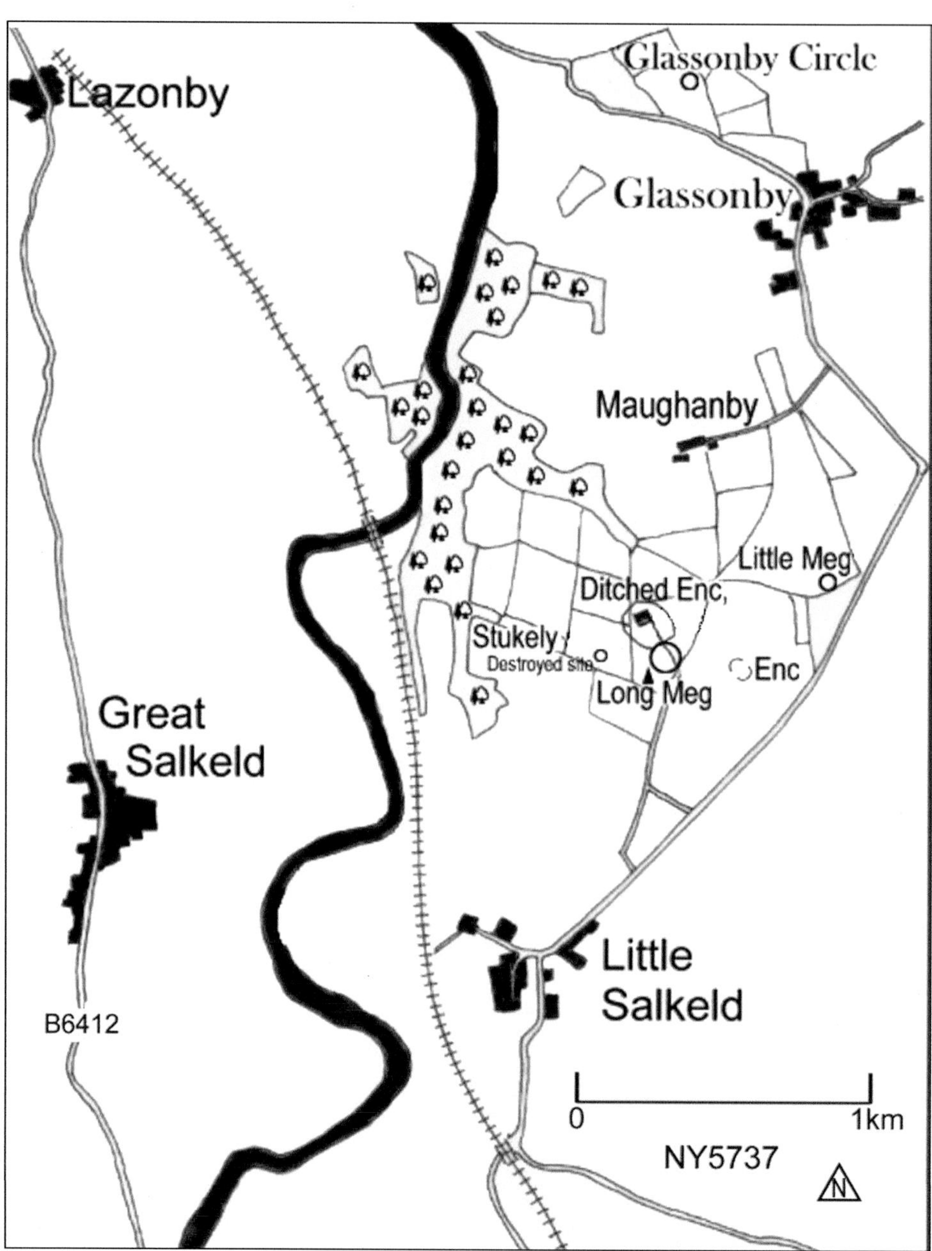

67 *The prehistoric sites of Long Meg, Little Meg and Glassonby*

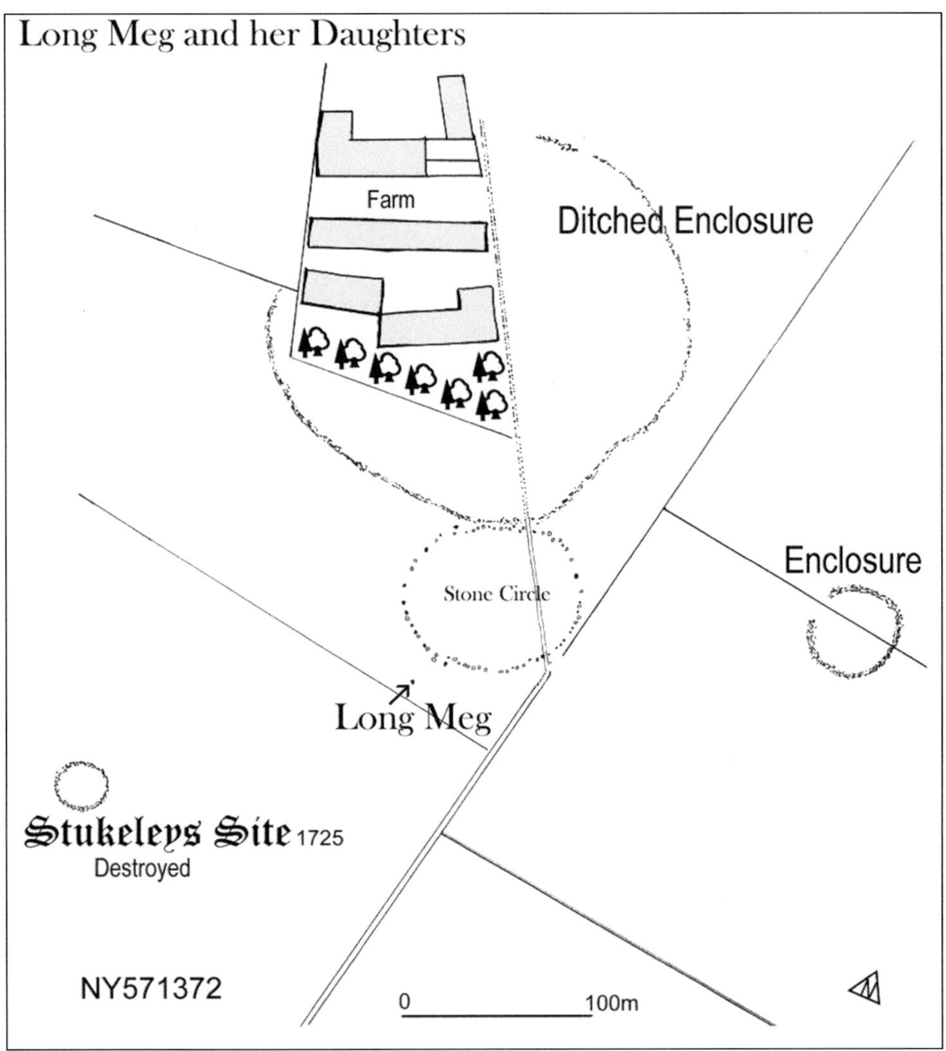

68 *Long Meg and hidden enclosures*

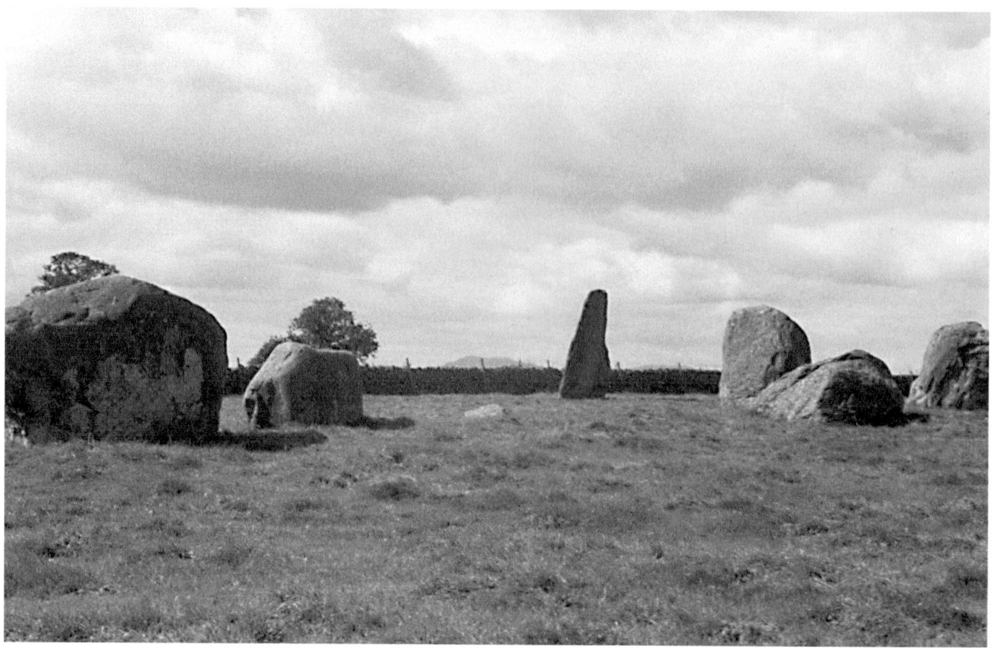

69 *Long Meg through the portal entrance, with the Lake District mountains beyond*

The question of the chronological relationship between Long Meg and her daughters remains open, because the stone could have been brought in, already marked, from elsewhere to add further significance to the stone circle; but Burl's argument is convincing.

The motifs

There have been reports of markings on Long Meg since 1835, when Sir Gardner Wilson observed the cup and concentric rings. In 1867 Sir J.Y. Simpson of Edinburgh included it in his *Archaic Sculpturings of Cups, Circles, &c.* The drawing is included here. In June 1940 a survey by Harvey revealed three groups.

Not many people have appreciated the full extent of the motifs because they are difficult to see unless the light is strong and coming in at an angle that throws the grooves into deep shadow.

The central section

The most obvious motif is a cup at the centre of three rings, with a groove meeting the circumference at a tangent. There is an additional concentric arc at the top, and the beginnings of another. Much fainter are two ovoids that meet the arc.

Slightly less visible below is a spiral of four turns that rotates anti-clockwise. It has a thin arc above it that meets two very faint concentric circles that lie between the spiral and concentric circle motifs. This group includes a tentatively pecked-out (unfinished?) figure of two concentric arcs that form around a line of small cup- or pick-marks.

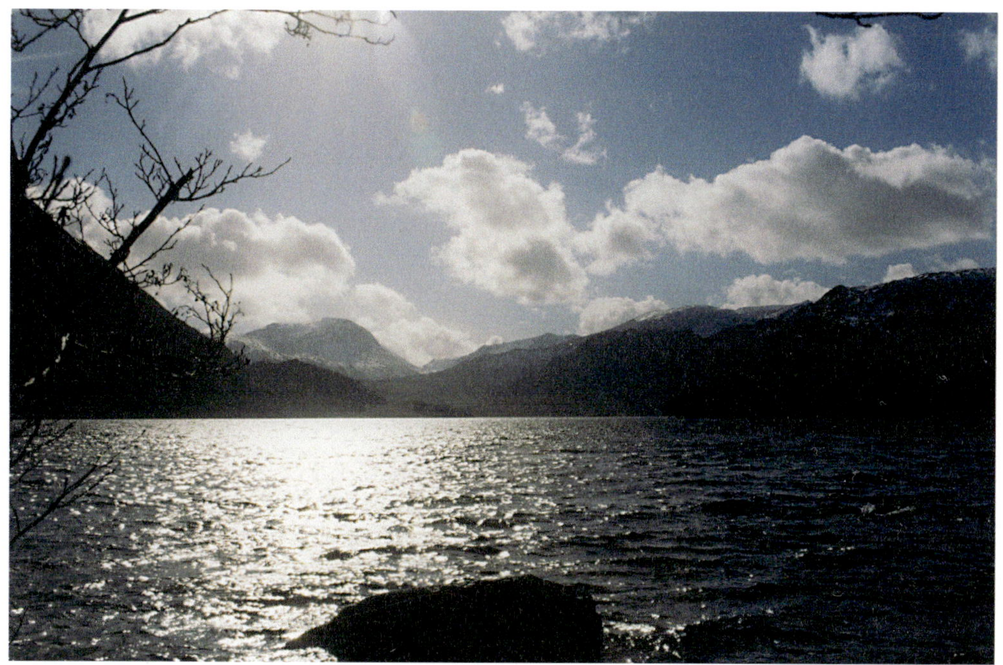

1 Ullswater

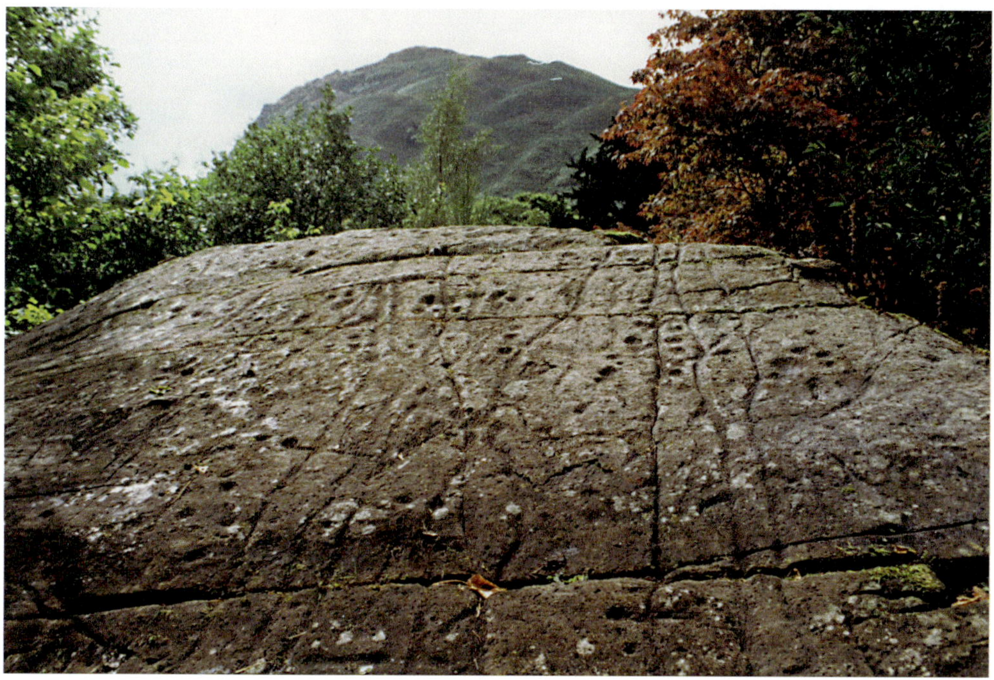

2 Patterdale site 2

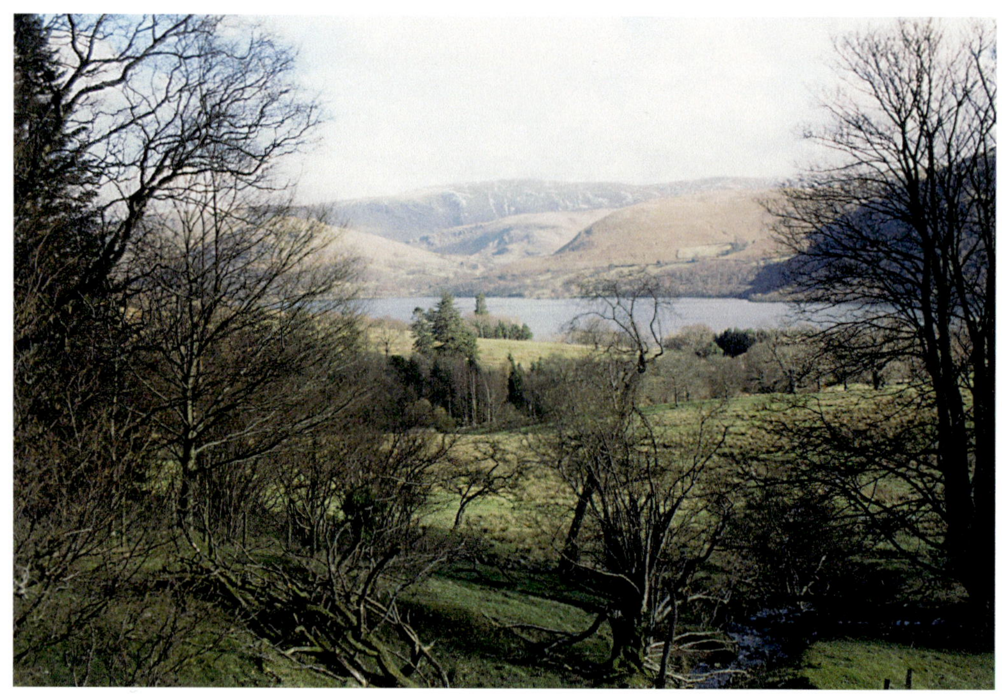

3 Ullswater valley

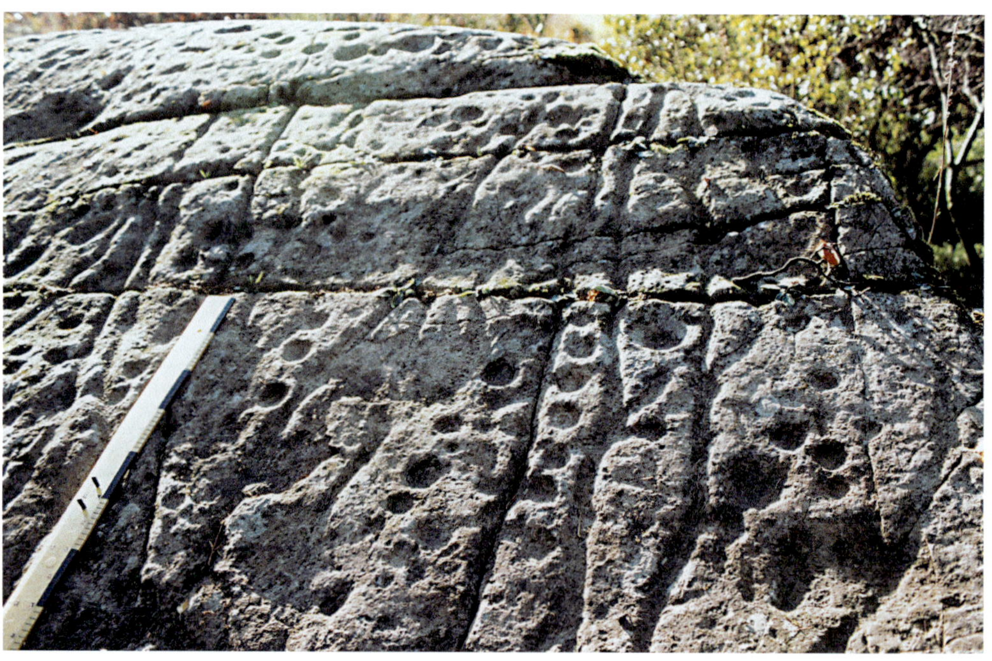

4 Patterdale site 2

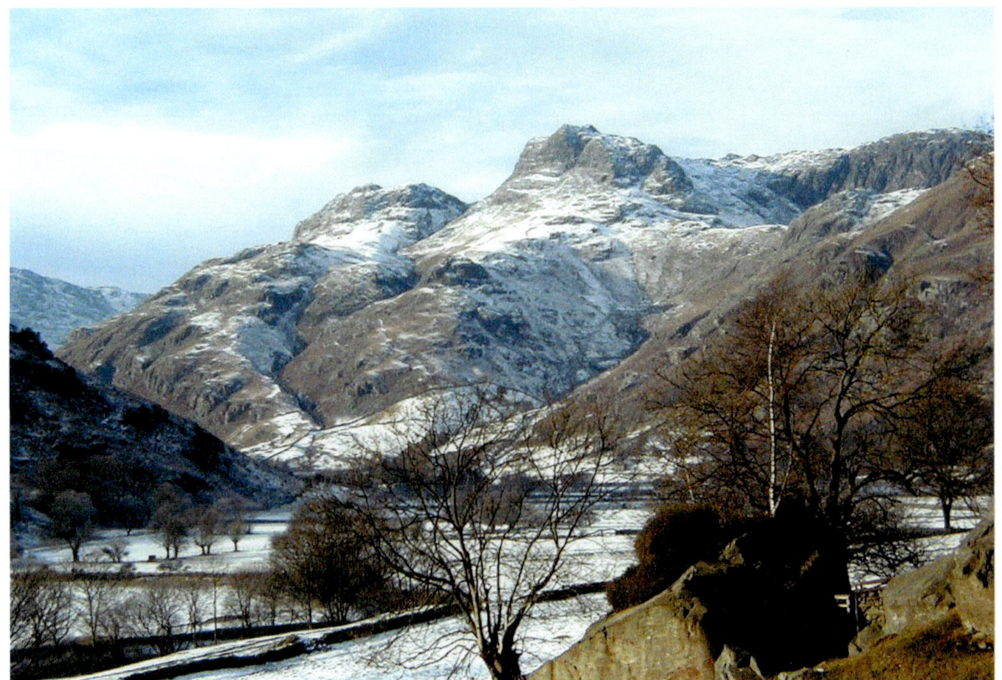

5 *The Langdale Pikes from the rock at Copt Howe, Chapel Stile*

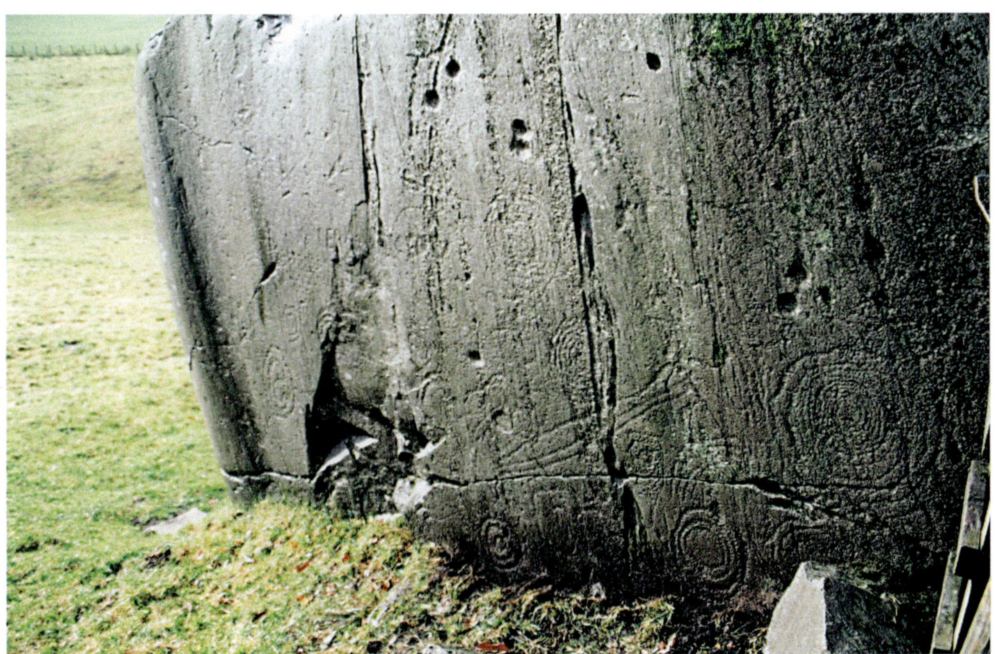

6 *The marked rock at Copt Howe, east face*

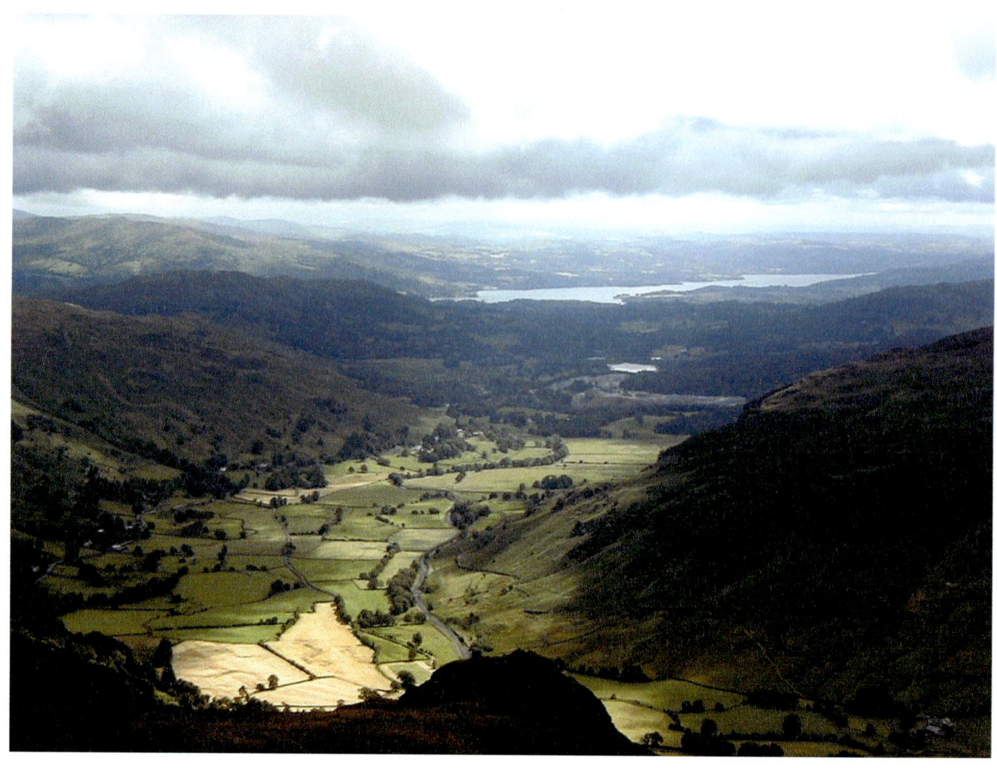

7 The Langdale valley and Windermere

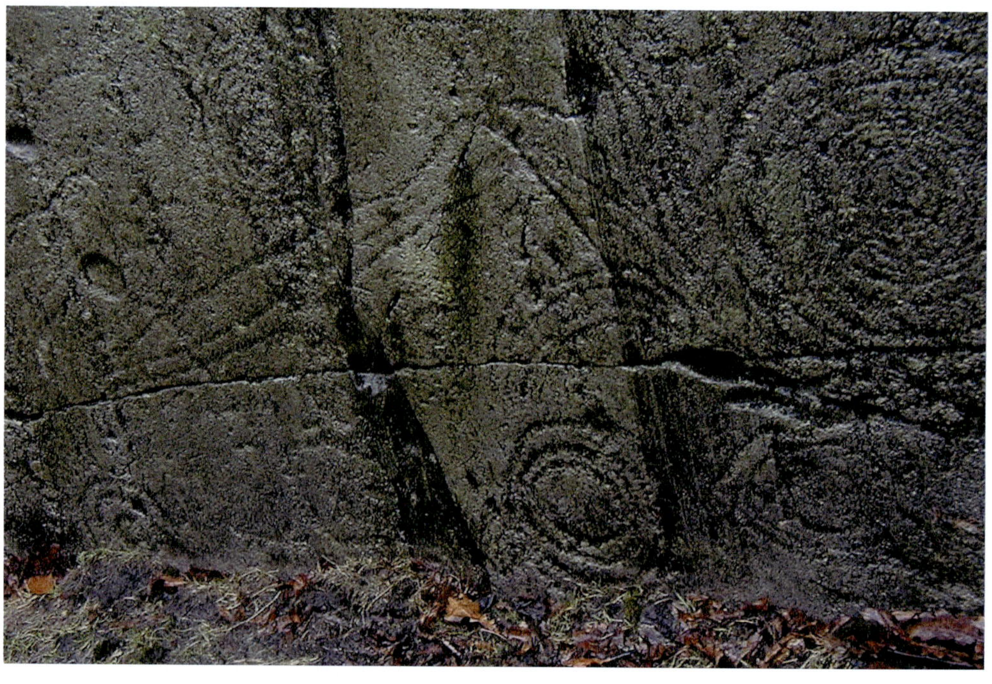

8 Detail of part of the Copt Howe rock

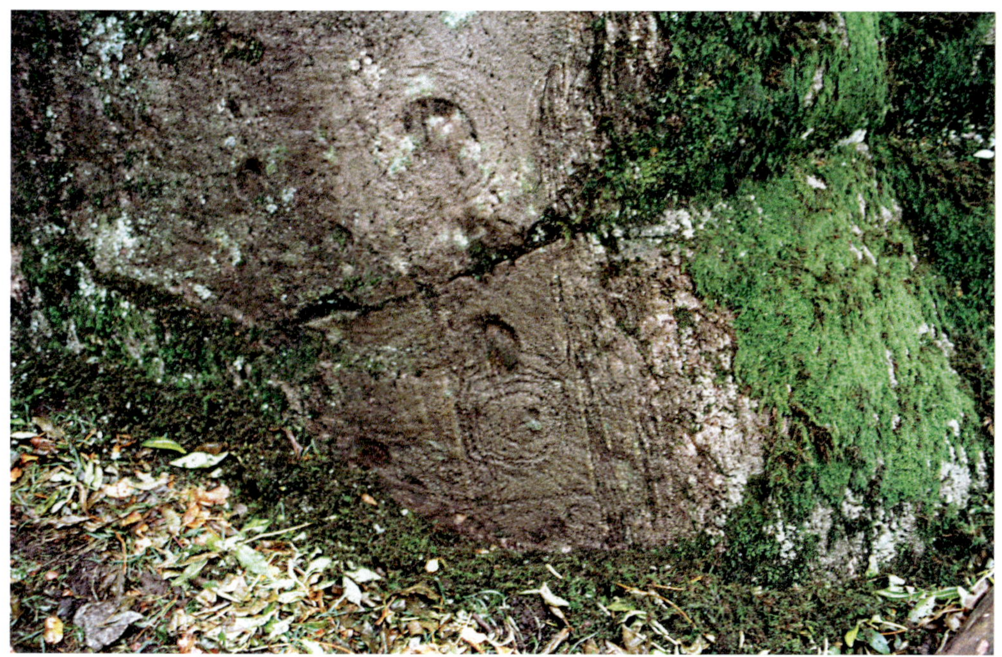

9 Copt Howe: the most northern markings

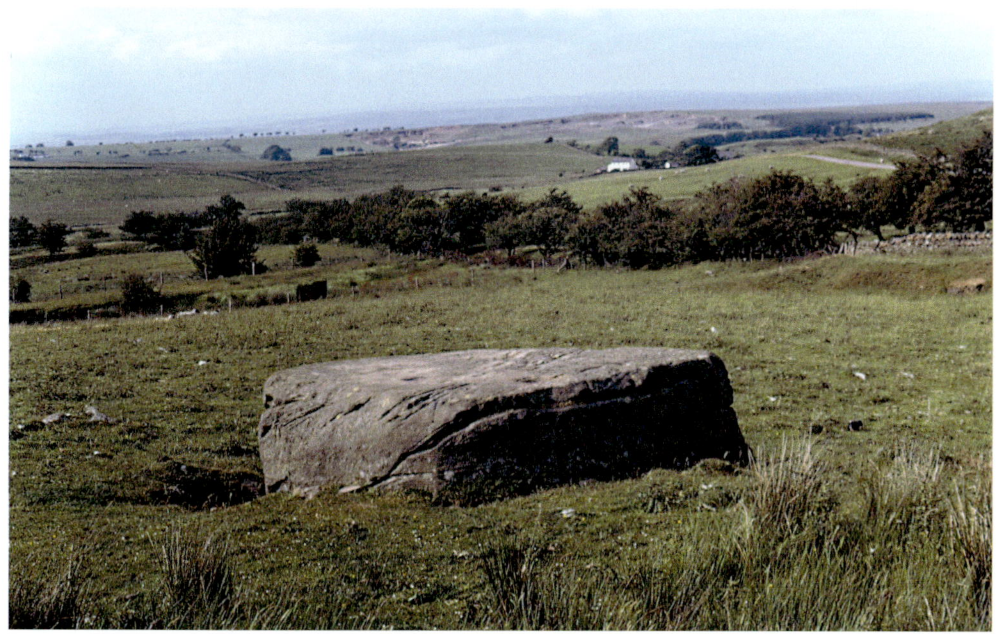

10 Tortie Cottage: rock 2

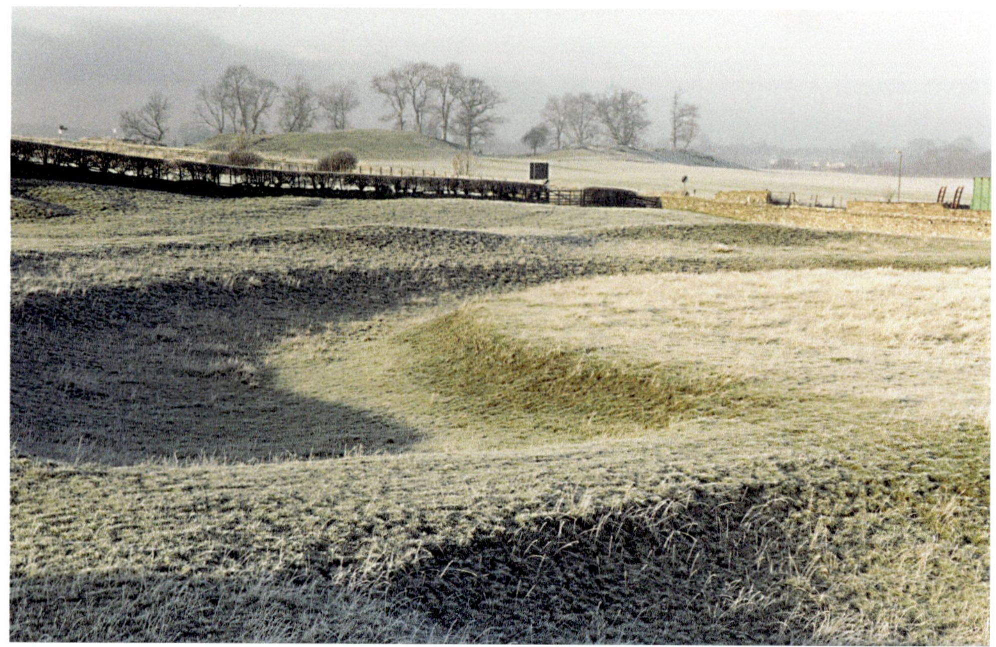

11 King Arthur's Round Table and the Mayburgh Henge

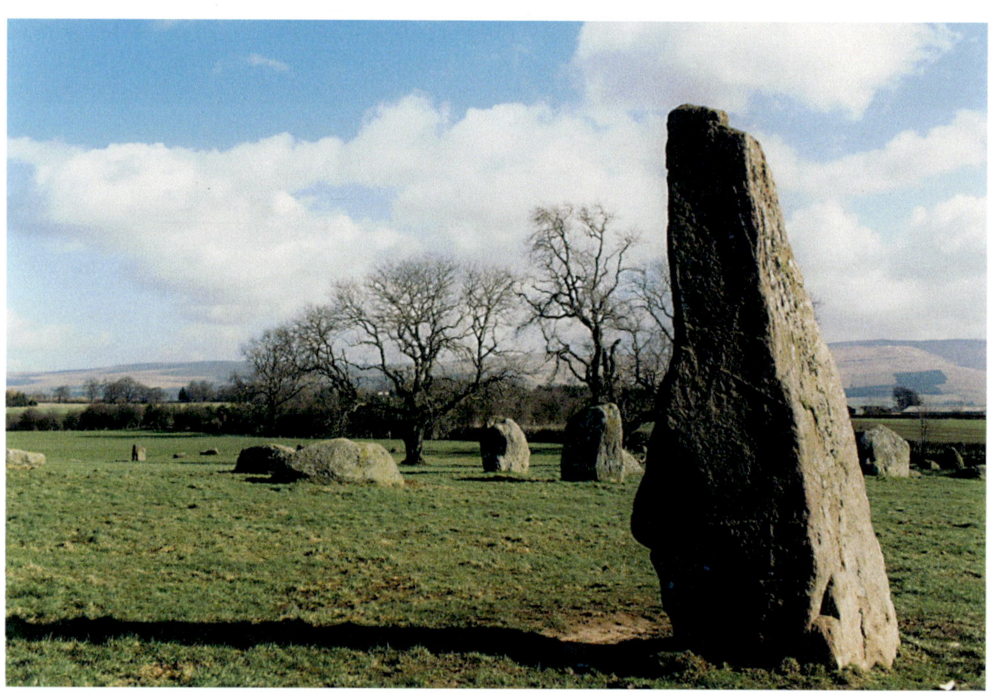

12 Long Meg: the unmarked face

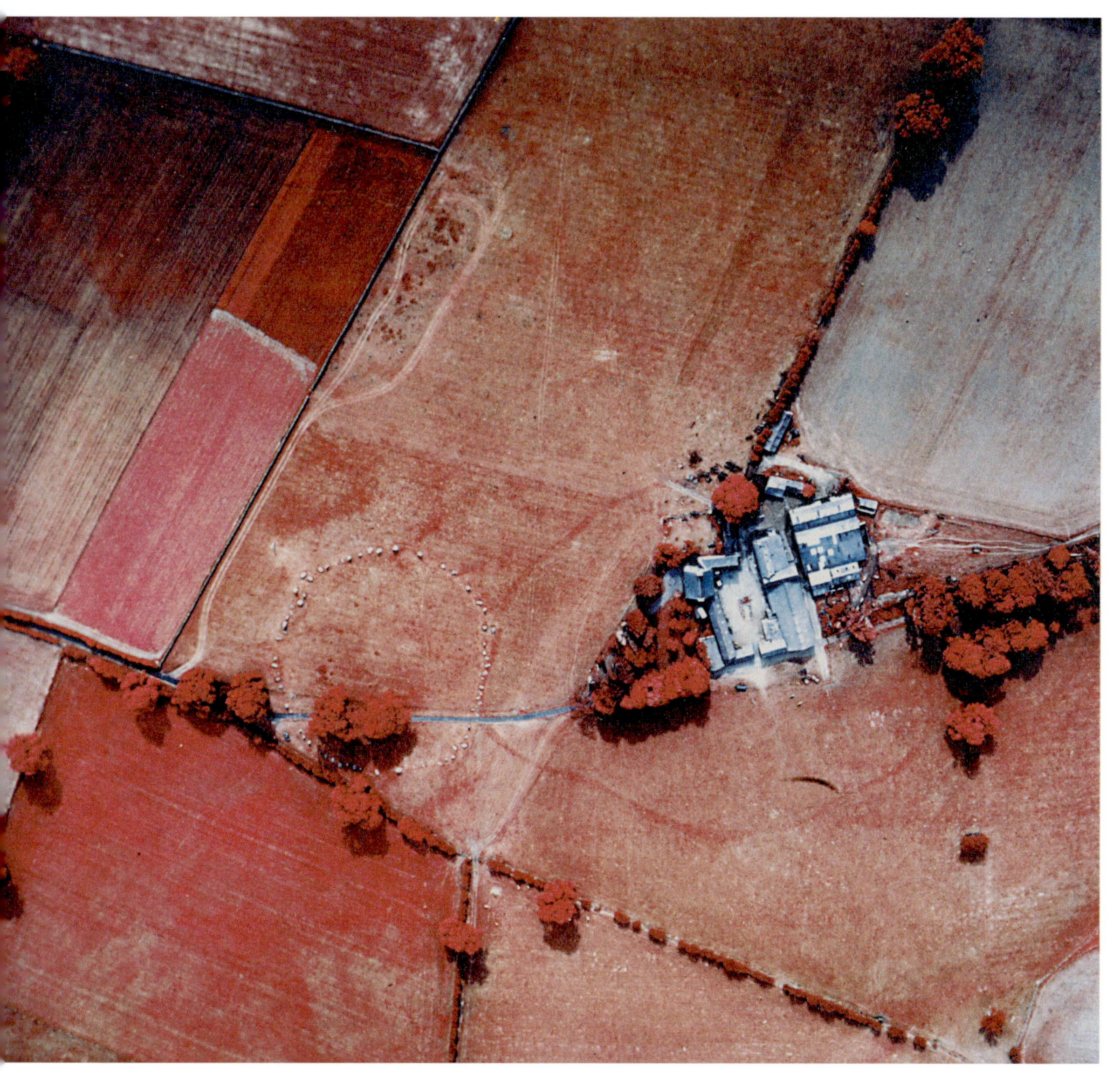

13 An infra-red aerial photograph of Long Meg and the hidden ditches. © English Heritage

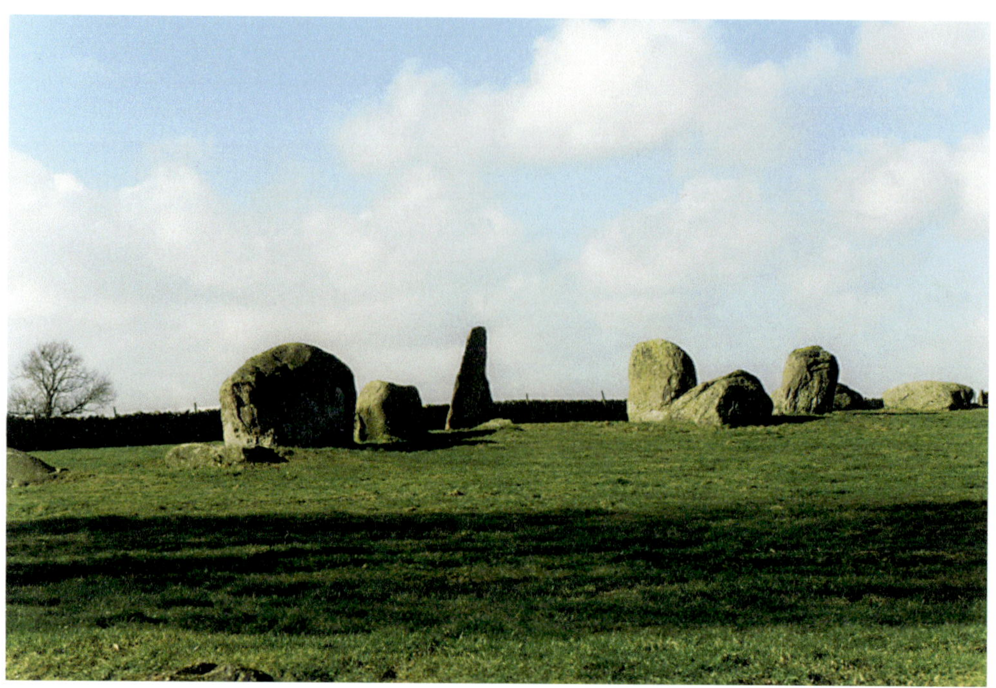

14 Long Meg with the portal entrance

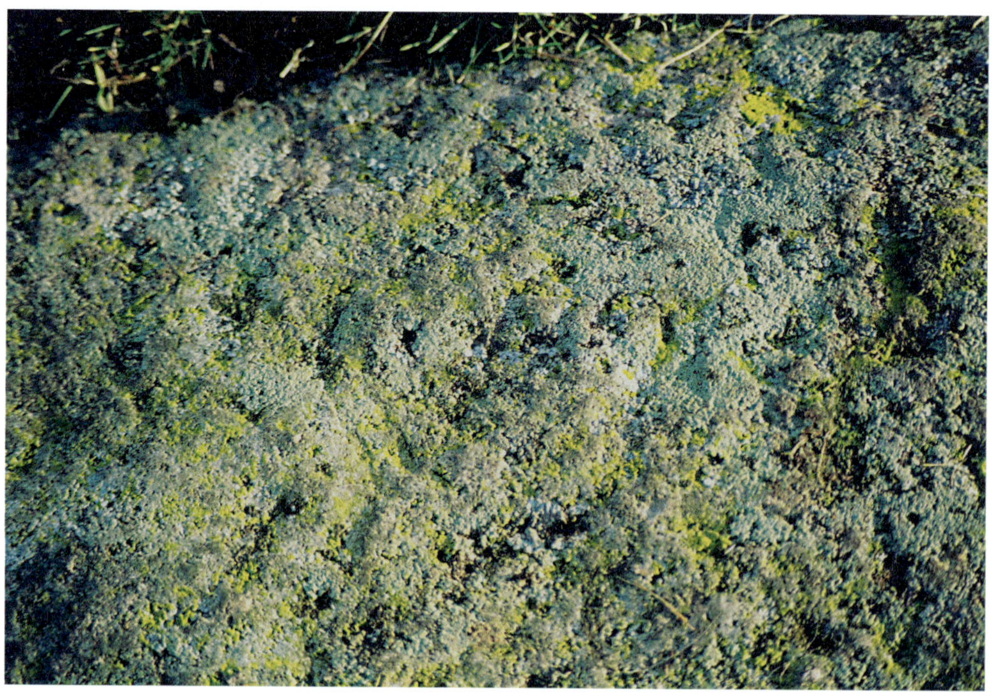

15 Faint spirals on a fallen stone to the north. Steven Hood and David Hankin

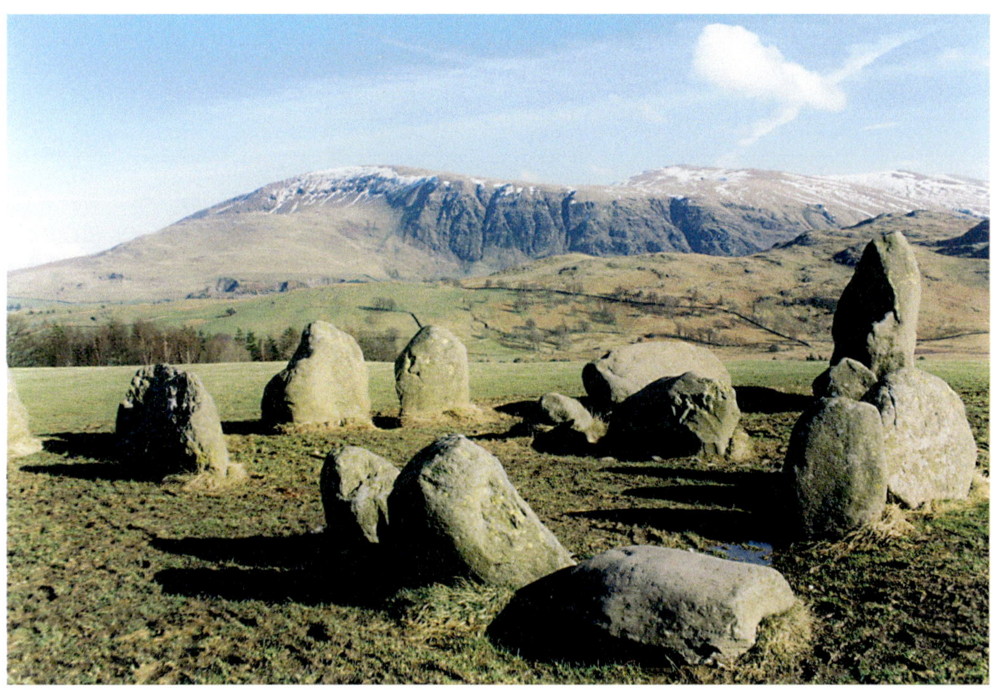

16 Castlerigg: the rectangular setting

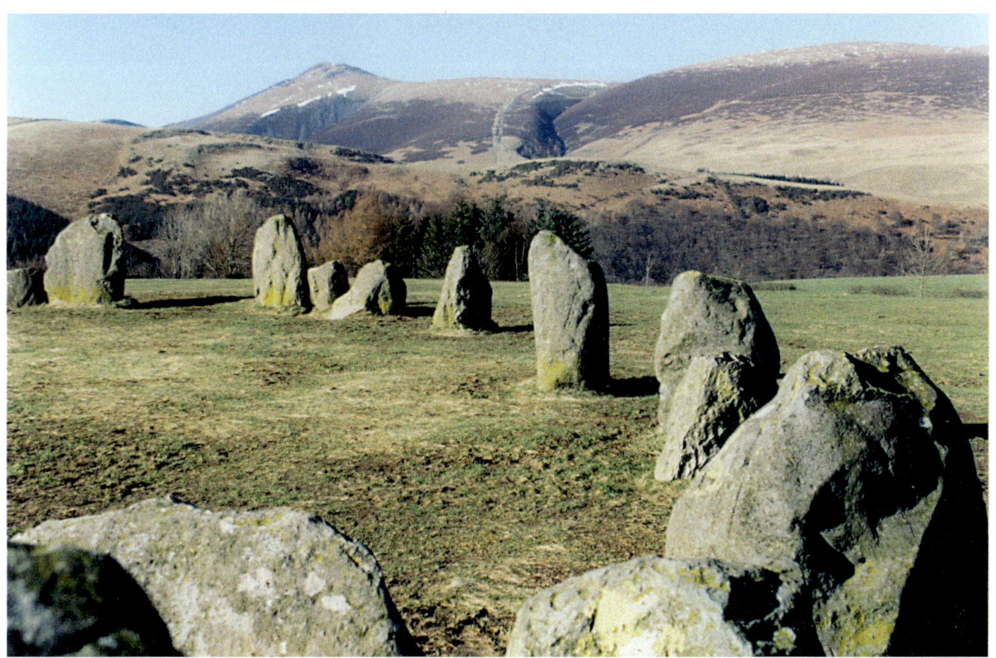

17 From the rectangular setting to the entrance to the circle

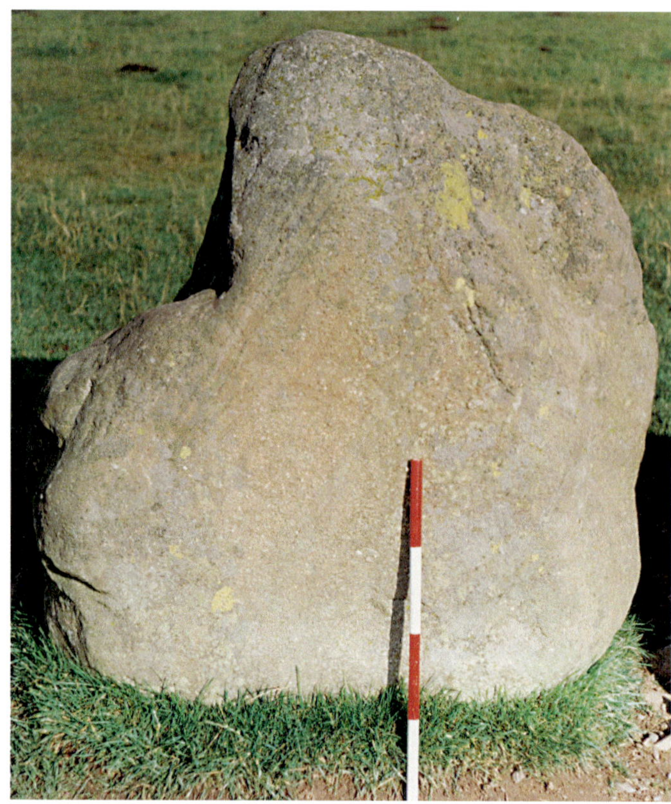

18 The spiral.
© Neil Stevenson

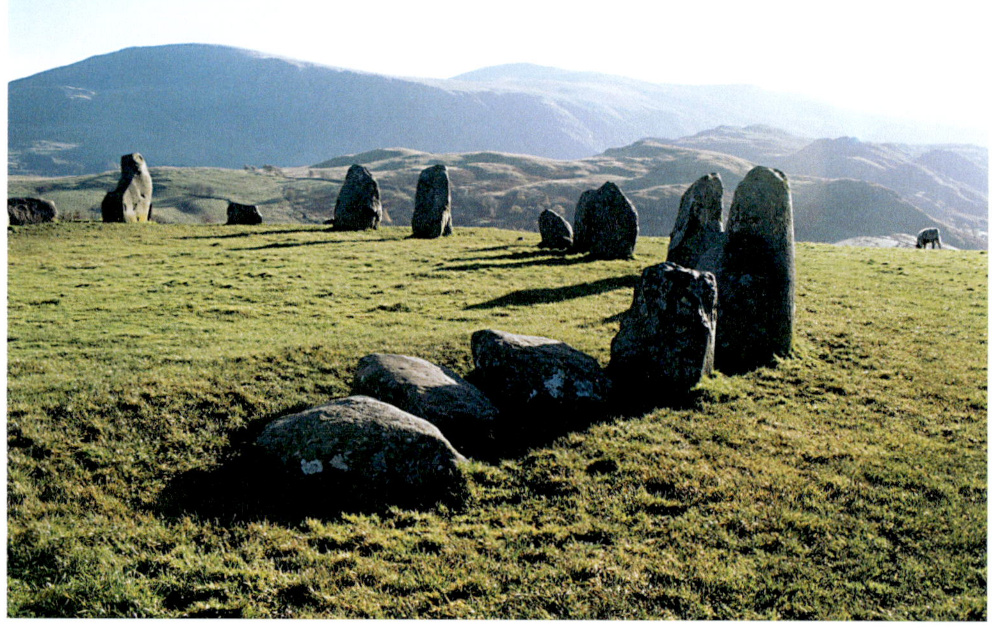

19 The south-west part of the circle

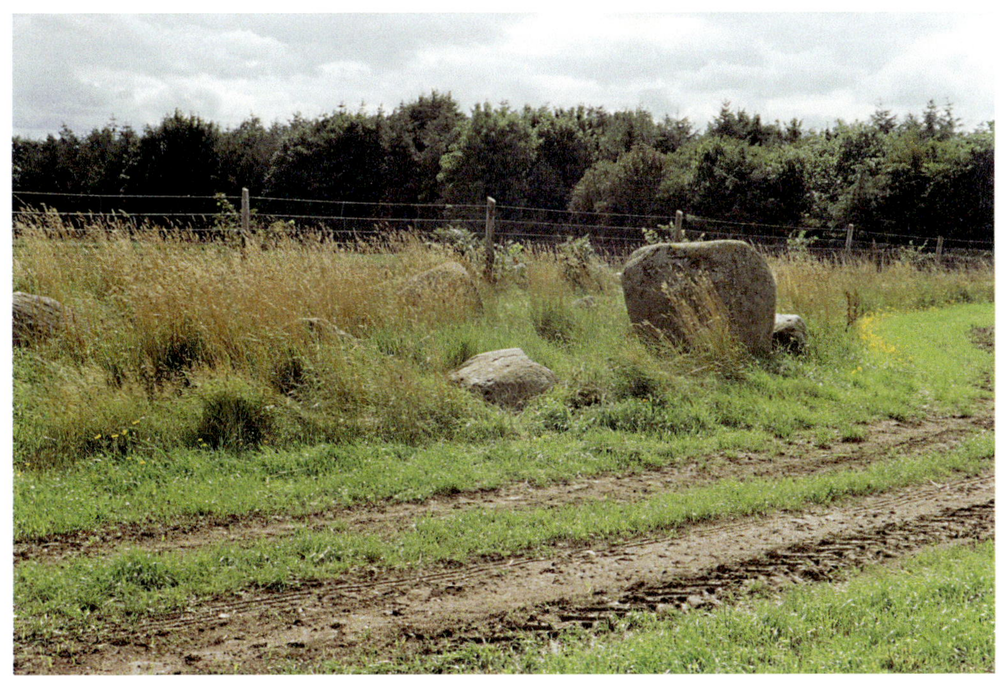

20 Little Meg

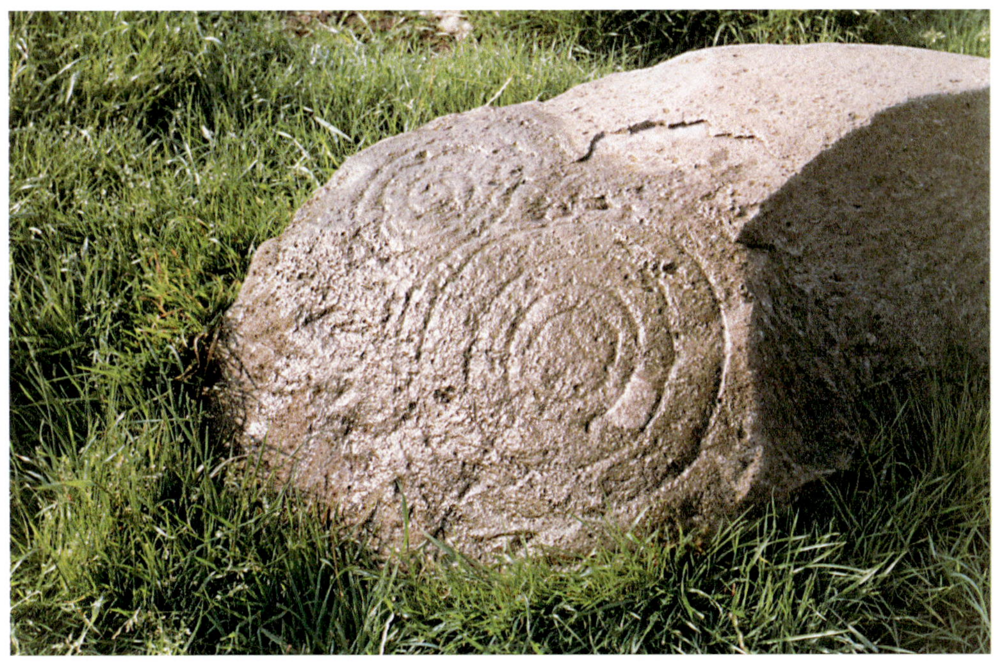

21 Little Meg

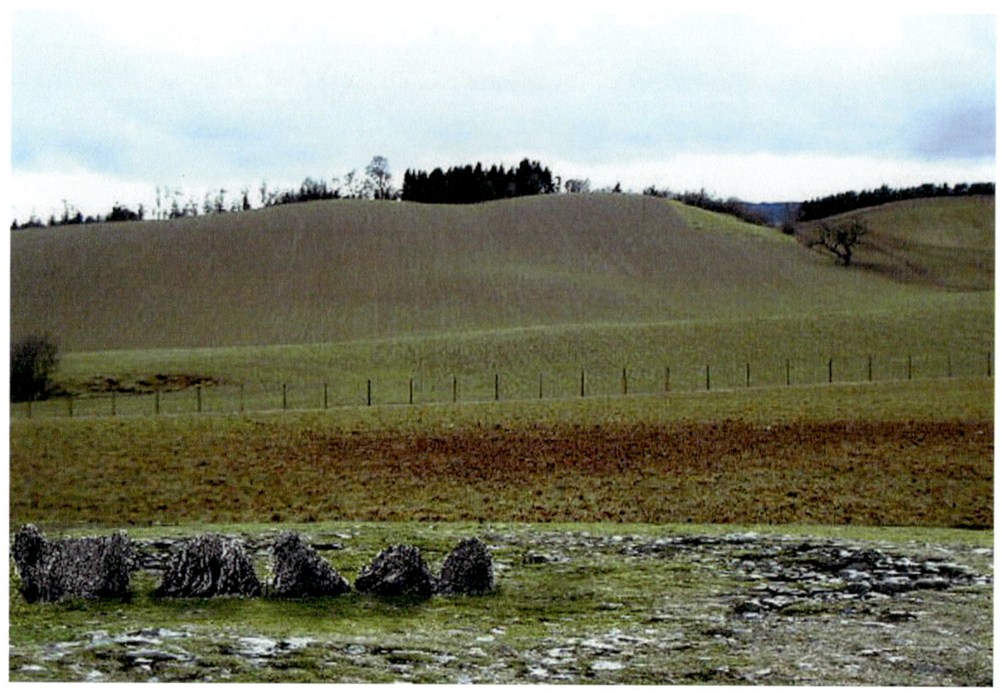

22 Old Parks: a digital reconstruction of the site of the demolished mound. Paul Brown

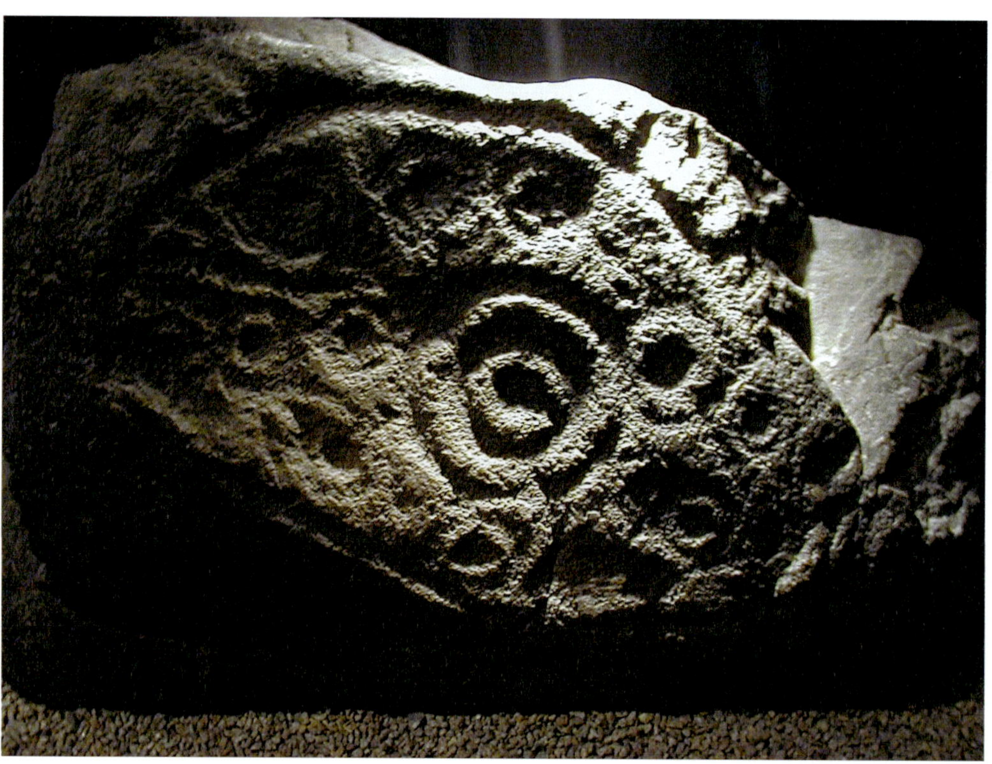

23 Honey Pots Farm stone

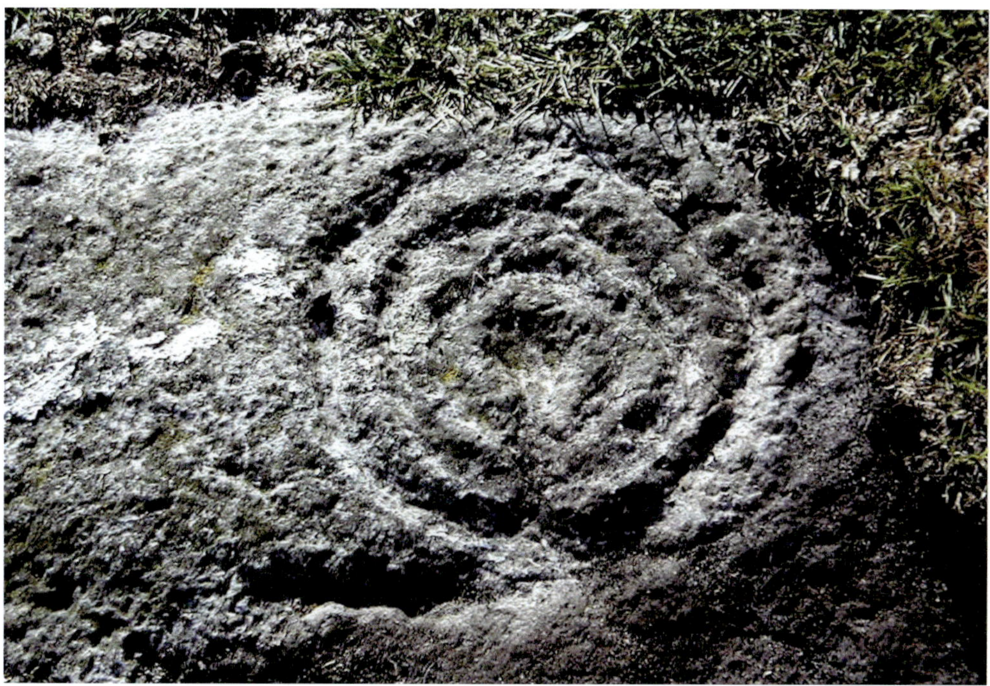

24 Leonard's Cragg. Paul Brown

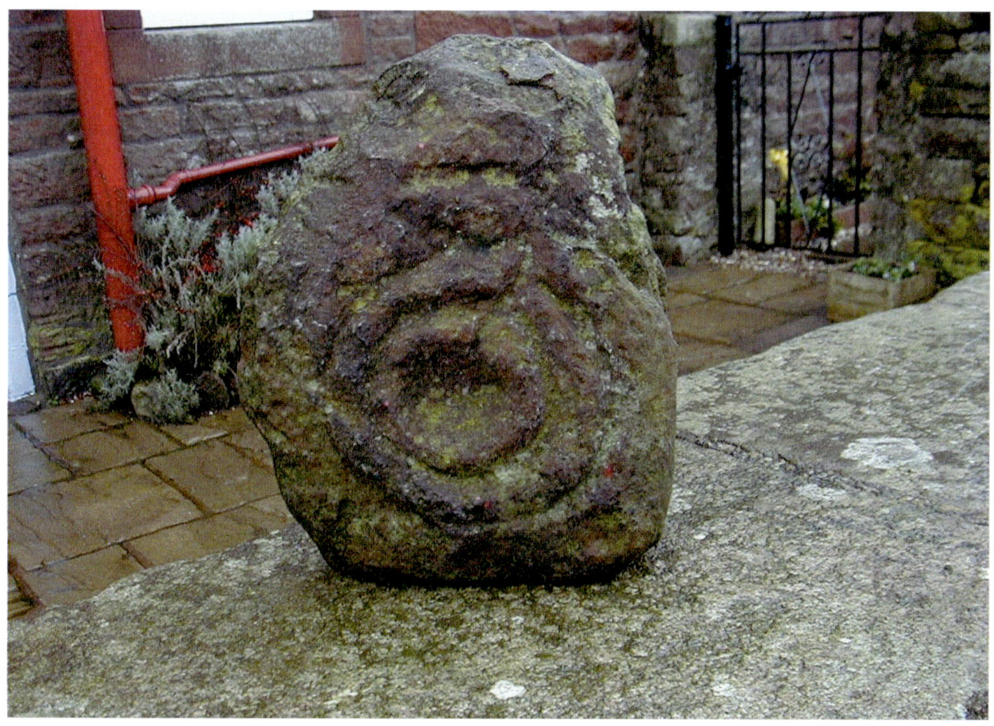

25 Ruckcroft, Armathwaite

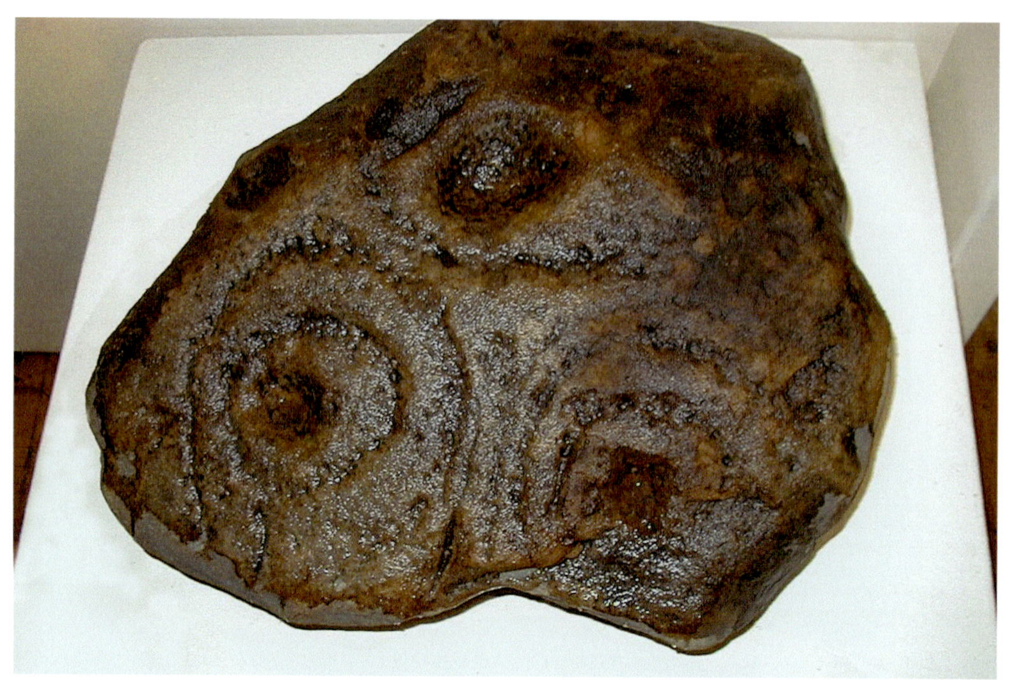

26 *Stone from the Little Meg cist, on display in Penrith Museum*

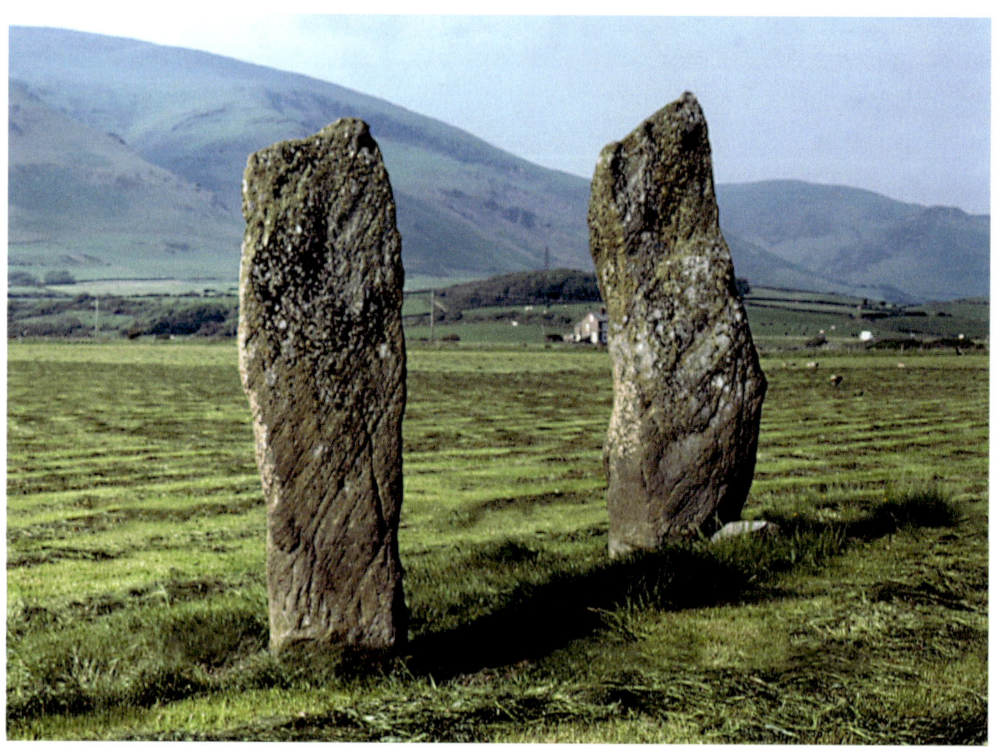

27 *Kirksanton: the Giant's Grave*

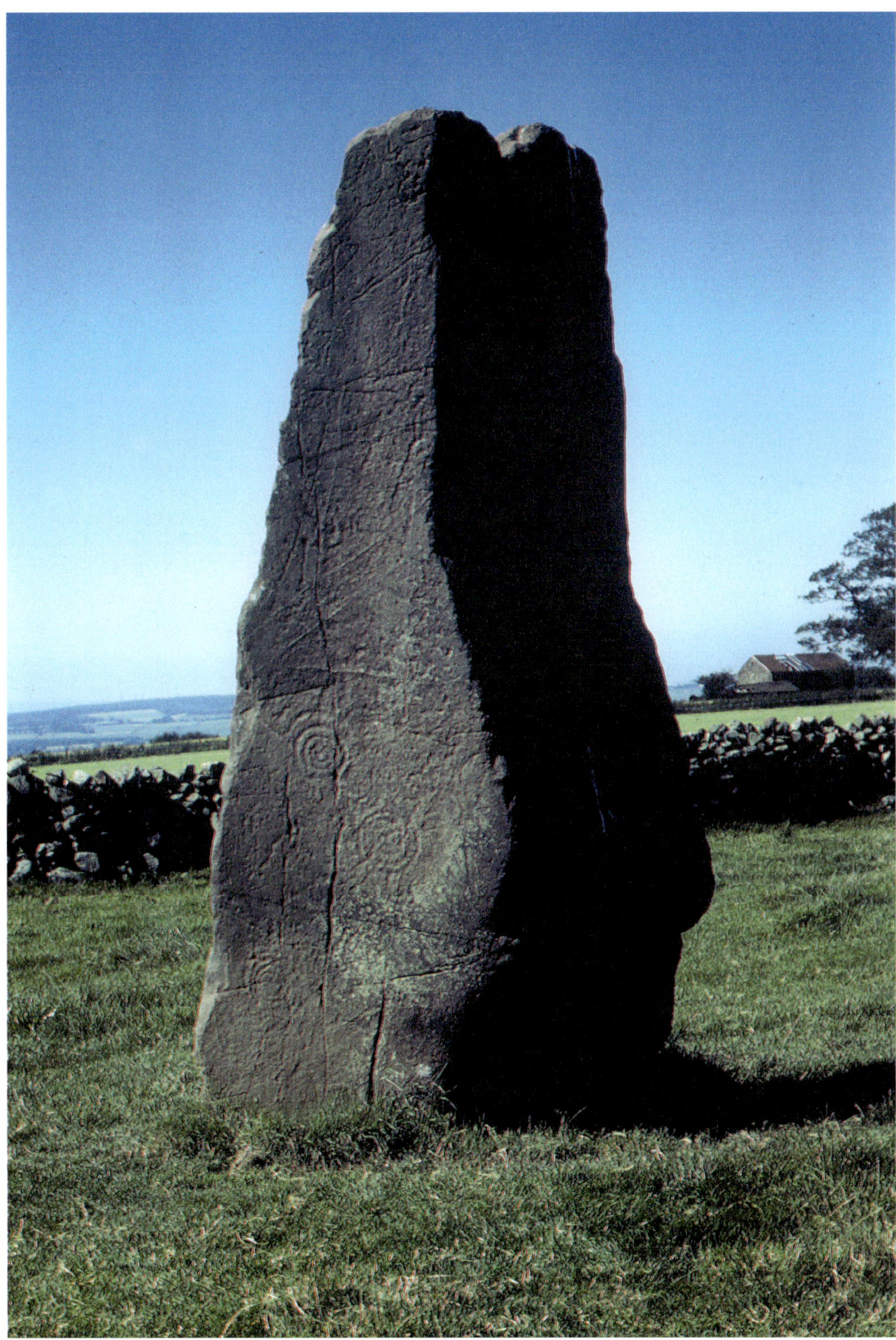

28 Long Meg

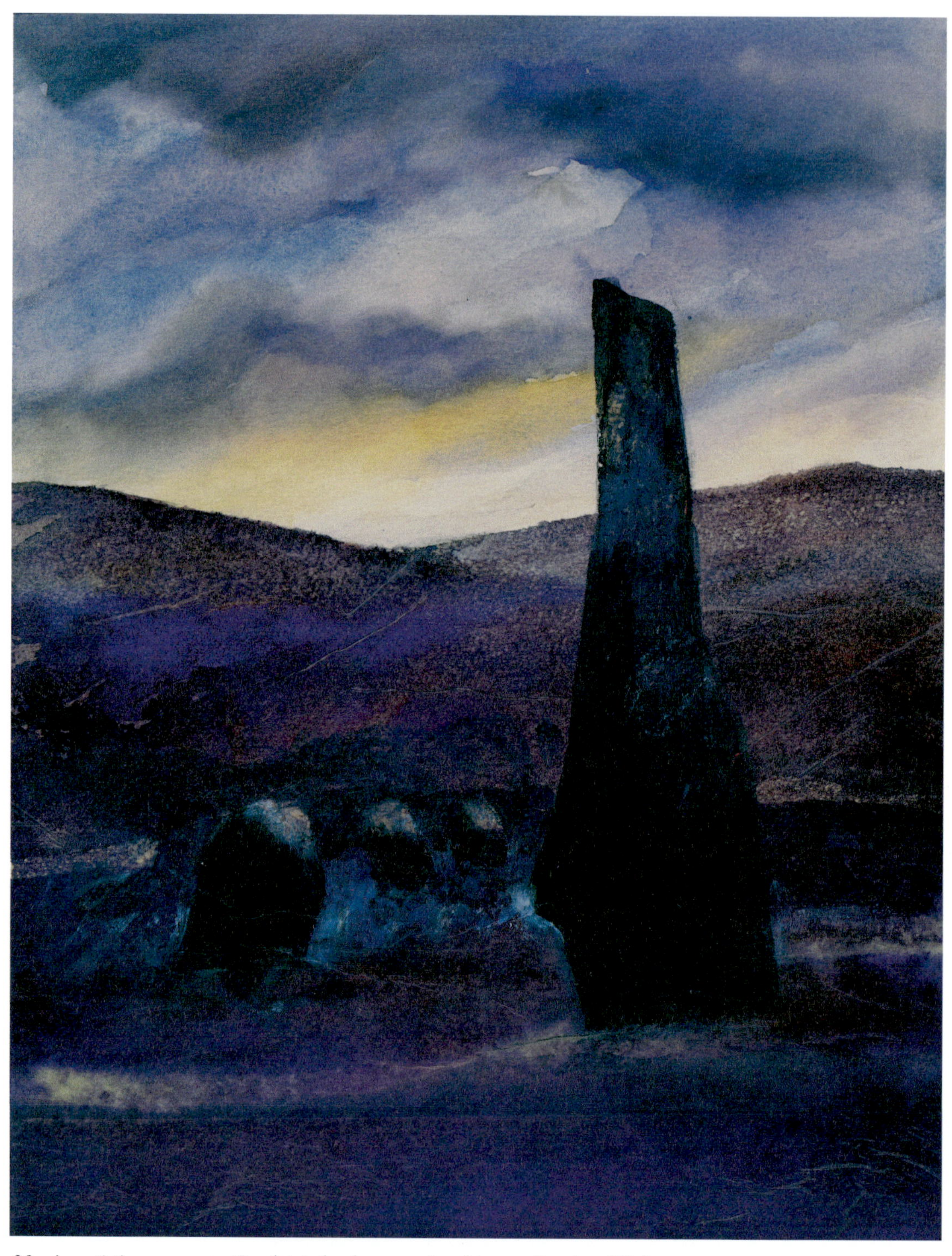

29 *An artist's response to Cumbria's landscape and prehistory.* Gordon Highmoor

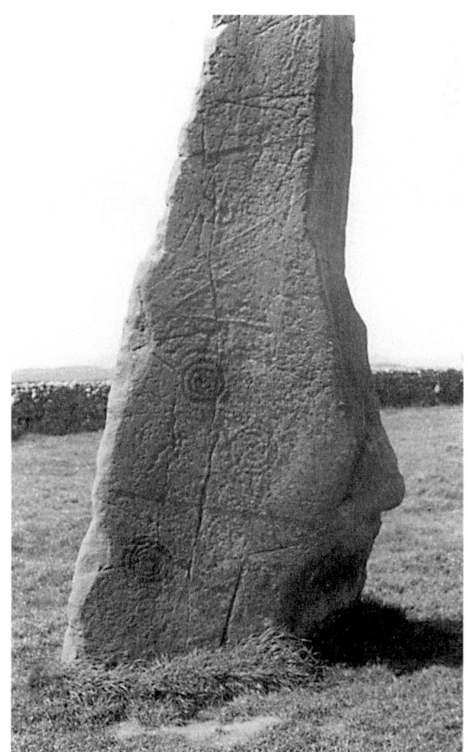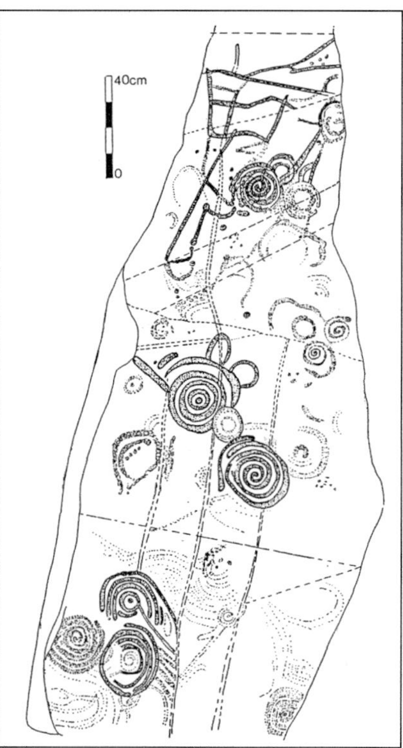

70 *The Long Meg decorated surface.* Photograph by Paul Frodsham

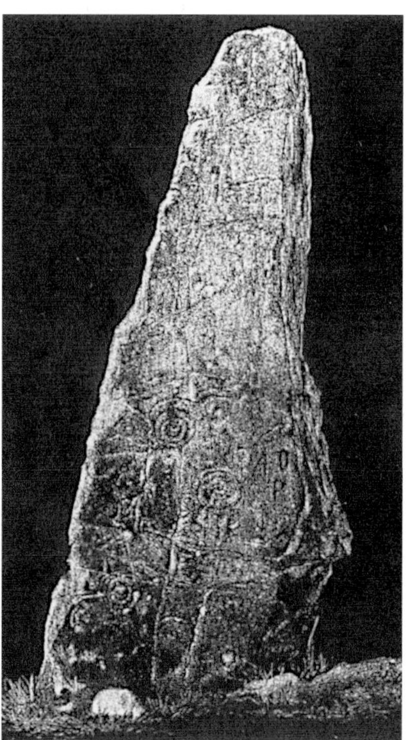

71 *A. Ritchie's lithograph of Long Meg, from Sir J.Y. Simpson's* Archaic Sculpturings, *Edinburgh, 1867*

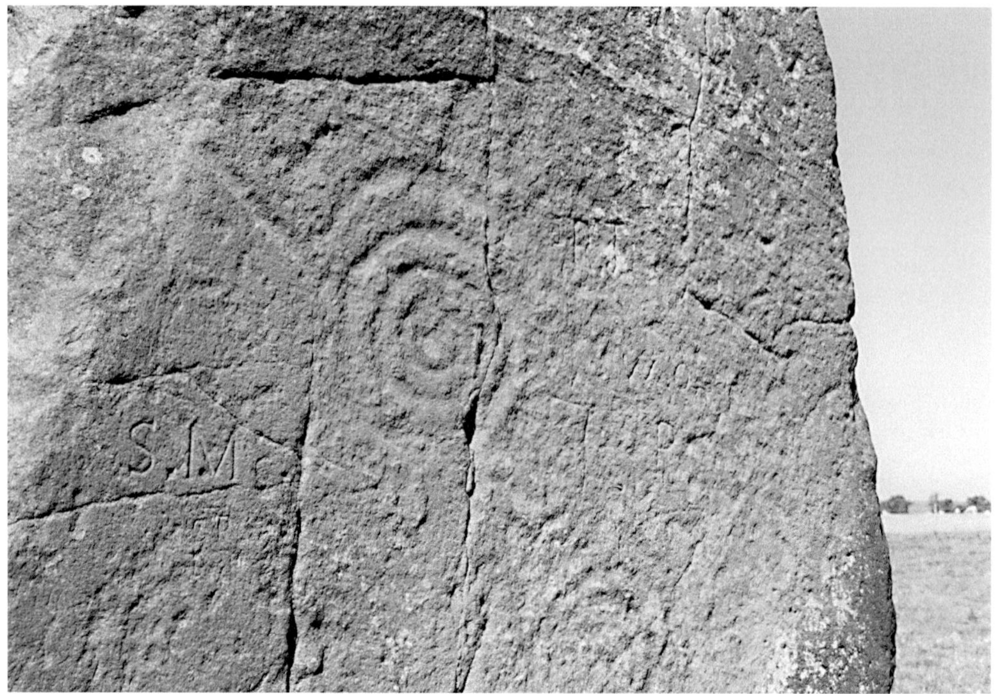

72 *The central section of the Long Meg motifs*

Two roughly horizontal natural strike lines that are crossed by three natural vertical cracks enclose this central section. The middle vertical crack runs the length of the pillar. Within the central section are other faint peck-marked motifs that include the beginning of another anti-clockwise spiral, a smaller similar spiral on the line of the top crack, and some pick marks and arcs.

The lower section
There are three faint figures at the left-hand corner that may be unfinished. On the edge is an anti-clockwise spiral. Above is a cup and ring and three concentric arcs, one of which runs in to the vertical crack. At the bottom is most probably a spiral or a series of interrupted concentric rings. There are other faint marks in this section including arcs. Sir J.Y. Simpson writes:

> Lately I had the opportunity of examining this stone, and found, not one, but several series of concentric circles carved upon it, three of four of them low down on the stone and much faded.

The drawing that he made of these (*Plate VII*) is of great interest, as his observations seem to have been almost entirely ignored since then: my drawing has rediscovered, albeit very faintly indeed, some of his motifs.

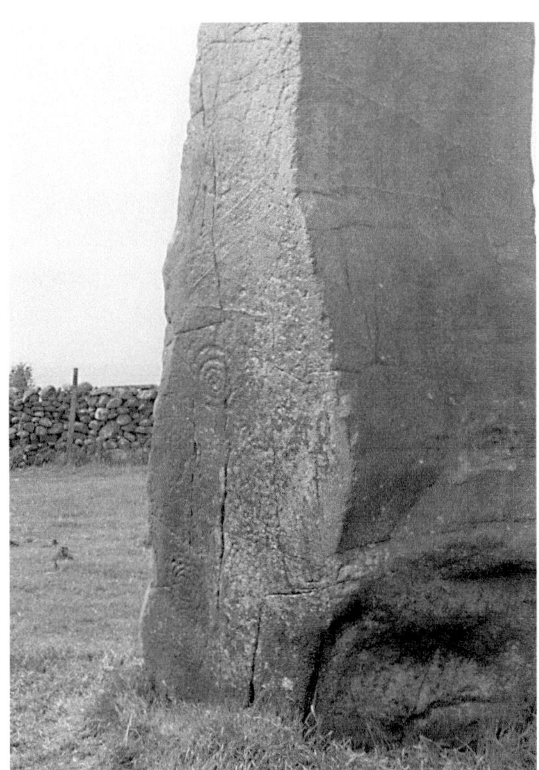

73 *The middle and lower section*

74 *The upper section*

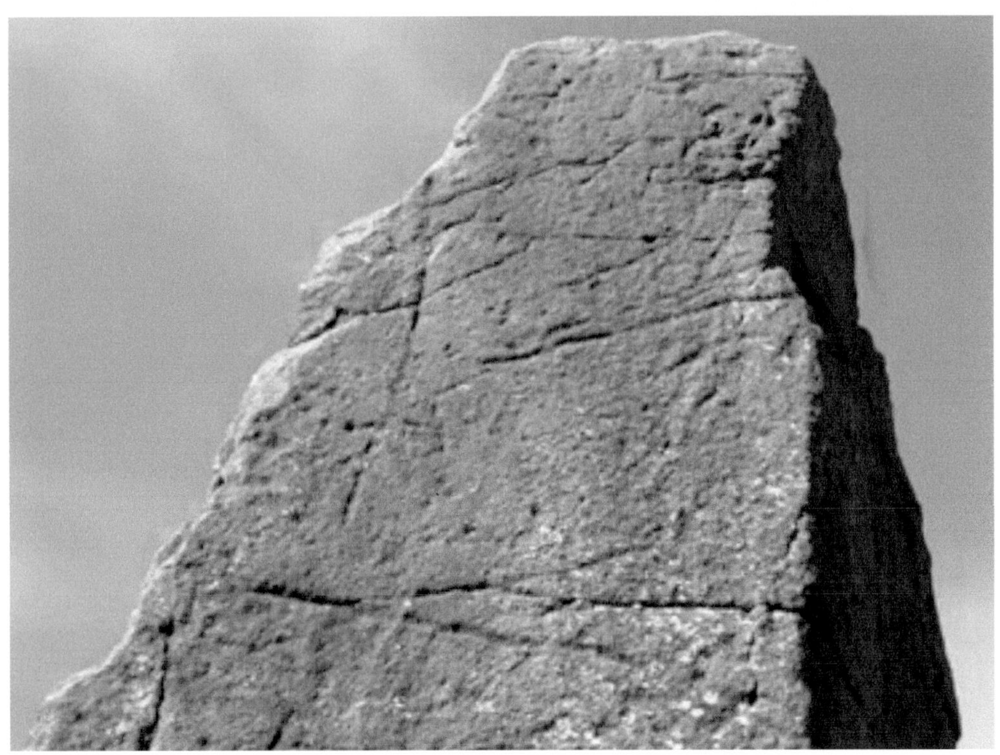

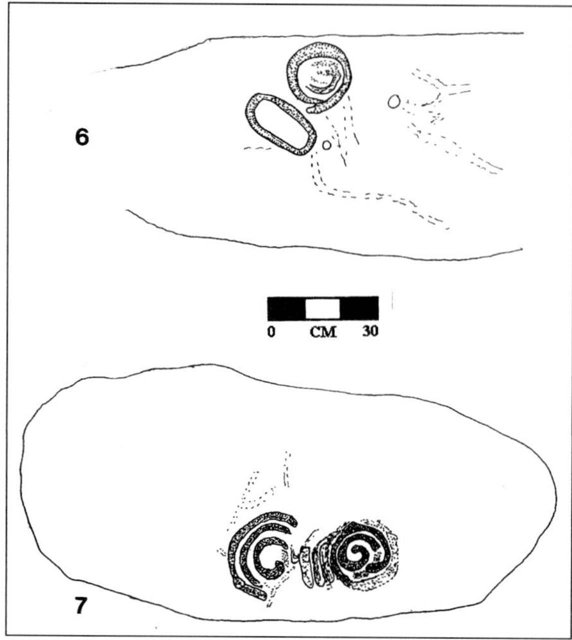

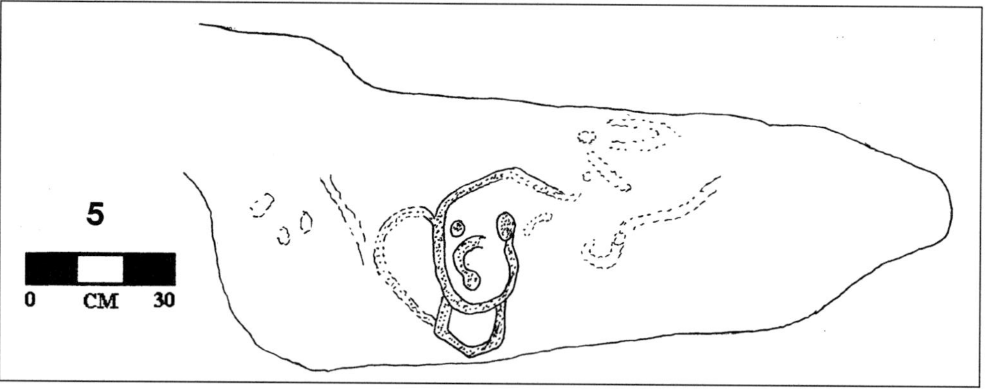

75 *Marked fallen stones 6 and 7*

76 *Stone 5*

The upper section

It is important to distinguish between artificial and natural features on this part of the rock, as there are some mineral veins that form lines across the surface. There are some quite complex linear features made with a pick, as the drawing shows. There are faint spirals, rings, ovoids and half-ovoids scarcely visible, but revealed by delicate wax rubbing and photography.

As Simpson says: 'Other more indistinct appearances of portions of circles are traceable higher up the stone.' Very significantly he then added:

> I found no traces of human art upon the surface of any of the 67 stones of the Salkeld circle, except one, a large block placed on the opposite side of the circle from Long Meg, and which has the doubtful appearance of a faded circle upon its western face.

Other marked stones

In January 1999 Stephen Hood and Dave Hankin from Workington discovered a spiral on one of the fallen stones of the circle close to the metalled road that leads to the farm. It was seen in the morning, and the finders noted that it was not visible during a late winter afternoon. They counted the two marked stones to the west of the road that runs to the farm, numbers five and seven from the road. I was asked to investigate this, which I did at once, and made rubbings of four fallen stones in the same group.

The stone that they had discovered indeed had a spiral, here drawn from my rubbing. Although it is faint, it is possible to pick out its anti-clockwise spiral centre, but after that it does not appear to be well-formed. Either it has been damaged or it was not completed and left as a rough-out. What also appeared is an interrupted ring with two concentric arcs next to the spiral.

Other stones were rubbed, and one revealed what may be a tentative spiral and a rectangular groove with rounded ends. A third stone has some linear enclosures.

That there are some artificial marks on these stones is without doubt, but care has to be taken about 'patterns' on rocks that rubbings reveal, as the actual natural structure of rocks may produce markings that appear to be artificial. This is not the case with the spiral here, nor with the large spiral at Castlerigg stone circle (see below).

It is better to acknowledge that there may be other motifs on all sorts of prehistoric structures that no one else has noticed, waiting for the right light and the keen observer to record. There are now some doubts about the use of wax rubbing as a means of recording (for it is said to remove tiny grains of the surface), and the use of a good-quality digital camera may be the immediate answer.

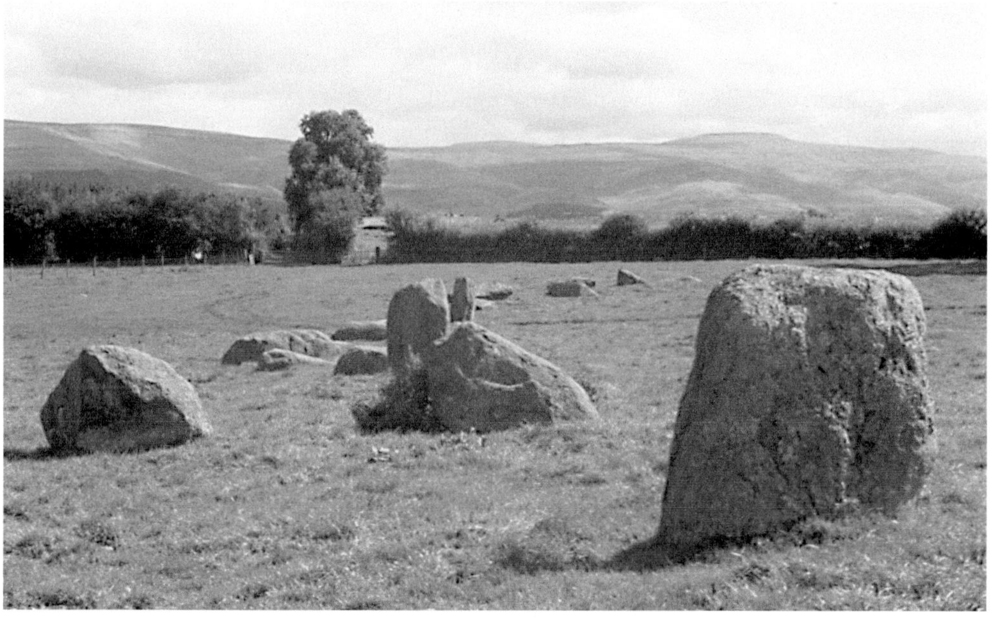

77 *The northern part of the stone circle, with the Pennines as background*

The motifs on the Long Meg stone circle include many spirals, in various stages of completion, and this tradition links them to (for example) the Temple Wood stone circle in Argyll (NR826978), which is well excavated and recorded. It has a double spiral linked on two faces of a kerbstone, and a history of use over 1000 years. Burials at the centre in the early Bronze Age effectively closed it as a stone circle. Temple Wood and the other rich monuments in the Kilmartin area are all linked in their ceremonial use, but this use changes to meet new beliefs. As there has been no excavation at Long Meg, such information remains hidden. Fortunately, its status as a protected monument will save it from some threats. In the late eighteenth century the local landowner, Colonel Lacy, was about to blow up the stones with gunpowder when a violent storm and the panicky retreat of his labour force made him change his mind – or so the story goes.

For those who visit, the signposts point to 'The Druid's Circle'. This, of course, is legend, as the Druids do not impinge on history until the Romans make us aware of them. It became a convenient label for something no one understood, an alternate to attributing monuments to Caesar or the Devil. The Stonehenge ceremonies are just a bit of diverting theatre.

Castlerigg Stone Circle (H001123   NY292236)

Our experience at Castlerigg stone circle demonstrates that even the most visited sites have rock art that has been overlooked. Chance favours a prepared mind! Until quite recently the Castlerigg stone circle was without any recorded rock art. I recorded a cup marked stone in a wall nearby, and then two students from Newcastle University, Nick Best and Neil Stevenson, photographed a spiral on one stone in the late afternoon winter sunlight of 1995. Other archaeologists were present. This discovery was amazing, as so many people visit the site each year, and have not observed any markings. It is also understandable, as motifs can be so faint that they only appear when the sun casts shadows in the right places!

Also in 1995, a few days before the Autumn Equinox, Hanna Casement of Eskdalemuir had been at the stone circle for a few hours with some friends, during which time they had not seen anything unusual about this stone. I let her tell her own version of the events that followed:

> We decided to wait for the sunset, and as it began we were facing away from the stone watching the setting sun. It was purely by chance that I glanced behind me towards the stone, and saw that it appeared to be glowing orange and had this huge spiral coming out of the rock. It was absolutely unbelievable, as it had not been apparent all day. It seemed that it was only visible as the setting sun hit the rock. We were all completely amazed at the way this spiral seemed suddenly to appear, and tried to see if we could feel it carved into the rock. We couldn't feel anything very definite, but we could definitely see it, and took photographs to prove it.

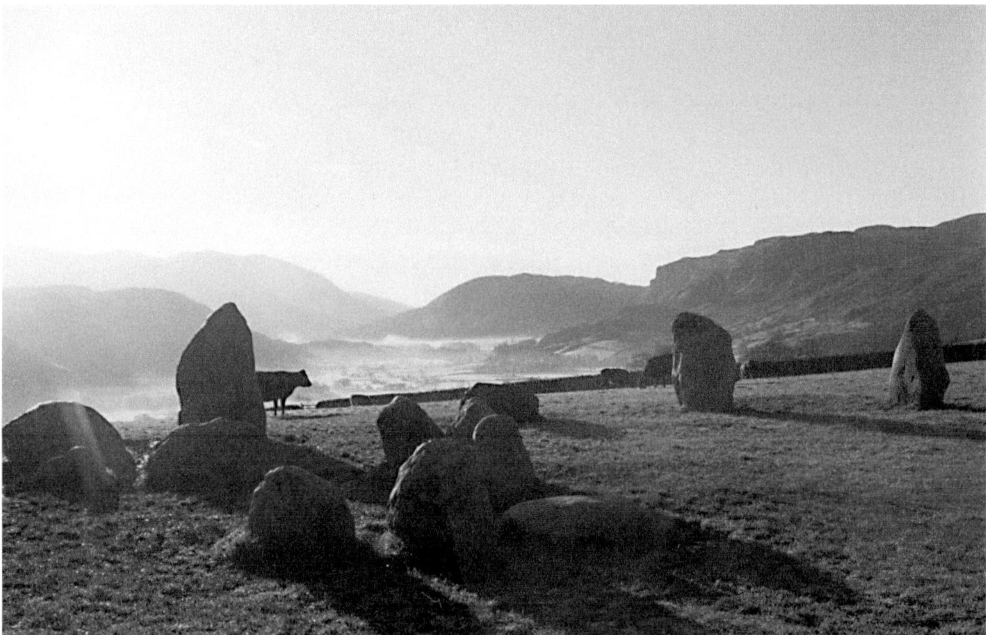

78 *Early morning at Castlerigg stone circle*

I have returned to the circle many times since to try to see the spiral again, but have never seen again what I saw that day. Nor have I been sure that I could feel the outline of it. But the memory of that extraordinary experience and discovery will remain with me forever, as the spiral seemed to be glowing out of the rock as the sun hit it. In the photographs the rock has an orange tint to it, from the setting sun, whereas it is grey ordinarily. It seemed that it was the contrast of the orange on the grey that allowed us to see this wonderful spiral.

Castlerigg is different from Long Meg. It is smaller, but it stands on a summit that commands views of the mountains all around, whereas the bulk of the stones at Long Meg are on a slope. It is like a circle within a circle; one looks at a 'circular' landscape of mountains and valleys from the inside. It is also a natural centre for routeways, and as such would be another focal point for the scattered farming communities in the area. Within the Lake District it is one of the most beautiful places, especially in the early morning when the mist lies over lower ground.

Another difference is that it is not just a circle of stones. There is a rectangular box-like arrangement of spaced standing stones that project into the circle. Cairns have been reported from inside the circle when it was trenched in 1882. A small part at the west end of the rectangle had a 3ft (0.91m) deposit of black earth and stones, possibly with charcoal; no Cumbrian stone circle has yet been dated from carbon samples.

It is on the inward-facing stone at the centre of this rectangle, firmly based on the circle itself, that the spiral is to be found (1 on the map). The stone to the left of the

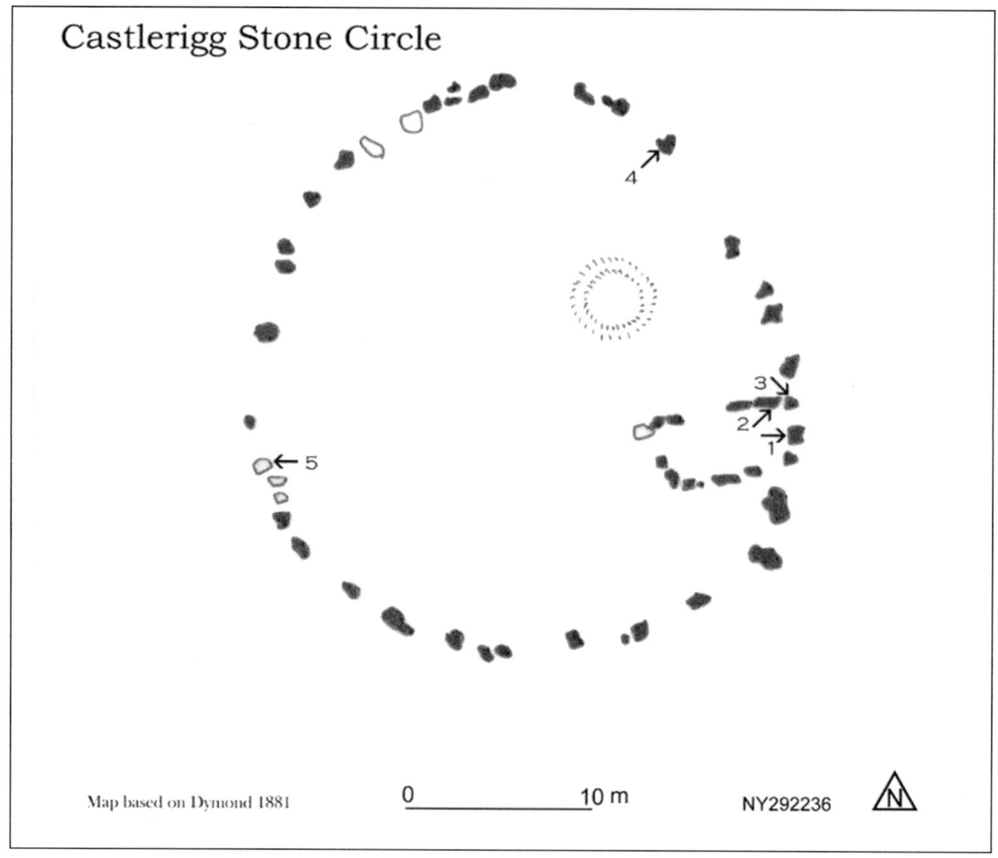

79 *Castlerigg site plan, with numbered marked stones*

spiral (3) as you stand in the enclosure looking outwards, has a lozenge motif incised or pecked on it. Next to that, into the rectangle, a long stone (2) has what may be the beginnings of a circular or spiral motif, discovered during a digital photographic survey of all the stones in 1999. Opposite the rectangular setting of standing stones is the recumbent stone 5, which also has a lozenge-shaped motif. Finally, stone 4 near the entrance has a small cup and incomplete ring.

The discovery of these motifs carries with it an important lesson. We find very often what we expect to find; we approach sites and problems with a bias. No one *thought* that there was any rock art at Castlerigg, so no one looked carefully enough. Richard Bradley's discoveries in the Maes How chambered tomb on Orkney demonstrate the point, as he and his team found a series of crossed and parallel scratches. The discovery of the motifs also emphasises the unique character of the rectangular enclosure attached to the inside of the circle. Similar motifs appear on the Neolithic houses at Skara Brae.

I have looked carefully at all the stones in the field wall that encloses the monument, without finding any other markings. One stone did appear to have some, which I think are natural.

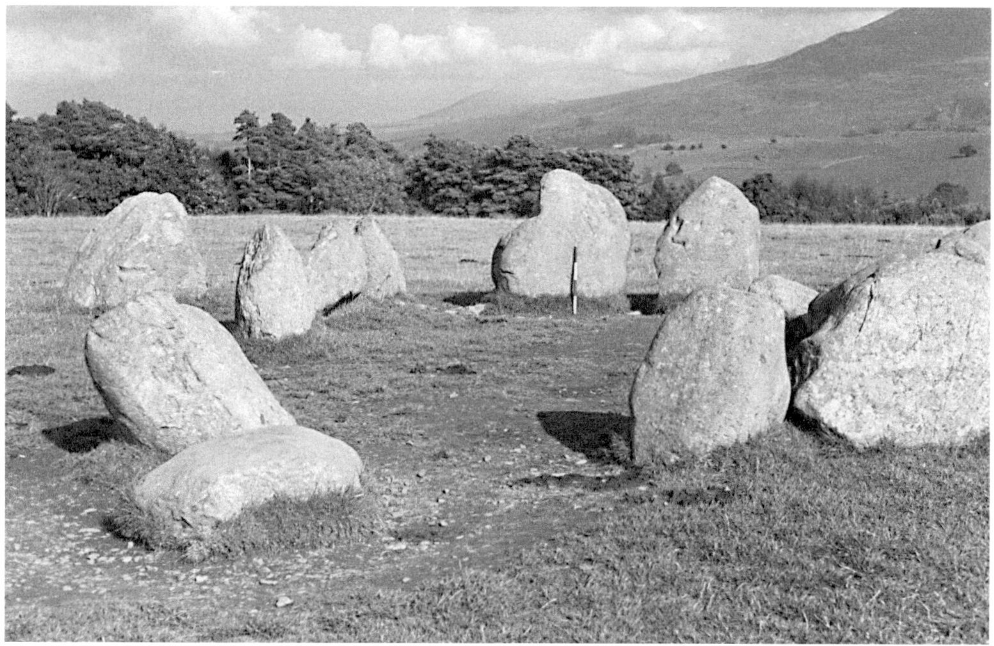

80 *The rectangular stone setting.* © Neil Stevenson

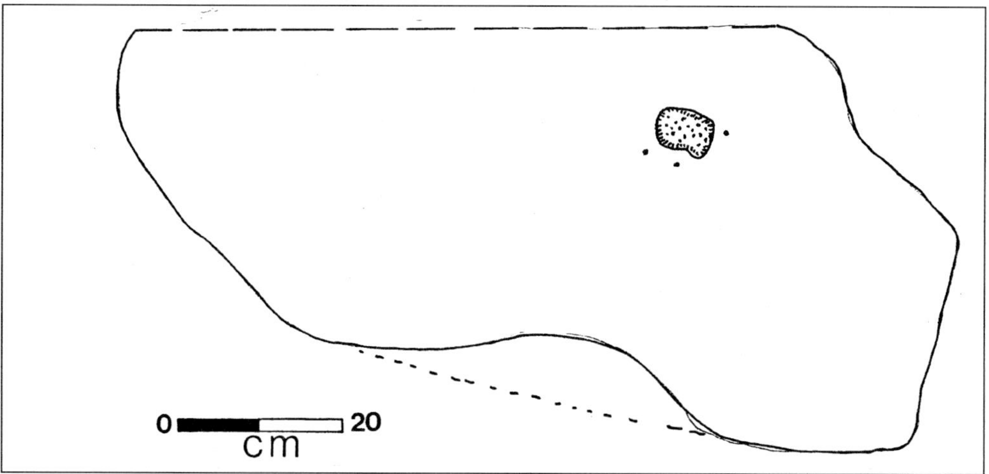

81 *A cup marked stone embedded in the field wall*

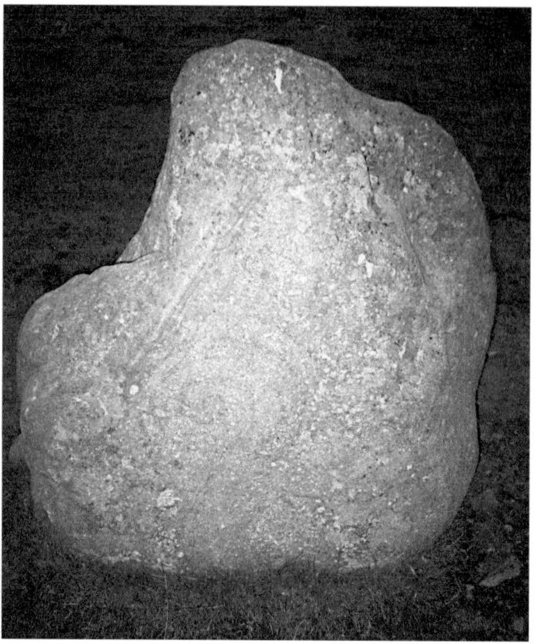

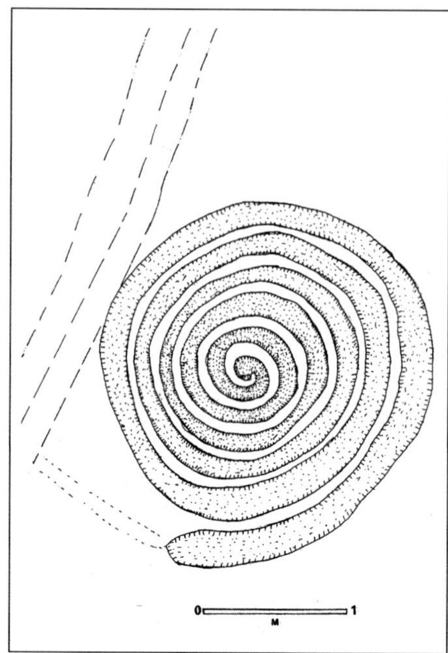

82 *Hanna Casement's photograph of the spiral in 1995*   **83** *A drawing of the spiral*

Motifs

The spiral on stone 1 is clockwise, the outer curve running up against the natural strike lines of the rock. This configuration is the opposite of spirals at Long Meg and Little Meg. The pecking is very light on a hard surface that has tiny pinpoints of minerals. The spiral was revealed after many attempts at rubbing the surface gently with wax on thin, strong newsprint, although the motif remained unseen. I have made other rubbings since, with the same result, and the original photograph accompanies the drawing. It faces directly into the rectangular setting of stones.

The lozenge on rock 3 is easily visible in low light. There are natural deposition lines in the stone, and the lozenge has been incised deeper into these. There is a similar, visible, lozenge on rock 5, a small rounded boulder. The cup and ring is pecked into the upright stone 4, and is visible in strong, oblique sunlight. In all cases, the existence of motifs has been confirmed by rubbings.

Next to rock 3, and part of the rectangular setting, is an elongated stone 2 on which a ring was recorded by digital photography. This too was confirmed by wax rubbing; although the outer circle is clear, and the groove appears to be curling into a spiral form, the centre is on uneven rock and may be unfinished, spoiled or natural.

It is quite remarkable that so much has been found recently, and it emphasises that there must be a re-evaluation of all the stones in stone circles in Cumbria to see if rock art is more widespread than previously thought. One of the sound observations made by the Rev. James Simpson in a paper to the inaugural meeting of the Cumberland and Westmorland Antiquarian Society in 1874 at Penrith was:

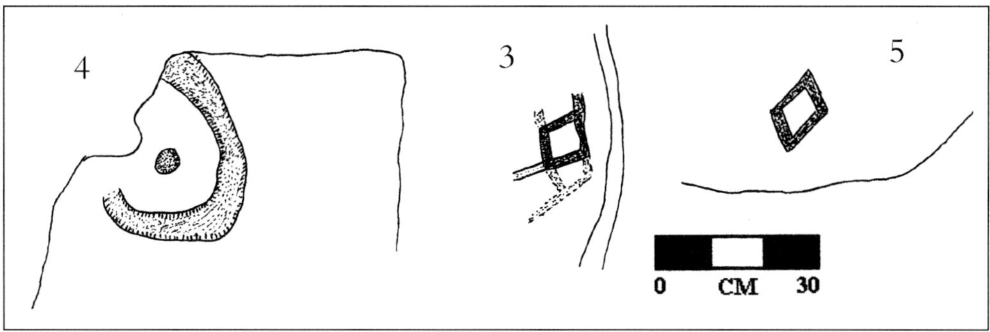

84 *Stones 3,4 and 5*

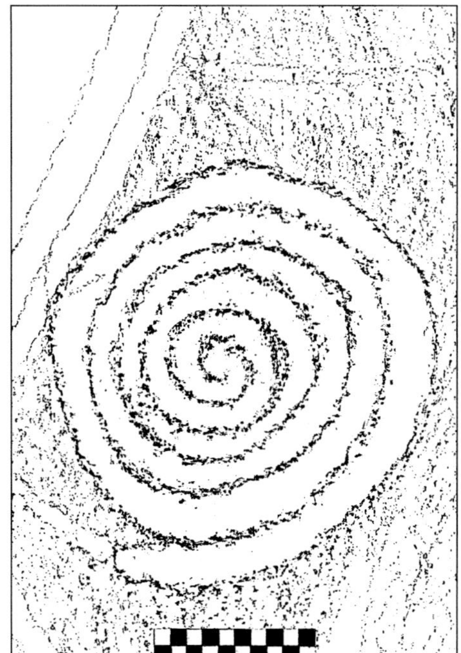

85 *One of many rubbings made of the spiral*

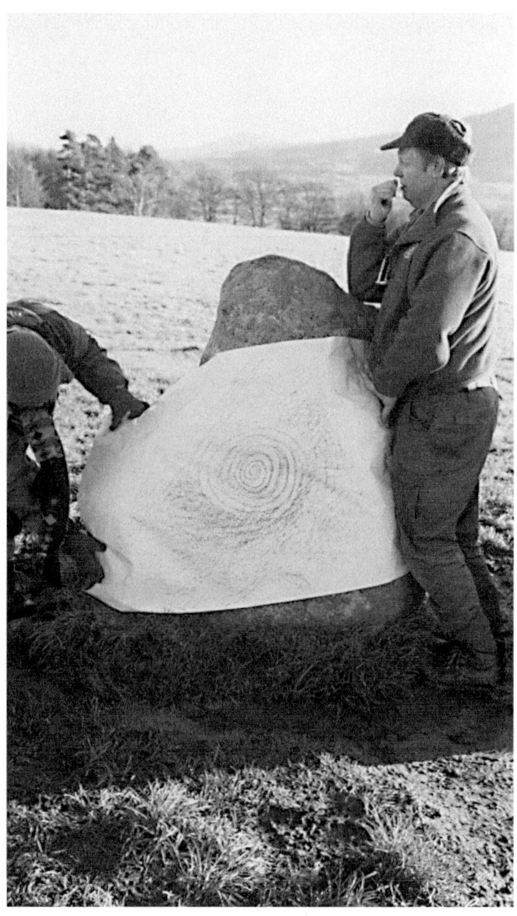

We shall do well – each in his locality – to keep his eyes open and examine these upright stones – whether in a circle or standing alone – to see if we can find any such marks upon them.

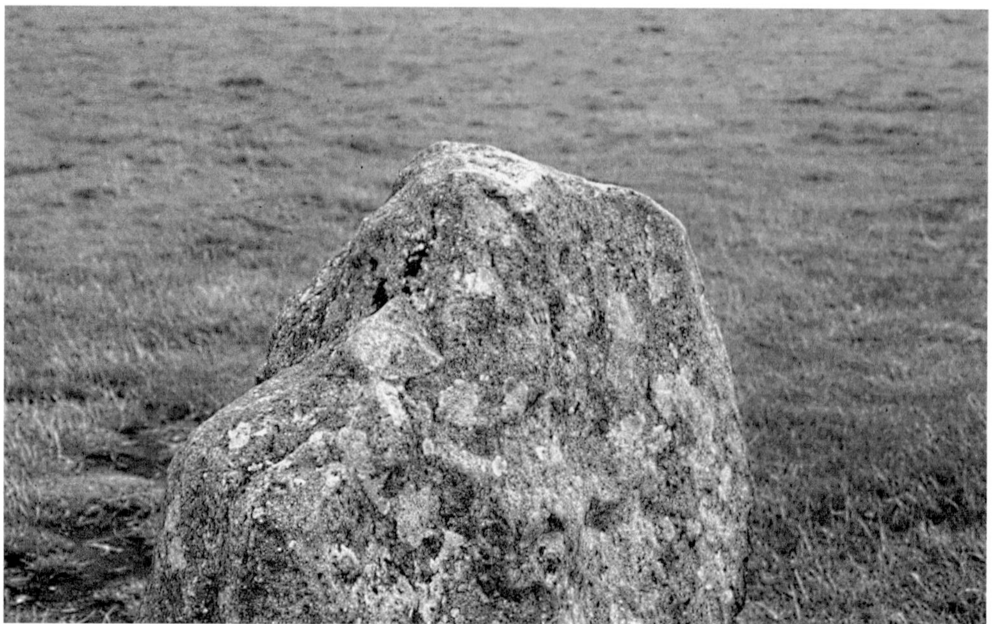

86 *A cup and part of a ring on stone 4*

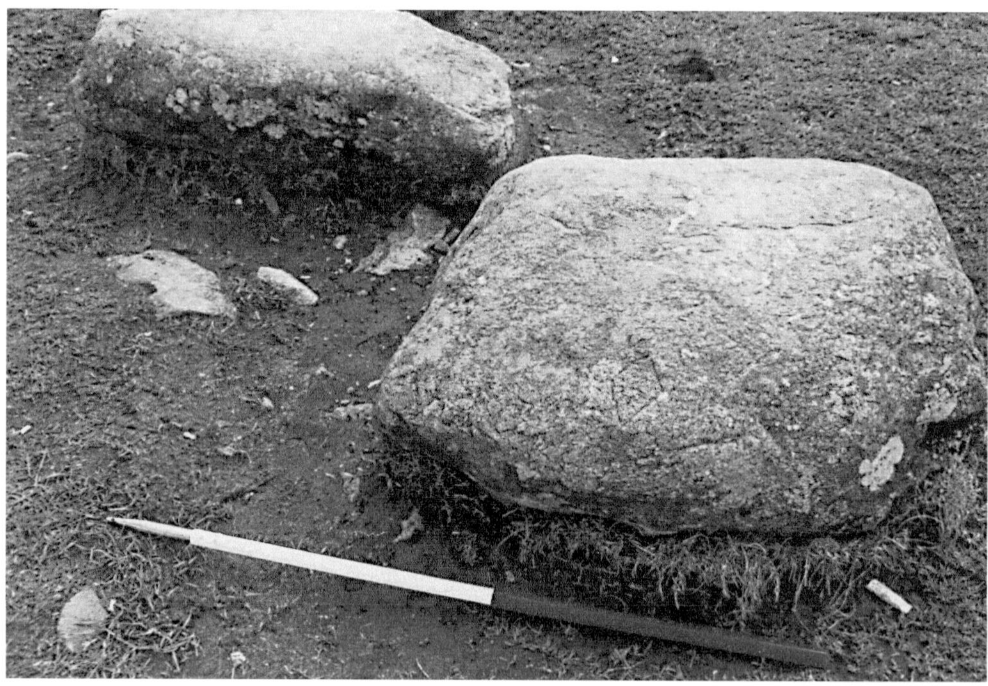

87 *Rock 5.* © Neil Stevenson

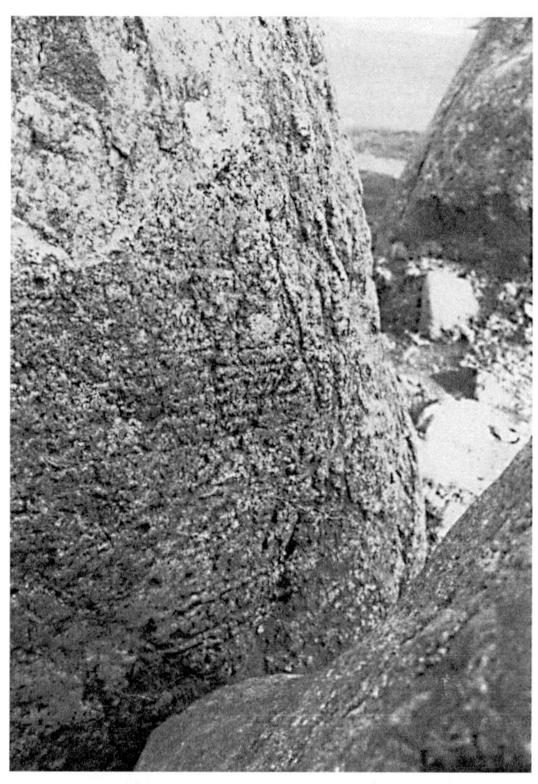

88 *Stone 3.* © Neil Stevenson

89 *Stone 2*

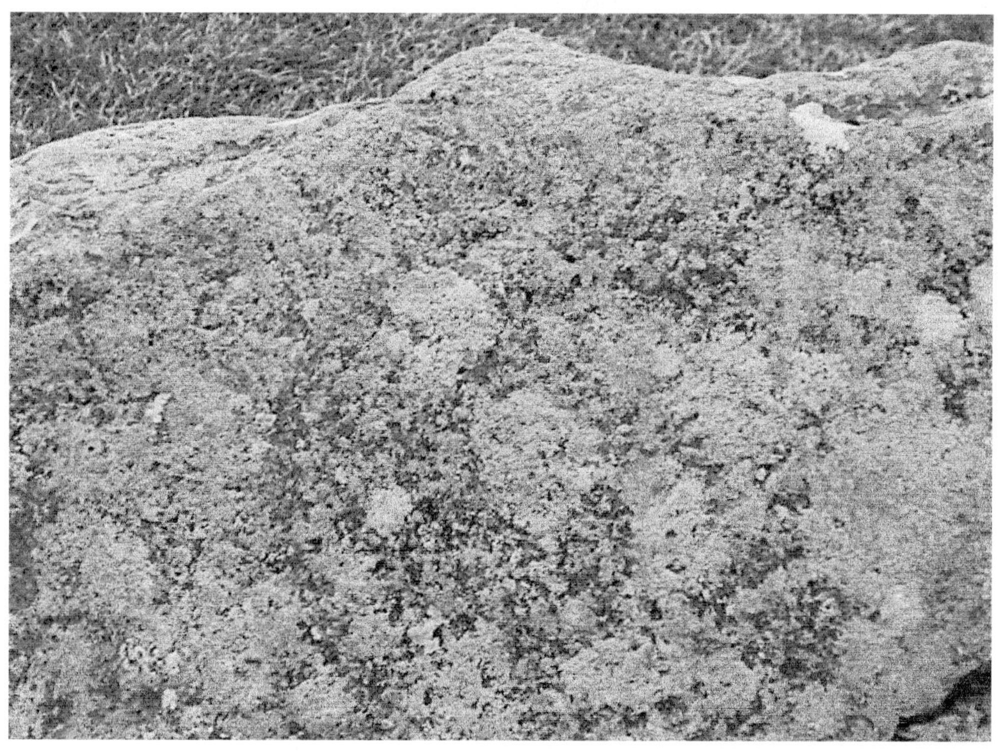

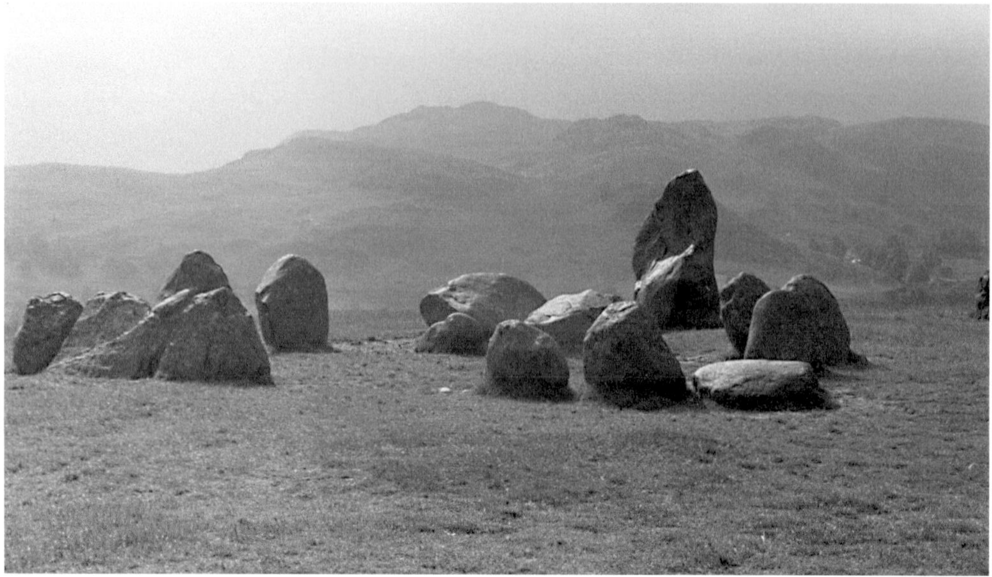

90 *The rectangular arrangement of stones adjoining the circle*

Chapel Flat, Dalston

The most northerly of Cumbria's stone circles was at Dalston, south-west of Carlisle. Today there is nothing left, and the only account of it is sketchy. In 1860:

> There was formerly a circle of rude stones, ten yards in diameter, near the village, supposed to be the remains of a Druidical temple; and at a little distance from it, was a tumulus, 3 yards (2.74m) high and 8 yards (7.31m) in diameter.

An eighteenth-century account describes it in roughly the same way, and what all the written evidence amounts to is a 27m diameter circle of stones that were 1m in diameter (and presumably unworked), and four large stones east of the centre of the circle lying on top of each other. The latter could have been a disturbed cist or 'cove', or a dolmen from a Neolithic barrow. Another reference says that one of the stones had 'a sort of circle, very crudely cut out, or marked, near the top.'

4 Burial contexts

We now turn to monuments, some of which have been classified in the past as 'stone circles', that are kerbs of stones containing burial mounds.

Little Meg (The Maughanby Stone Circle) (H01102 NY57693749)

The popular name of this site is appropriate, as it is close to Long Meg and considerably smaller. Maughanby (pronounced maff-anbee or moff-anbee) comes from Welsh and Scandinavian, meaning 'Merchiaun's settlement'.

It lies on the edge of a field called Whins, which usually means that there was gorse or dolerite stones there, but it now alternates between arable and pasture. There is a gate by the wide grassy verge south of the house, and a path skirts the field to the stones by the fence. The largest stone is upright, but the others may have been toppled. They give the impression that they have been pushed to one side. The marked stone is furthest into the field, with clear motifs, especially when the sun is low. The circle can be seen as part of a larger group of monuments, linked to Long Meg, Glassonby and Old Parks.

It was first recorded by the Rev. Canon James Simpson, who wrote of 'Eleven stones around a cist, situated a few hundred yards from Long Meg.' In 1866 he said that 'the barrow not only filled the enclosure, but partly covered the (standing) stones'.

The Rev. James Simpson was a friend of Sir J.Y. Simpson, whose book gave an account of the site. He mentions 'ring cuttings' on

> two boulders, forming part of a circle of eleven stones placed around a short cist in a large cairn . . . I have seen them along with him. Two or three cairns or tumuli existed locally till lately in the same locality. One of them, of large size, stood on land belonging to the free school of the township of Maughanby. After removing from its central mound or barrow a quantity of cobble stones mixed with earth, several large stones, one of them only erect, were found arranged in a circle about eighteen feet in diameter. Several of them were buried beneath the projecting edges of the barrow. In the centre of the circle was placed a semi-ovoid cist formed of rough stones, and measuring only three feet nine inches in length, two feet four inches in breadth and ten inches in depth. The cist contained an urn, burnt bones and charcoal. The only ornament upon the rude urn was a raised line near the top. No ornaments or weapons were detected, though careful search was made for them.

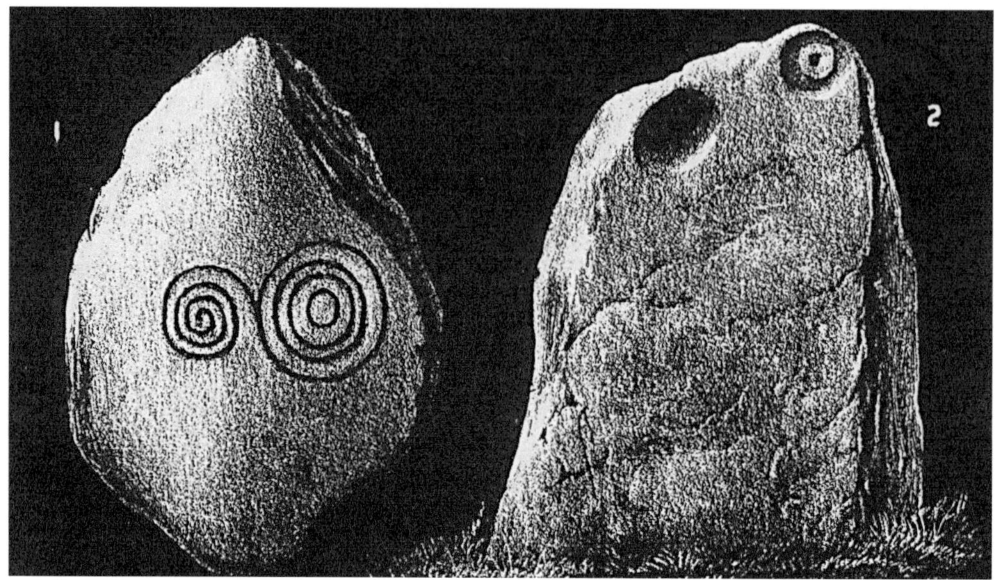

91 *Little Meg, from Sir J.Y. Simpson, 1867*

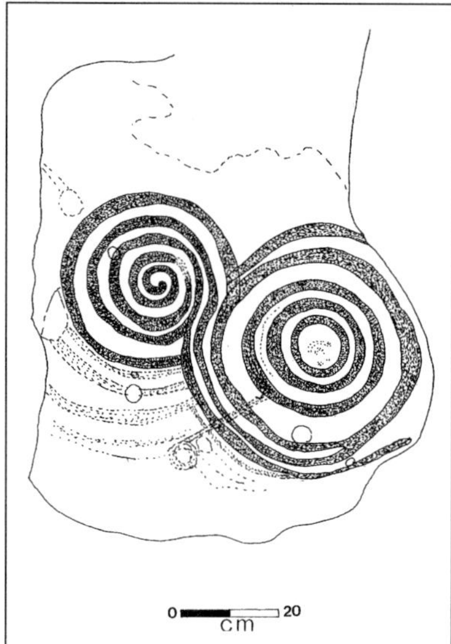

92 *Little Meg: linked spirals and concentric circles on a kerb stone*

On the inner and upper side of a large whin boulder, forming one of the eastern stones of the surrounding circle, is cut a spiral line which makes four turns or circles, the outermost having a diameter of ten inches. Alongside of it is a group of four concentric circles without any cup-centre or radial duct. The diameter of the innermost circle measures four inches, that of the outermost nineteen inches. The outermost edges of the volute of the concentric circle touch and meet at one part.

On top of the second stone on the western side are two circles, both about eight inches in diameter. The lower has its centre cut out; the higher encloses within it the remains of a small central cup, with a ridge around it.

The descriptions are illustrated by two sketches (**91**).

Assuming that it was an 11 stone circle, the centre would not have been very large, and it could be that the internal cairn was part of the original structure. A reference to the site in 1901 again speaks of 'a semi-ovoid cist with an urn and burnt bones within a circle of stones'. The Rev. Canon Thorley goes on to say that 'One of these stones, or part of it, was shown to me by Mr George Watson in the Penrith Museum', on display.

On site we have the boulder on which there is a very good spiral carefully linked into multiple concentric circles. The design was executed in one go, as the integration of the two sets of motifs shows. We can also see other faint peck marks concentric to the motifs. The shape of the boulder was considered to determine how the motifs should be applied. The markings on a second kerb are not visible today.

In Penrith Museum are two cup and ring marked stones from the central cist. How they related to the construction of the cist we do not know. Had they been placed inside the cist as part of the structure, to support a capstone? There is no mention of one. Were they placed in the cist as grave goods? Were they broken when they were removed?

The larger stone is roughly triangular-shaped with twin motifs at the base. They are concentric penannulars arranged around single cups. Above them is a large faint cup and arc, and there are various pick marks, a small oval, cup and part of a cup. The smaller stone has a cup and incomplete ring around it arranged centrally. The ring ends with an oval that points away from the line of the arc.

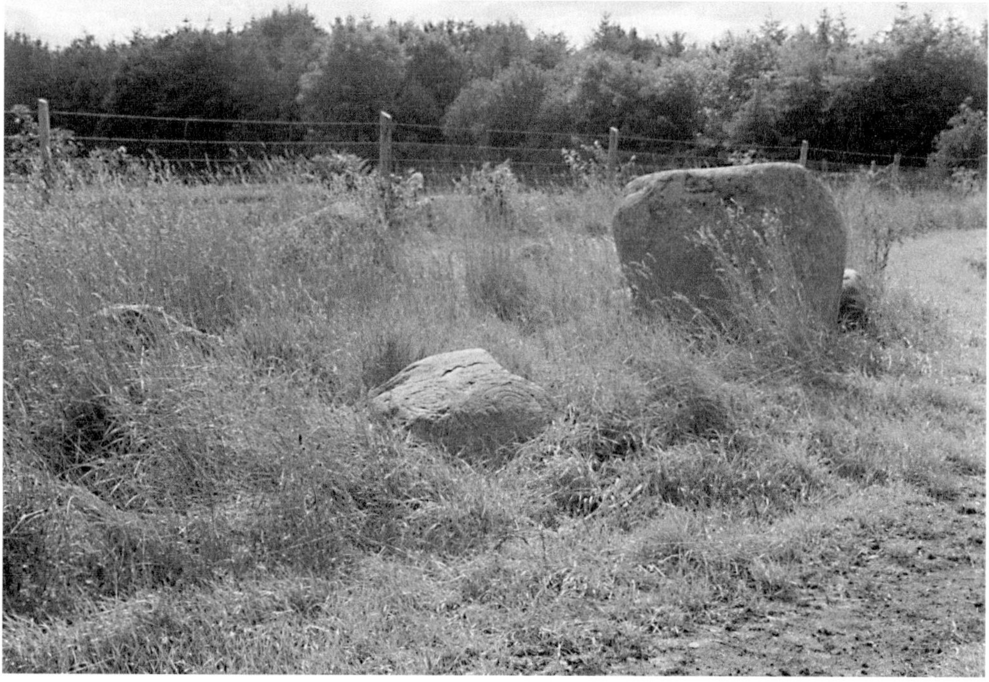

93 *The remains of the cairn*

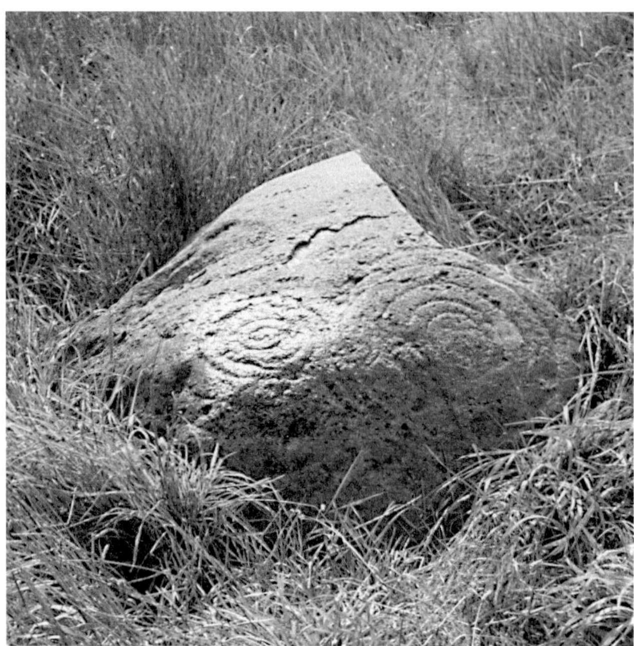

94 *The motifs*

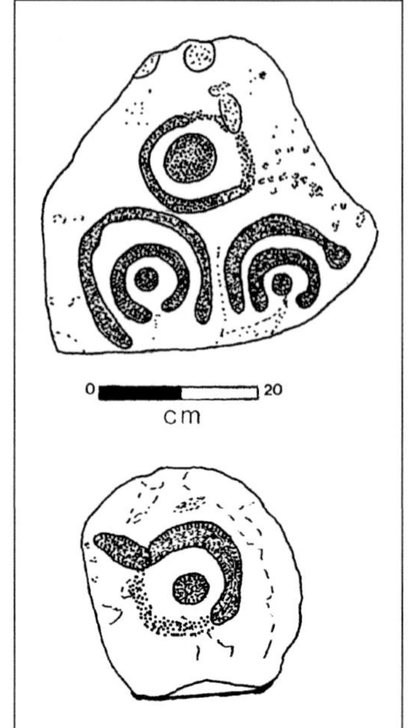

95 *Little Meg cist stones*

It could be that the motifs were made especially for the cist, or that they were brought in from elsewhere. Their *use* may be later than the circle that surrounds the cist, but they could have originated in the same period. The small stones are of sandstone, which is easier to mark than volcanic rock, and the spiral and concentric circles on the kerb boulder were not only more difficult to pick or incise, but they are more skilfully presented. The concentric circles are centred on an unmarked surface, a tradition that we have seen at Chapel Stile, and will see again at Glassonby, whereas the stones in the cist are cup-centred. These appear to be two different traditions of rock art, and strengthen the idea that the cist was inserted at a different time from the construction of the kerbs.

The Rev. Canon Thornley refers to a possible third stone from the cist: 'An old resident, Mr Thomas Glaister, remembers to have seen ring markings on a stone now lost, but once filling a gap at the SSE or SSW side.' It is unlikely that a circle only 5.49m diameter made up of ten recumbent and one standing stone can be regarded as a 'stone circle'. It is a kerbed cairn, the centre of which was filled with cobbles and earth over a buried semi-ovoid cist that contained an urn (what sort?) and cremation, and two marked sandstones. The centre of the mound was packed with enough material to cover the kerbstones, so that only the tops of some showed through. On a much larger scale, the Temple Wood circle in Argyll has spaced standing stones that were later closed with horizontal slabs between them, and the site used for cist burials, covered over to the tops of the monoliths by cobbles. Excavation there showed a long succession of uses of the site, and this may be the case at Little Meg, on a much smaller scale.

82

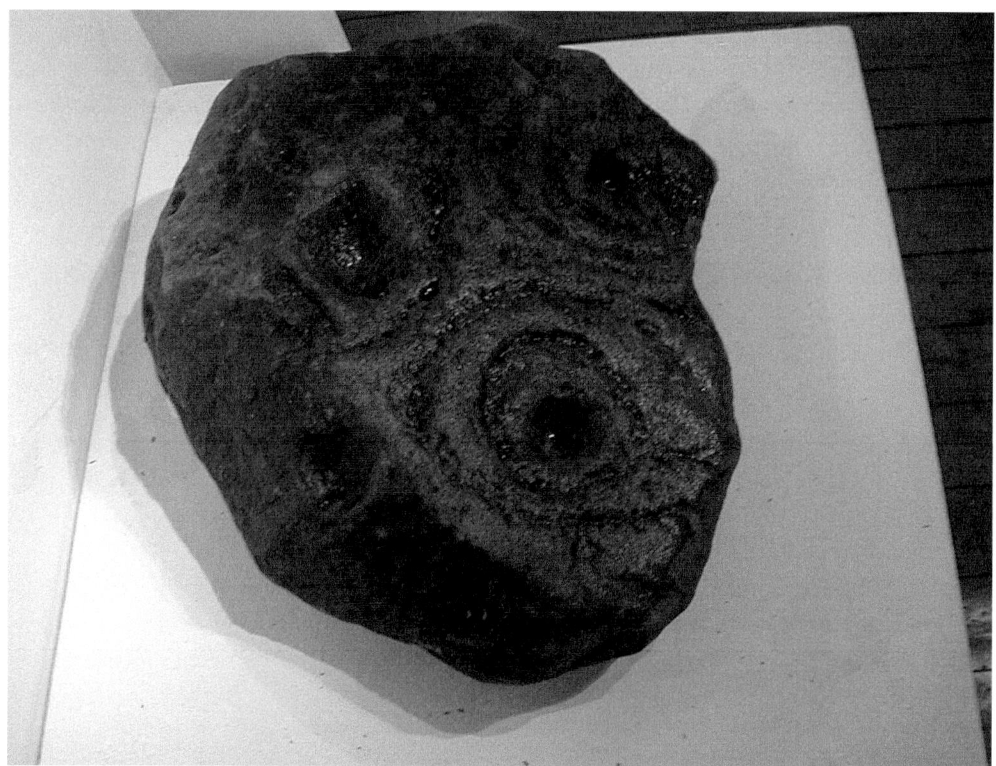

96–7 *Little Meg cist stones*

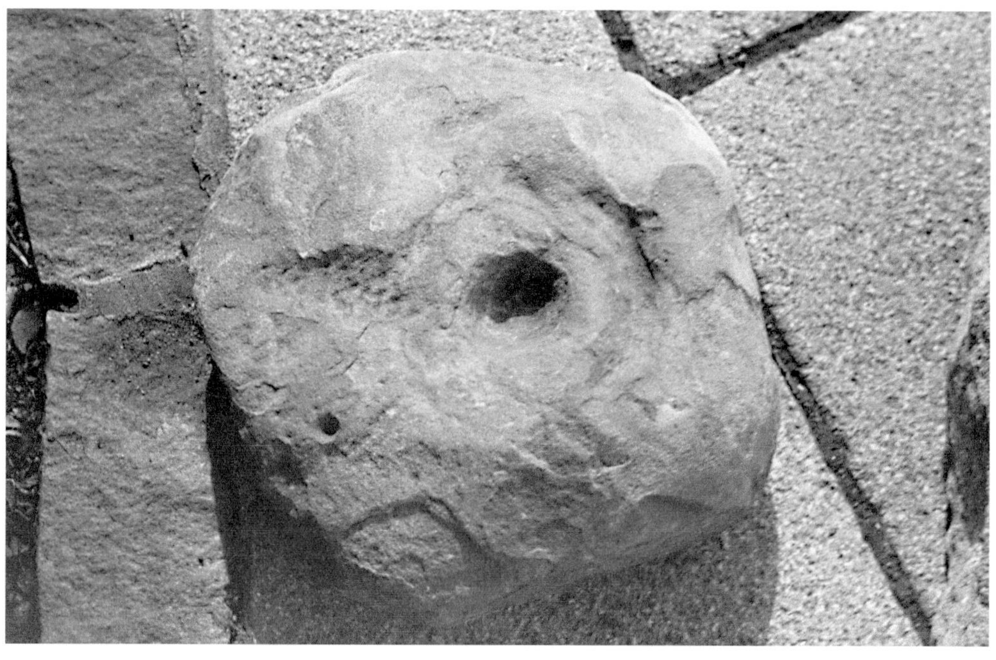

I noticed in December, in looking again for Simpson's elusive cup and cup and ring on a large standing stone, that the inner face of the large stone next to the spirals and concentric circles has some very fine incised lines, one an elongated oval. The problem is that it is sometimes difficult to distinguish natural features from artificial markings.

The Glassonby circle (Grayson Lands) (H01115 NY57293934)

Whereas Long Meg and Little Meg are well known to visitors, the Glassonby circle is not, probably because it is on private land and permission has to be sought to visit it. It can, however, be seen if you lean over the gate at the roadside, where a track leads downhill towards the site.

On the way down to the circle, which lies at the end of a sloping field, there is evidence of a very important buried feature revealed as a mark in the soil (spotted by Nick Best and Neil Stevenson): part of a cursus monument with a very clear ring ditch at its terminal. This is still being investigated; what it may demonstrate is that the Glassonby circle may be part of a more complex ritual area. A cursus is a sacred area enclosed by two parallel ditches, and may extend for hundreds of metres across the landscape. We have already seen that at Long Meg there are buried ditches, not of the cursus type, that could well have an important ceremonial function.

From the monument the views include the river valley and the Pennines, including Cross Fell. Fences and a small wood confine it to a corner of the field, and a ridge blocks the view back to the road.

Glassonby has an Irish name as its first element, and it means Glassan's settlement. It is also called 'Grayson Lands' or 'Graystone lands', which means grey horses, referring perhaps to the stones themselves, a common tradition (e.g. Gray Mare, Gray Yauds).

Today what you can see is an interrupted kerb of stones that encloses an oval cairn that has been robbed of some stone and added to by field clearance. The kerbstone with the motifs, still in situ, has the markings facing inwards, and they are so faint that they are almost invisible. Ploughing has taken place right up to the kerbs.

The site had been disturbed before the local antiquarians dug it at the turn of the century, and it is in reports of 1901-2 that we have to turn to make sense of what remains. The authors of these reports, W.G. Collingwood and the Rev. Canon Thorley, refer to the earliest mention by Canon Greenwell, Dr Rolleston and Chancellor Ferguson, who said it was 'a stone circle or fence'. It is, in fact, a kerbed cairn made of cobbles, and not a stone circle. The excavators claim to have dug to the 'natural' base of the field, which they described as 'undulating'. The mound surface was fairly uniform. They also referred to some of the cobbles being smashed up to make the mound compact.

Their drawings show that at the time of excavation there were 30 kerb stones, with gaps, including red sandstone, blue whinstone, greenstone, brecciated greenstone, granite, 'grey cobble', and hard white sandstone. Such stones were brought

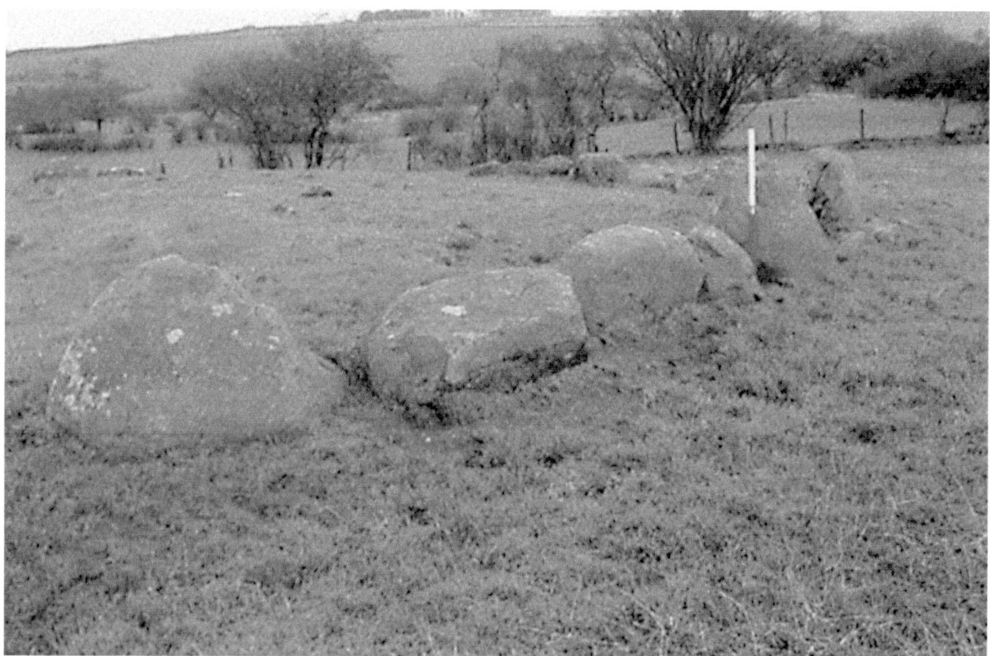

98 *The Glassonby circle*

down by glaciers, shaped and dumped. The stones, apparently, did not have sockets and were set vertically, but many had fallen. They varied in height from 2-36in (0.05-0.19m), in length from 20-85in (0.51-2.16m), and were between 6-36in (0.15-0.91m) in thickness. They were said to be continuous and touching. Some were missing, but no one bothered to ask whether the natural surface beneath the stones bore evidence of their weight and size.

The plan shows the position of the surviving marked rock (stone 28), still in situ. In 1875 a red sandstone block (over 3ft/0.91m long, 6in/0.15m thick, 2ft/0.61m high) 'with a spiral or concentric circles, like the figure on Long Meg, incised on its side' was found between stones 5 and 6 or between 30 and 1. The former is the stronger candidate, as it appears there on the plan, although it is marked outside the kerb.

So there is enough information here to define a near-circular kerbed cairn, two stones of which had motifs in the form of concentric rings or spirals and semi-ovoids. Some of the kerbs have been toppled from their vertical positions. A good photograph of stone 28 and its markings, by Mr F.W. Tassell of Carlisle, shows that there were many cobbles outside the kerb area; either the ritual area had been extended outwards, or the excavators had dumped material from the cairn outside it. More about that later.

Clues to the use of the site depend upon the same report, and the cist inside it shows that one use was funerary. All four sides of the cist were made of red sandstone, an ideal choice for making slabs, although as we have seen at Long Meg it may have had another significance. A cist is a pit lined with stone to make a box

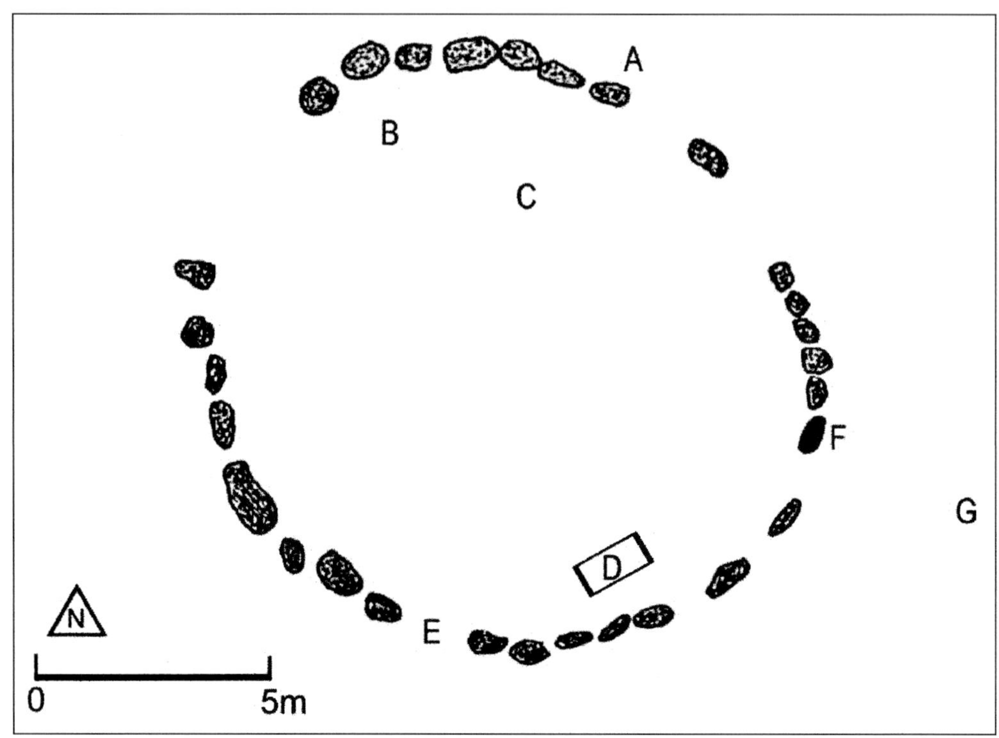

99 *A sketch plan of the Glassonby site. Key: A bone; B bead; C burnt area; D cist; E missing marked stone; F marked stone; G urn*

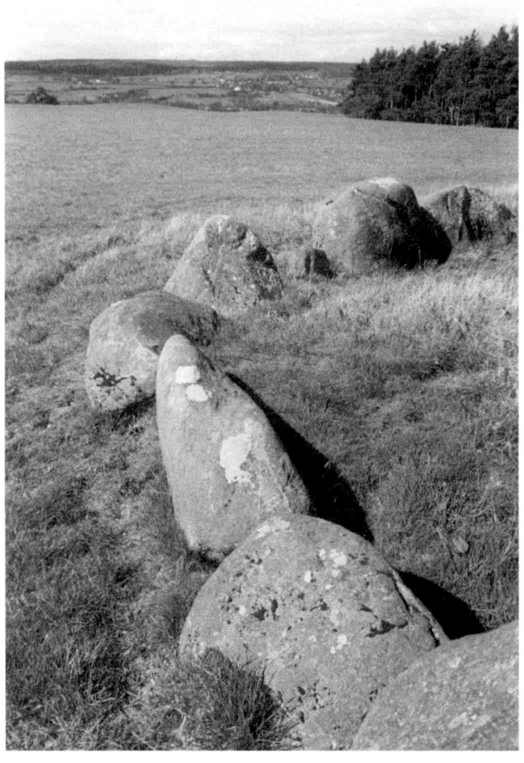

100 *Glassony kerb to the north*

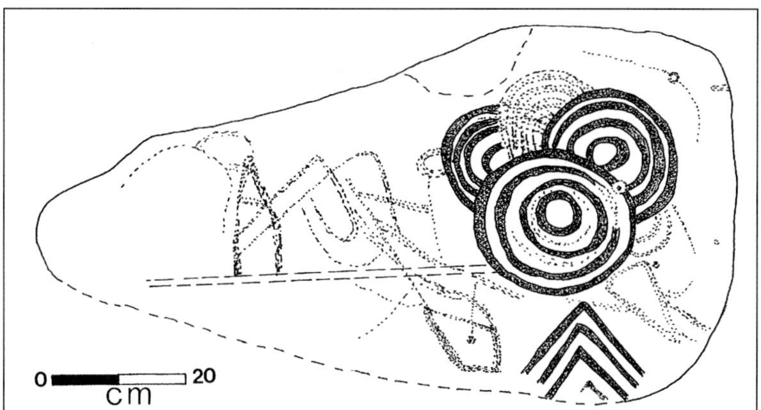

101 *Glassonby motifs still in situ*

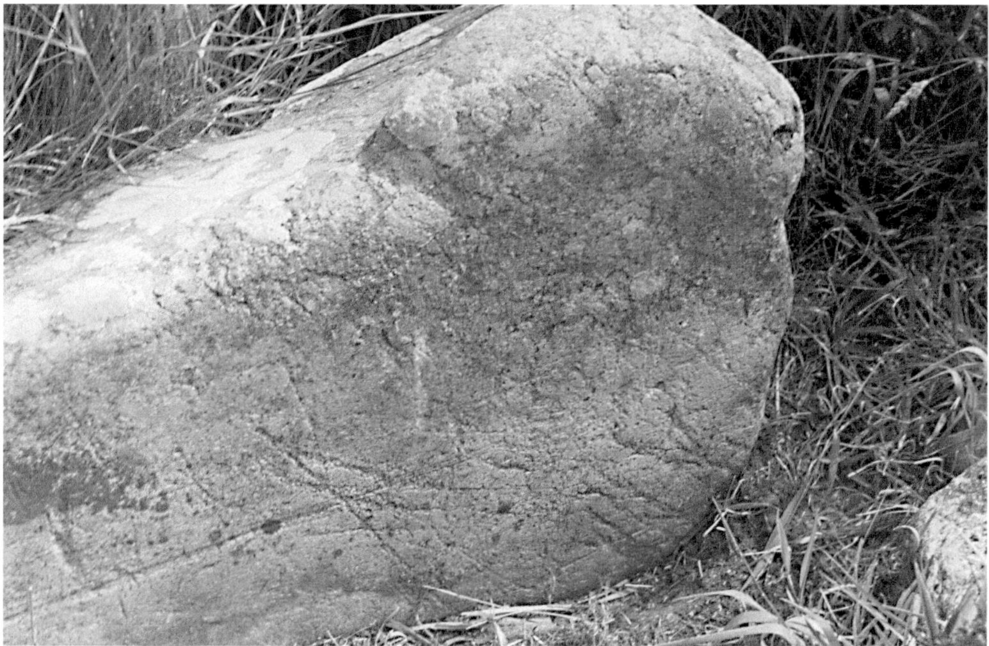

102 *The Glassonby stone*

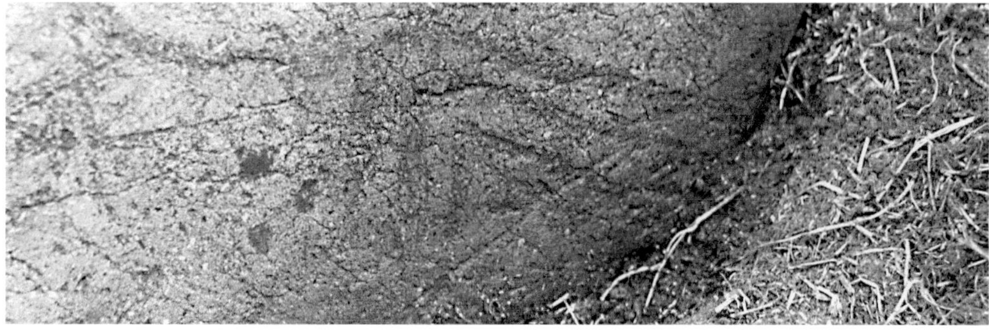

103 *Detail of the chevrons*

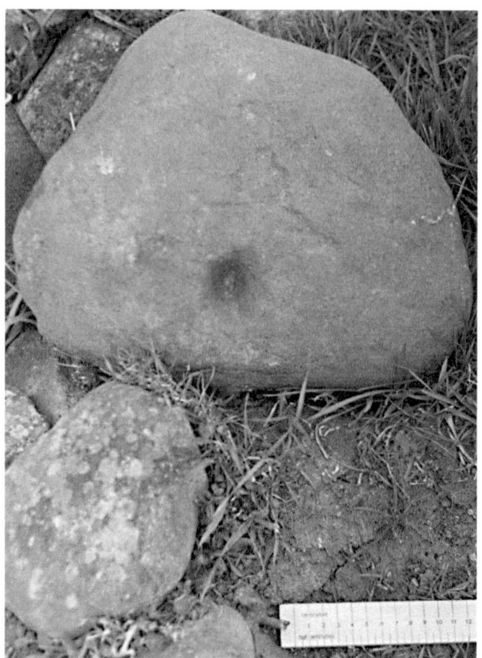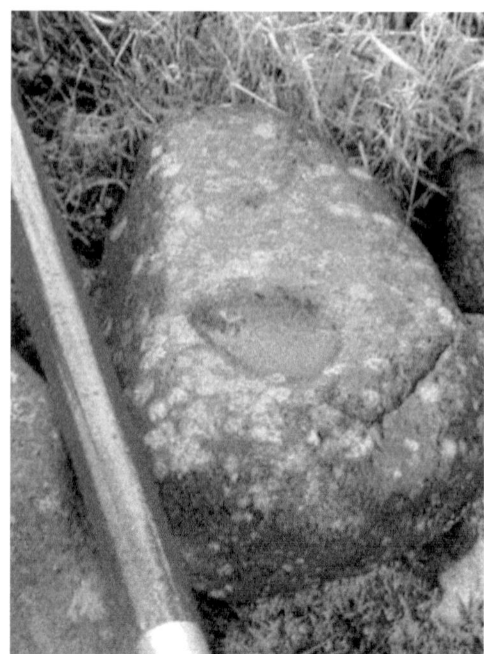

104–5 *The two cup-marked cobbles near the cairn*

for burial. The grave was dug into the natural base at a depth that kept the capstone just below the base, the capstone completing the sealing of the cist before the stones were piled on top. It had been robbed or disturbed probably at a time when bits of old bone or pot were disappointing finds. Within the mound was a patch of charcoal 'on the original floor'.

A bead of light blue transparent glass, with decoration, also inside the circle, could be a later votive offering at a site still visible and which retained a reputation for sanctity.

Outside the kerbstones were burnt bones and an urn. These could have been covered with a secondary wall of cobbles outside the kerbstones to bring them into the ritual area, although at the time of the excavation it was said that it had no cover, even though a photograph at the time shows stones in a shallow heap outside the kerb. How deep did stones have to be to make a 'cover'?

The collared urn is late in the tradition of prehistoric burial, both in its type, well known elsewhere, and in its position outside the circle. It is safe to say that there was cremated bone inside the urn, and that the urn was inverted. We are not told what covered the urn, or whether it lay in a scoop in the ground. It certainly contained bones and charcoal. Dr Henry Barnes and Professor William Turner identified 24 teeth; the largest bone was part of a thigh, and the remains were of a man. The second cremation was unurned, smaller in quantity, and the bones were assumed to be those of a woman younger than the man in the other burial.

To turn now to the marked stones; a second report, by Rev. Canon Thornley in 1902, covered a number of sites, but added some interesting pieces to the Glassonby story.

He located the place where the missing marked rock had been: 'a ring-marking on a stone now lost, but once filling a gap in the SSE or SSW side'.

He described the stone that is still there as 'hard cobble-stone' with 'concentric circles, one group of four complete and plainly marked circles, above which are two groups of four circles or curves each, springing from or intersecting the ring below'. A touched-up photograph accompanies the description. He calls the motifs 'rudely and lightly hatched'.

The motifs

The rock is not 'rudely' marked; the pecking on it, executed with a finely pointed implement, produces narrow grooves quite skilfully.

No one has drawn attention to a novel chevron at the base of the stone (people tend to copy the last drawing!). It was a very difficult design to draw, and took many hours. The surface was lichen–free at the time of recording, and its position protects it from erosion. It is tough and smooth rock.

In type, the motifs bear some similarity to those on Irish passage graves, and there is an affinity with the Gavrinis tomb in Britanny. It is not in the common British 'cup and ring' tradition, and there are no spirals.

There are three ovoids that join the central group of concentric circles, but in parts they are so faint that only the most painstaking wax rubbings brought them to light. Elsewhere on the rock, what may have been seen as plough or harrow scratch marks are grooves made of tiny peck marks close together; they do not make any recognisable pattern. Thus the rock surface has been extensively used, some parts with curves and others with thin straight lines.

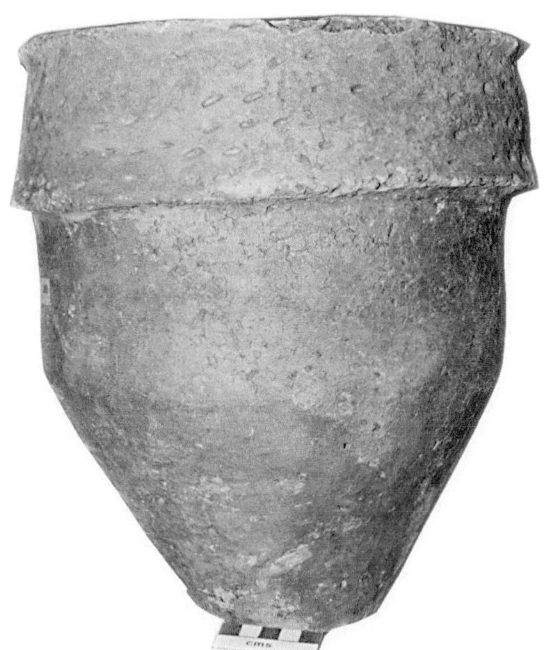

106 *The Glassonby collared urn.*
Tullie House museum

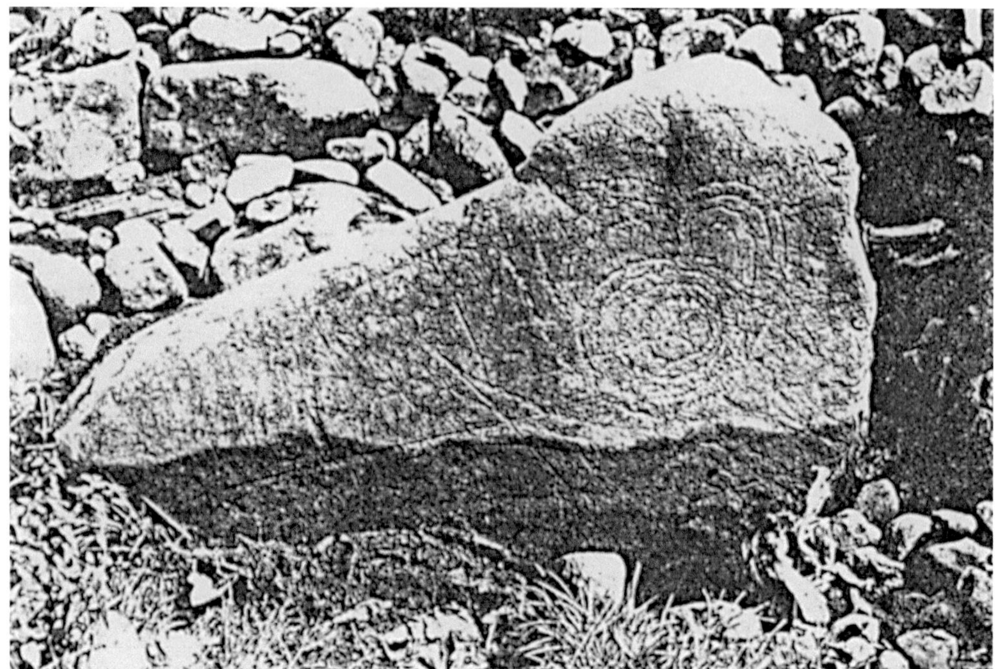

107 *A touched-up photograph that appeared in an early report*

The fine linear grooves link it with Long Meg, but the missing red sandstone with its spiral or concentric circles provides a stronger link. The concentric rings round an uncupped centre link it with the Chapel Stile rock, and so do the very rare chevrons.

Is the stone that is still in place earlier than the cairn, and brought here because of the importance of its previous context? The site has been reused, perhaps many times in prehistory; cist, bead, pot and cremations all point to a secondary use of the cairn in the early Bronze Age.

There are many cobbles scattered around the field boundaries. Two have cup marks on them. It is very likely that the burial mound was made up of cobbles that were lying around on the surface or used from field clearance. Now the reverse has happened: some of the cobbles have been taken from the mound and scattered. A thorough search might locate more.

Old Parks, Kirkoswald (H01103a–c NY56993988)

Kirkoswald means King Oswald's church. There is nothing to be seen now at the site. This section attempts to reconstruct the history of the site in words and sketches before dealing with the rock art in detail. Two of the three decorated stones from the site are now on display at Tullie House Museum, Carlisle, alongside the Honey Pots Farm stone. The site is in Low Field: 'hlaw' means a burial mound.

90

The story begins in 1892 when Cumberland County Council bought a heap of stones in this field to use as road metal. It was assumed to be field clearance until the finding of an 'incense cup' prompted an archaeological interest. (The term 'incense cup' is no longer used, but is retained in this report.) By the time Chancellor Ferguson and the Rev. H.A. Macpherson got there, 30 cartloads of stone had already been moved from the north end of the mound. From there the 'incense cup' and fragments of large urn and some bits of calcified bone were found. These men 'dug onto the centre of the mound, where some large slabs of stone were lying about, and partially exposed a large earthfast stone'.

At first they thought it was part of a cist: 'On it we observed a curious artificial mark or grooving. Near it we found two or three vertebra and a fragment of a skull, none of which were human. We also found a very little charcoal, and some stone that had been subject to the action of fire.'

There was a pause in the Council's activities, but when further dismantling of the mound began, another 'incense cup' was found. This one had 12 beads inside, discovered when the farmer's wife, Mrs Potter, 'with the curiosity of the sex, got to poking in it with a hairpin'.

It was visited again in 1894, but 'much earlier' a photographer been sent to the site. Between 1892-4 about 600 cartloads of stone had been removed, and 'a considerable heap was still remaining on the west side, awaiting removal'. The stones were mainly sandstones.

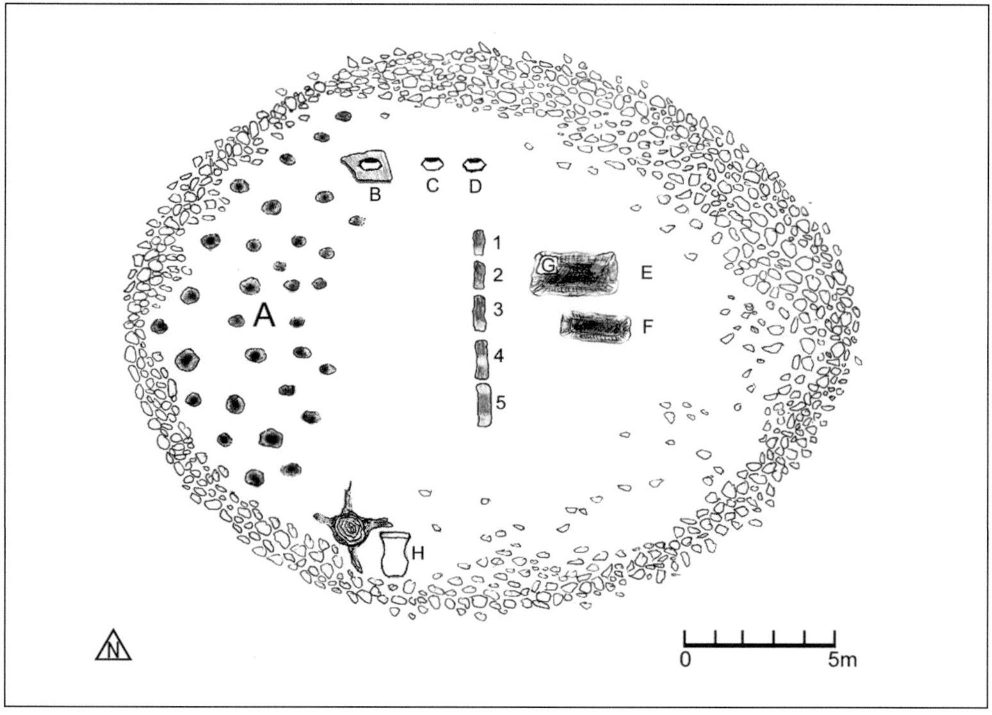

108 *A sketch plan of the Old Parks site, based on reports*

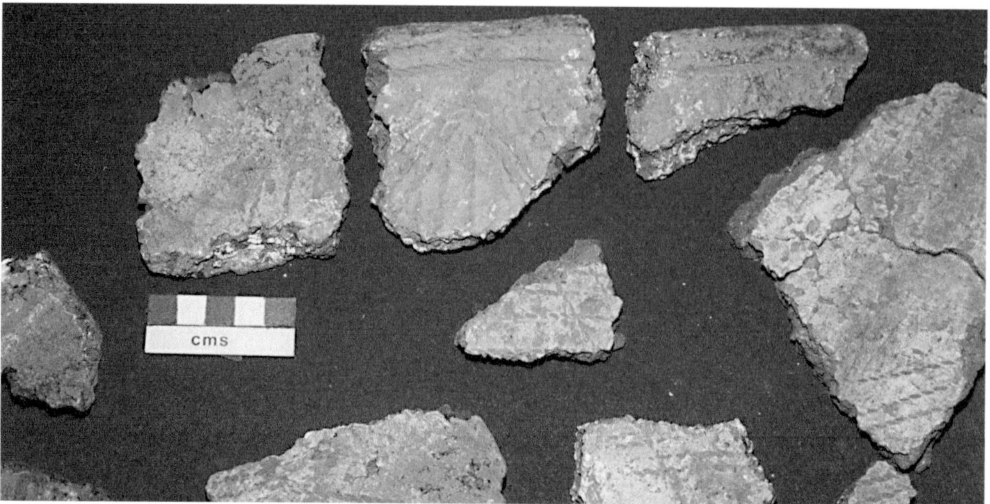

109 *Urn fragments at Tullie House*

The sketch map helps to make the 1894 report clear. The height of the mound was about 4ft (1.22m) and 'somewhat depressed' in the centre, which sounds as though someone had been digging into it before the commercial activity started. It had probably been used as a dumping ground for other stone, and a large tree had grown at the southern end within the circumference.

Structurally, the most important feature of the mound was a 14ft 9in (4.5m) long row of five slabs of stone that ran in a straight line north to south, set in shallow scoops in the 'natural'. They were from 1ft 8in to 3ft 2in (0.51-0.96m) long, 1ft 11in to 2ft (0.58-0.61m) tall, and 4-8in (0.16-0.33m) thick. Two had motifs on their east faces and one on its west face. 'The markings continue into the ground and show that they were upon the stones before they were set up in their present positions.' The marks were fresh, and had therefore not been exposed much before.

The line of stones divided the mound roughly into two semi-ovals:

West: There were 32 'deposits of burnt bones' in hollows scraped out of the natural surface of the ground, accompanied in some cases by fragments of broken urns, and also by stones showing traces of fire. Could the cremations have been done on the spot? This is the second reference to burnt stone.

The two 'incense cups' were found in the same area near the north end of the dividing line. The interments were 'dotted around the area of the semi-oval, but mainly towards the circumference. Under the roots of the tree, stated to have been growing on the south side of the mound, a large burial urn was found, full of burnt bones.'

'Fragments of similar urns were found among the bones of some of the interments, and also of urns of similar smaller and thinner paste, being possibly of the class known as drinking cups.' By this they meant 'Beakers'.

92

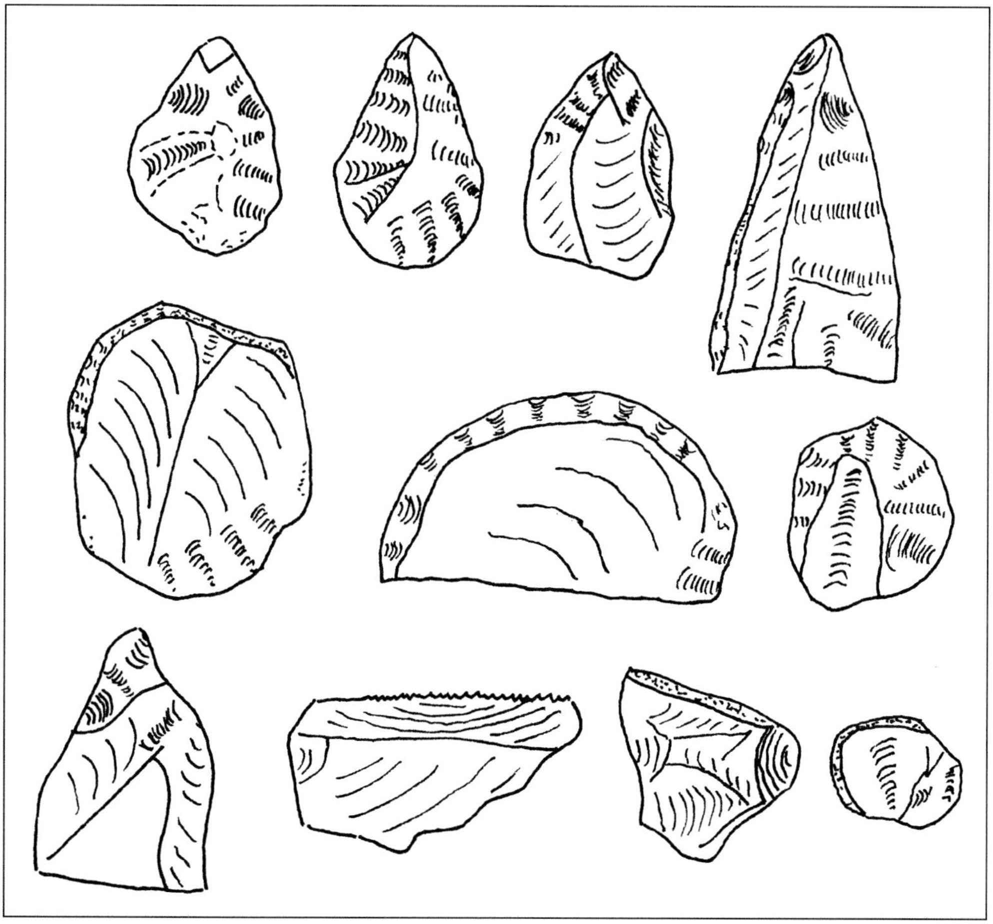

110 *Flint implements found in the area around the mound (now in Tullie House). Actual size*

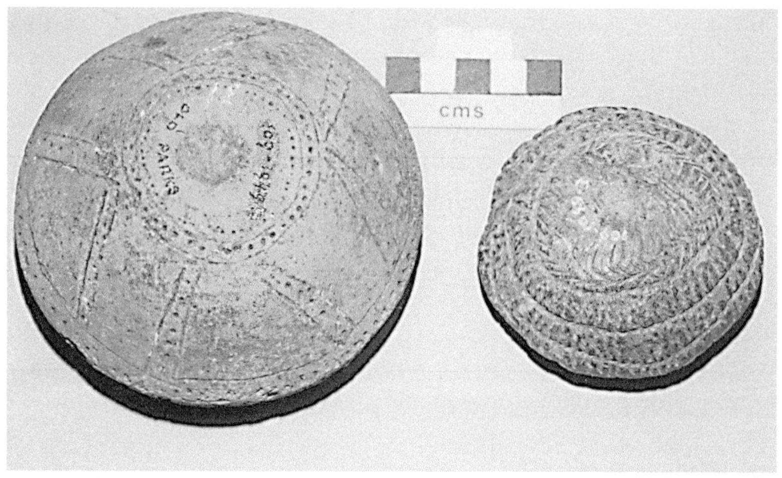

111 *Two 'incense cups' from Old Parks in Tullie House museum*

East: The description of this sector throws up all sorts of questions, because it contained 'no interments.' There were two trenches for graves, aligned east to west. The larger was 8ft 3in x 4ft 9in x 4ft 3in (2.51 x 1.45 x 1.29m) deep; 'the other was smaller, about the dimensions of an ordinary grave of the present day, but had been filled up before my visit, partly by the workmen, but mostly by a violent thunderstorm. Both, when discovered, were filled up with cobble stones, and in the corner of the larger, under a flagstone, were some burnt bones and ashes.'

They regarded the graves as inhumations for which the mound had been originally built, and the cremation under the flagstones as a secondary burial, because the graves were cut over 4ft (1.22m) into the original ground surface.

Having dismissed the possibility of the cremations being 'wholesale slaughter of slaves and dependants at the time of the inhumation', he concluded, 'It would be more probable that they were made subsequently and at different times.'

This conclusion is the best way to assess the history of the mound. Much of the evidence was destroyed by the removal of stone, and violent thunderstorms would not have helped observation. If one assumes that the line of stones with their motifs was the earliest part of the structure, the addition of early Bronze Age burials and grave goods would not be uncommon. There must have been considerable interference with the whole mound to make these insertions. This constant re-use of burial mounds is echoed elsewhere in Britain on a large scale.

The two 'cists' are puzzling, but show a different use of the two parts of the mound divided by the five slabs. There are other factors: go back to the earlier part of the report where animal vertebra and skull fragments are mentioned, and slabs of stone that were lying about. Without making too much of this, it does suggest another destroyed structure, and perhaps deliberate burial of animal bone. The history of the mound appears to be Neolithic to early Bronze Age.

The motifs

We are left, then, with the certain position of the three marked monoliths, and the survival of two of them. We have a photograph of the missing one, and the stone may yet be found.

Part of stone 5 is displayed at Tullie House Museum conveniently for its stability, but half is missing, and the stone should be viewed as in my drawing. The dominant motifs I call *fronds* (or walking sticks) and rings. All are picked into the rock surface with a sharp stone tool, but some are more finished than others. This incompleteness of design or execution is common in Britain, and the act of making the motif must have been important in itself. There is no comprehensive design, but a series of fronds, which are the central beginning of spirals, that have their stems following the same general vertical direction of the standing stone. Some are right-handed and others left-handed turns (convolutions). One curls back upon itself and another runs into a circle.

The marked surface of stone 4, west-facing, has a confusing series of bending grooves and apparently unfinished motifs that do not make it a very satisfying design

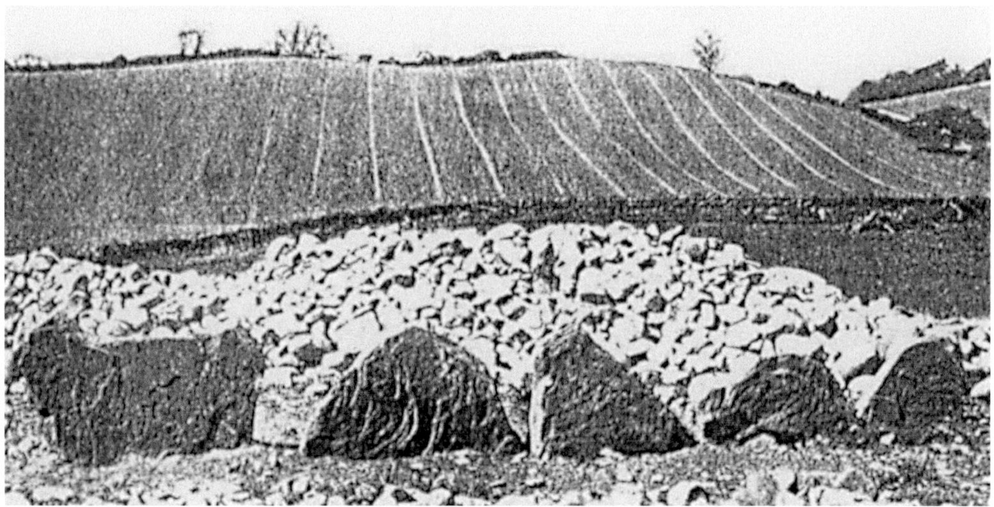

112 *An old photograph of the five stones in situ among the remains of the cobble mound*

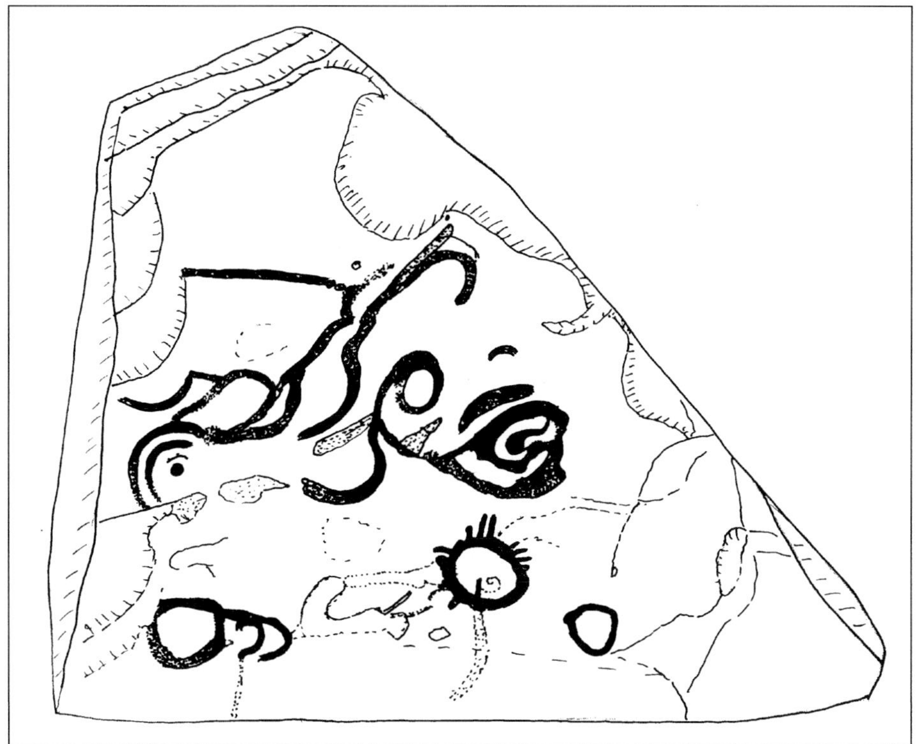

113 *Stone 3. As this stone is lost, the drawing has to be based on a photograph taken by Fred Tassell (see **116**). The motifs appear to be uneroded, and some may be unfinished. Some are serpentine grooves. There is what appears to be a deeply but crudely-cut interlocking spiral, a circle with incised rays (radiates) from its outer edge, a 'crook' with a long serpentine tail. Another has the crook joining the stem to form a ring, two concentric arcs around a cup, and two roughly circular enclosures near the bottom, one of which connects to two arcs or crooks*

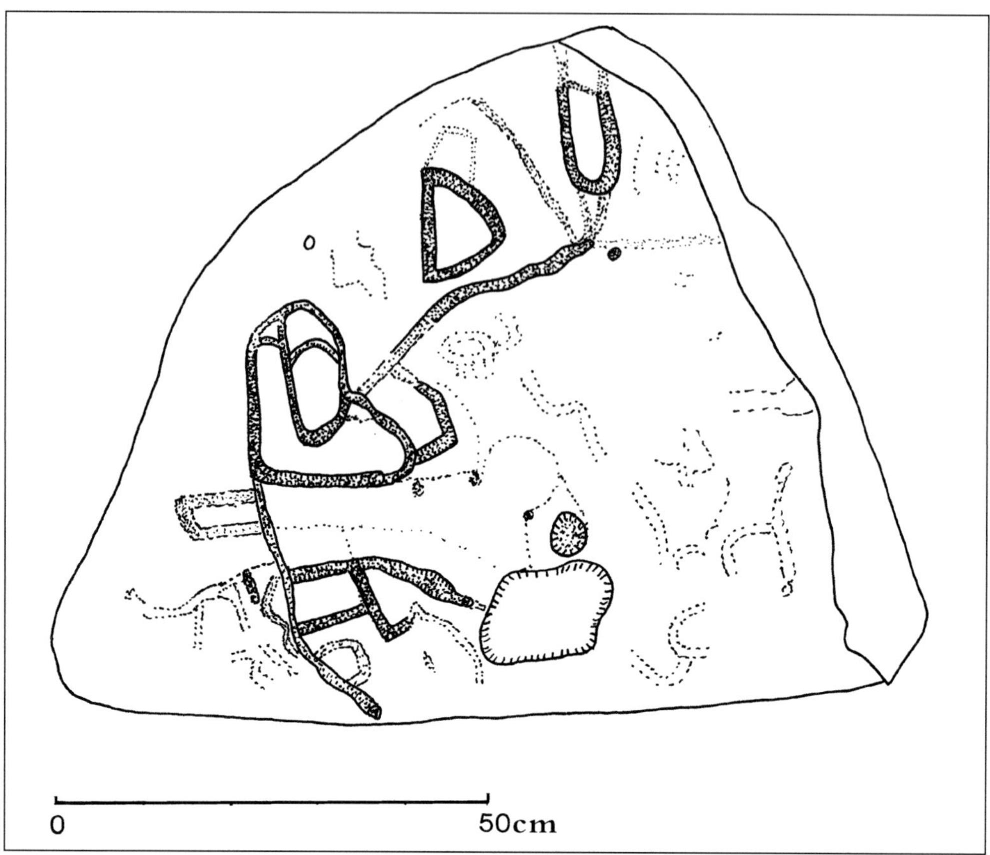

114 *Stone 4: now on show in Tullie House Museum. As all the pick marks are visible, it has most likely been buried and protected for thousands of years under a mound of cobble stones. It is displayed as it stood in a line of five, its flat base giving support. The motifs are largely angular, forming unusual enclosures. One figure is D-shaped. All are connected by long grooves. There are other marks, some artificial and others natural. The large depressed square appears natural, but may have been enhanced. It is a very strange display of markings, yet fits with those on the other two stones*

to modern eyes. Stone 3, from the photograph only, has two fronds, circles, and something that looks like a developing spiral. Again, there are tentative pick marks on the rock that suggest a try-out of some motif and its abandonment.

The three stones have the same motif characteristics, and were apparently all made at the same time for the same purpose. Freshly pecked, and under a mound, they follow the tradition in which there is a distinction between 'public' and 'private' use. In this case the motifs were meant for the dead. A rock like Long Meg is here for all to see, in the most prominent place. Inward-facing kerbstones in cairns of many periods, the use of motifs inside cists and on cobbles that make up burial mounds are continuations of a purpose that is hidden from the living.

Whatever the original structure of this site, it was considerably modified to allow other people of other centuries to intrude and share the mystique of the site.

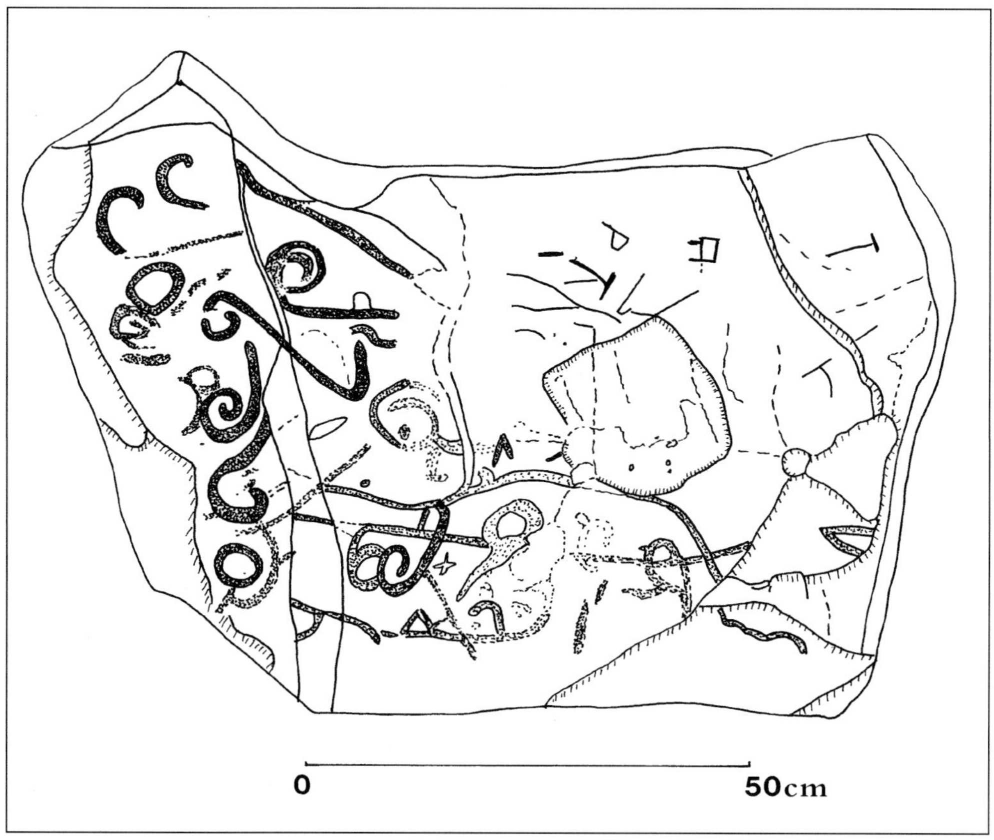

115 *Stone 5. A photograph by Fred W. Tassell of Carlisle at the time the mound was dug shows that only part of this has survived, and is now on display in Tullie House museum in a position different from its position on the site: what is now displayed as the 'top' was a side. The stone had been moved from its place in the mound to a wall, resting on its largest and flattest edge.*

The most prominent motifs are the 'crooks', the beginning of a spiral. On the left-hand side, running up to a natural, curved vertical line in the stone are eight of these, all with clear pick marks, some motifs more developed than others. In some the spiral curve has been continued to form a ring. The stems of three of these spirals continue beyond the line in the rock to link up there, but other new crooks and stems are developed too. These can be seen in the drawing.

What is unusual in the general arrangement of motifs is that there are scratches or incisions on a smooth part of the surface near the top, which could be recent or old. Although 'P.T.' suggests modern initials, this is not certain

The stone is the most elaborately marked of the three, and lies at the south end of the row. If the row of stones is the remnant of a kind of passage through a long mound, Stone 5 must have had a special significance. Stones 1 and 2, at the opposite end of the row, were unmarked, and presumably of less significance

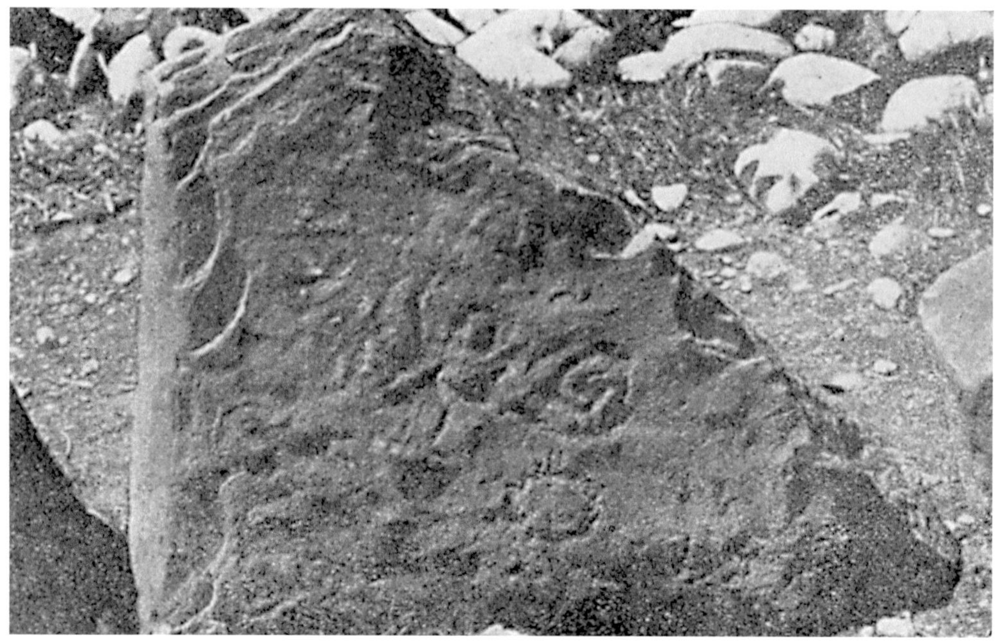

116 *Stone 3. This stone is now lost.* Fred Tassell

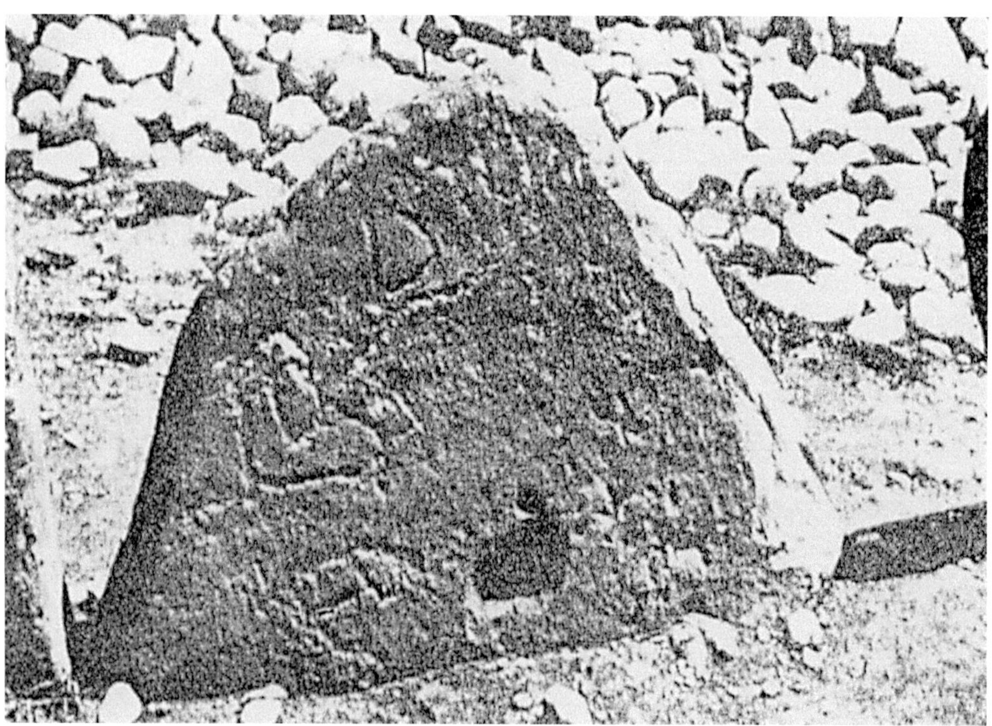

117 *Stone 4.* Fred Tassell. In Tullie House Museum

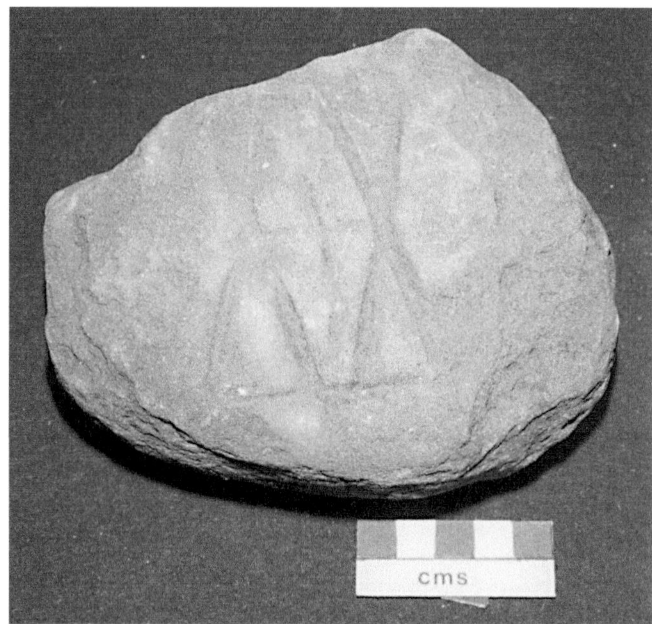

118 *Broomrigg.* Tullie House

Broomrigg (H01122 NY548466)

The continuation of this rich monumental landscape towards Brampton has important prehistoric sites at Broomrigg, including cairn circles and stone circles that have actually been planted over by forestry, and the remains of a stone circle called Grey Yauds.

The enclosure of areas for ritual purposes in Neolithic and early Bronze Age times seems to fall into specific high-density groups. At Broomrigg site B the smallest stone circle consists of seven stones, surrounding a robbed stone-lined conical pit that may have contained an urn. The excavator reported a small red sandstone with a crossed line pattern on it, but it has no certain context; it appears here as an unusual type of rock marking in a monument of roughly the same period as others in the area.

Definitely of the 'cup and ring' type of marking is the Armathwaite stone, described under 'Portables' (see below).

Redhills (H01118 NY50182777)

A good example of cup and ring art on a cist slab has been lost:

> The most remarkable cup-marked stone discovered in Cumberland and Westmorland was found in 1881 by Dr Taylor at Redhills, in the township of Stainton, in Cumberland, about 2 miles from Penrith. It is a large slab of freestone, 5ft 4in (1.62m) long, 3ft 6in (0.92m) in width at the centre, and it varies from 8-13in (0.20-0.33m) in thickness.

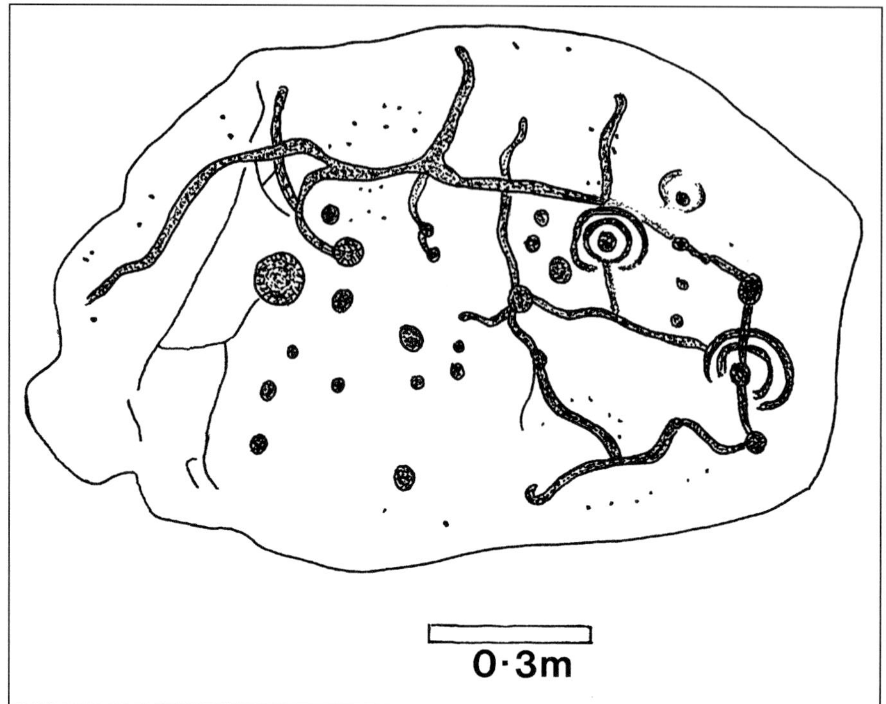

119 *The Redhills cist cover*

After a full description of the stone, Dr Taylor in 1881 gives details of where it was found: 'It formed the cover of a cist, which had contained an interment after cremation.'

This context means that the marked stone was either made especially for the burial, or that it was reused from another site. An important consideration is that it was reported on the *underside* of the slab, for in the early Bronze Age when motifs were incorporated into burials they were almost always facing into the grave. This means that they were not meant to be seen. The cist itself was cut out of rock and lined with cobbles. There were no grave goods reported, only charcoal and burnt bones.

As the upper part of the cist slab was plough-scarred, any cobblestone covering of the grave (if any) had gone. As we cannot see the stone, and as I have to reproduce someone else's drawing, I include Dr Taylor's description of the motifs:

> 24 cups of various depths and sizes.
> Two central hollowed cones surrounded by two concentric circles bisected
> by a radial groove.
> Hollowed channels running in different directions.
> Small pick marks.

He refers to it as both an unquarried 'white freestone' and as a soft sandstone. It was broken in several places by the workmen, 'but I have adjusted these and joined them together as carefully as possible'. He says of the largest cup that 'the chisel marks are distinct and fresh, as if done yesterday.' He observes that outside the cups and grooves are examples of diffuse pecking:

> There is another class of markings on the stone; these are little pits or peck–marks, small irregular holes picked in the stone; they are dispersed apparently all over the surface.

He supposes the marks to have been made with a mallet and chisel, and links the markings with stones from the Maughanby cairn (Little Meg), 'which contains a semi-ovoid cist with an urn and burnt bones. One of these stones is in my possession.'

His report is thorough and of great value, especially as the stone is now lost, and he makes another important observation, that although these markings occur in round barrows, the connection is rare. Compared with other examples of cup and ring art elsewhere in the north, it is not exceptional, and the range of motifs is limited, but its greatest significance is in its position as a cist cover.

The Moor Divock Ring Cairn (H01124 NY49402196)

Askham village (NY515236) is south-west of Penrith. Askham Fell, which includes Moor Divock, can be reached by public path west out of Askham, or via Helton along an unfenced minor road. There are many monuments, including the Copstone, and a disturbed burial cairn that had an inverted urn at its centre. Another disturbed cairn has a cist visible at its centre. The Cockpit is a circle of stones containing the remains of a wall, enclosing a large central area. If you walk south along the Roman High Street, climbing steadily to some superb views of lakes and mountains, then branch east, the Moor Divock area contrasts completely with it, like an enormous even plain. There are many sinkholes in the limestone. Beneath the bracken are lines of narrow rig and furrow ploughing, which show that the land has been cleared for arable farming, also showing that cairns, standing stones and circles are lucky survivors.

The cairn with rock art lies in one of the most visited prehistoric landscapes in Cumbria, but it was not until 1995 that I saw the cup and ring mark on a standing stone that formed part of the outer circle of the cairn. It was fortunate that I arrived there when the westering sun cast an oblique shadow of the cup and ring. It is possible to visit the cairn and not see the cup and ring, but the photograph and drawing are evidence.

The site was excavated by Simpson and Greenwell (Greenwell 1877, 400), who found a 0.6m (2ft) deep pit at the centre, and ashes and sherds of a broken vessel. A Food Vessel lay above this on the sand. There is a cup-marked cobble still at the centre.

The cairn is of the type dated to the late Neolithic/early Bronze Age, about 4000 years ago. Whether the marked rocks are contemporary with the burial is not known.

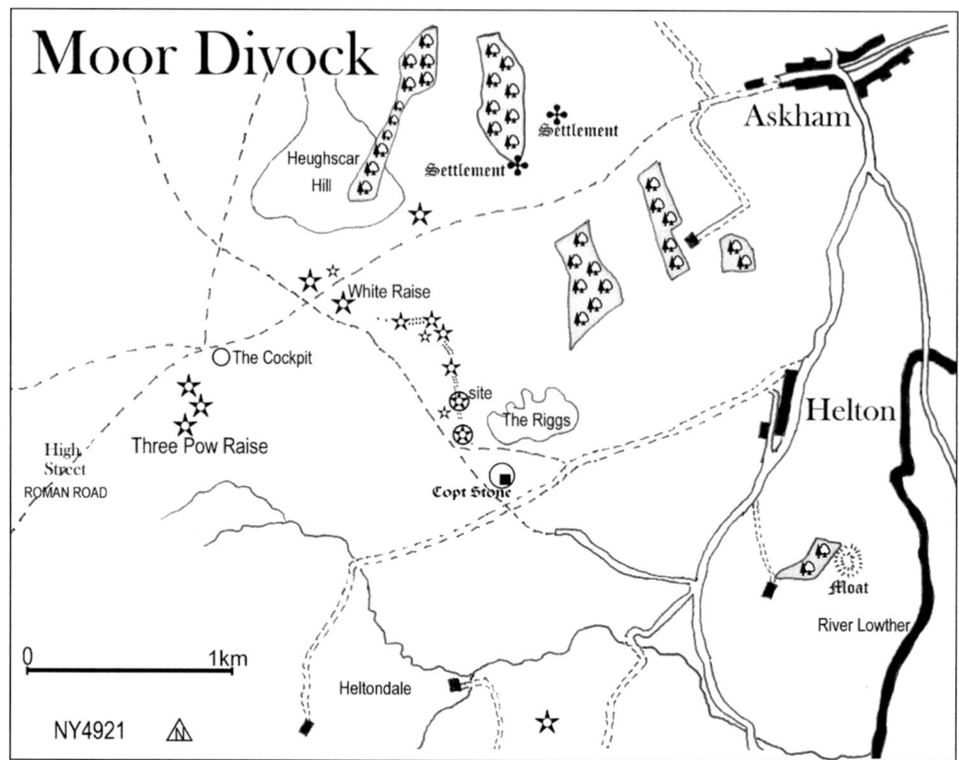

120 *Prehistoric sites at Moor Divock*

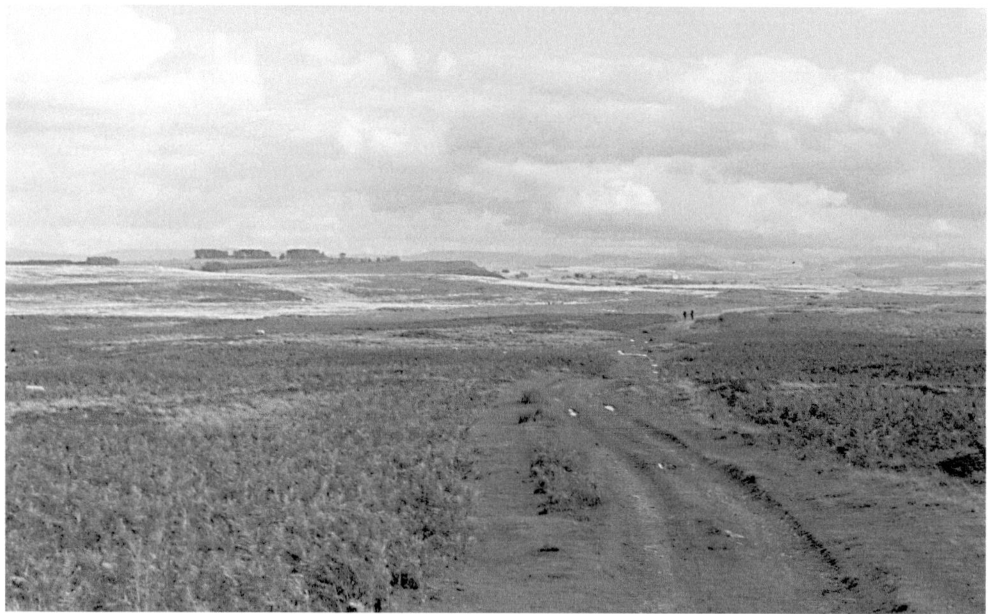

121 *Moor Divock, looking south-east*

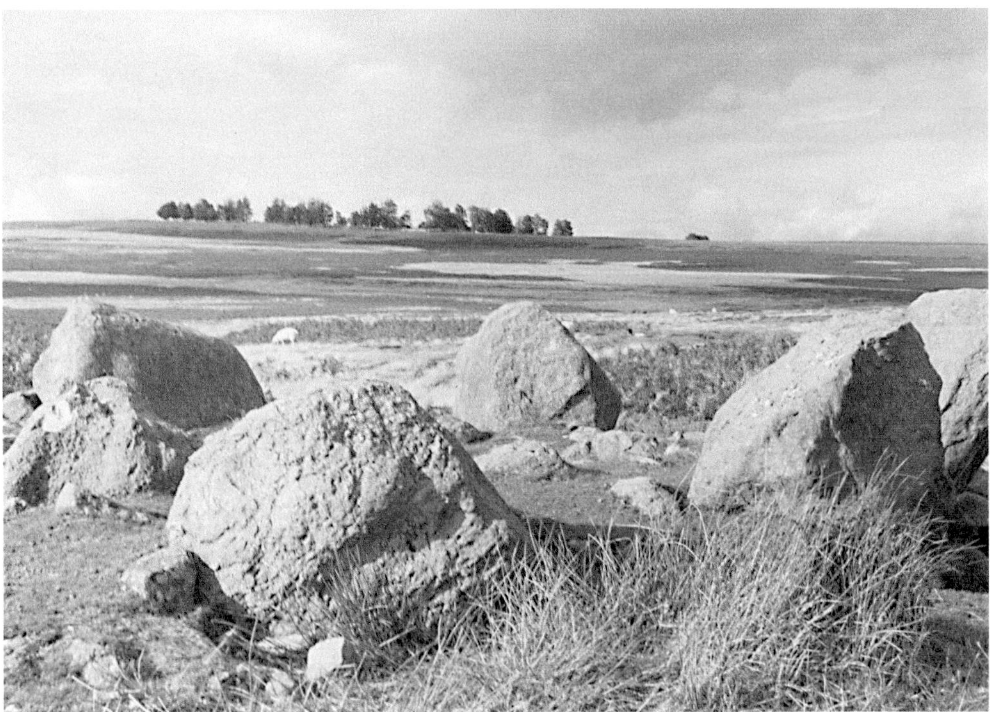

122 *The cairn with the marked rocks*

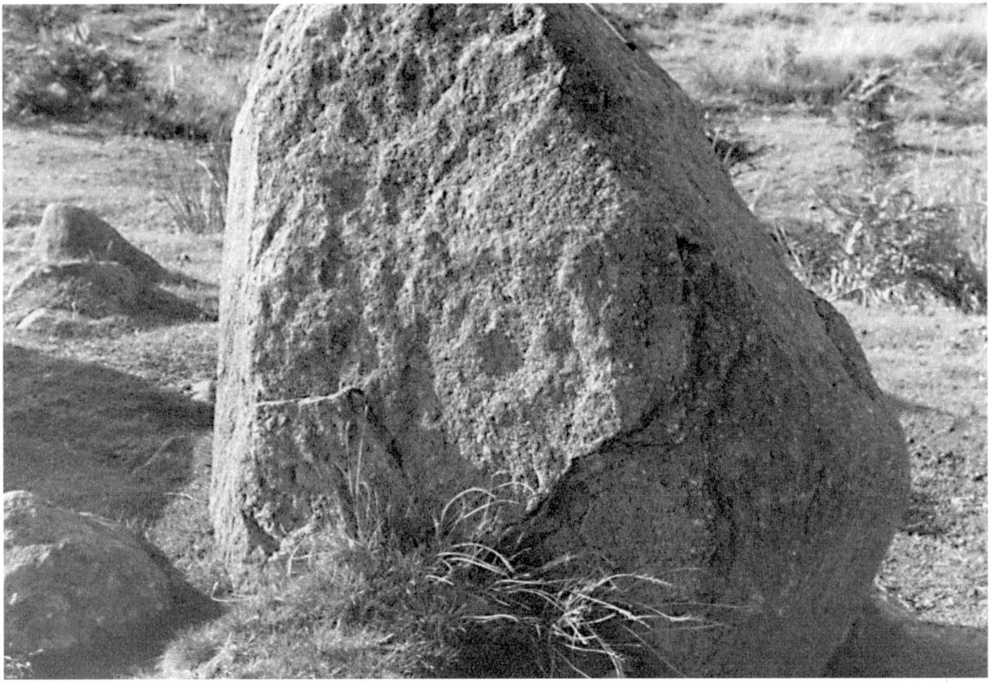

123 *The cup and ring mark revealed in low sunlight*

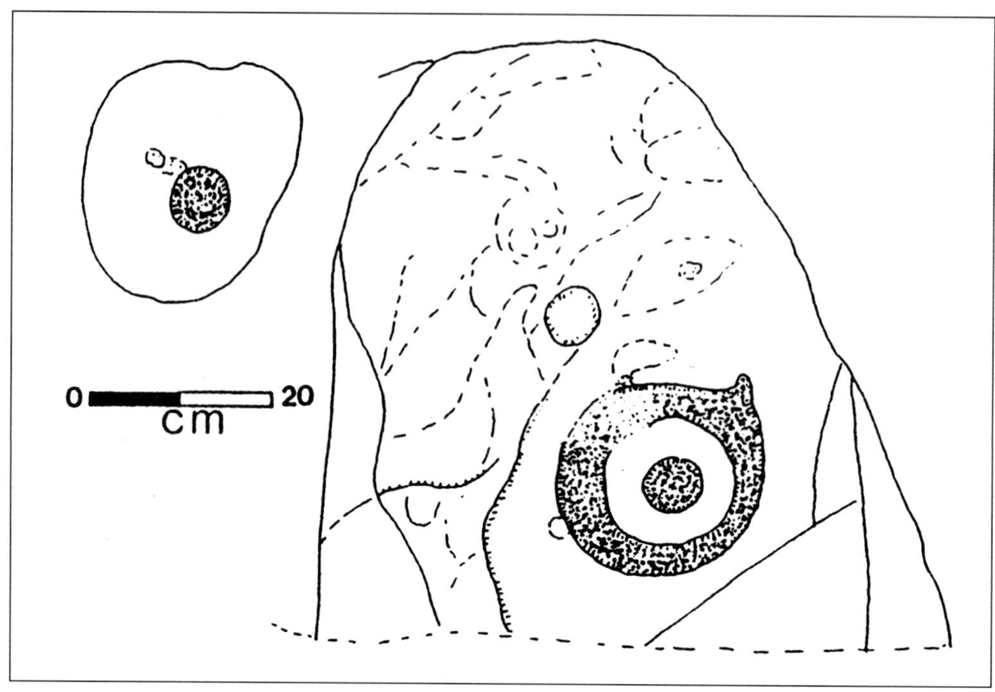

124 *The marked kerbstone and the cobble at the centre of the cairn*

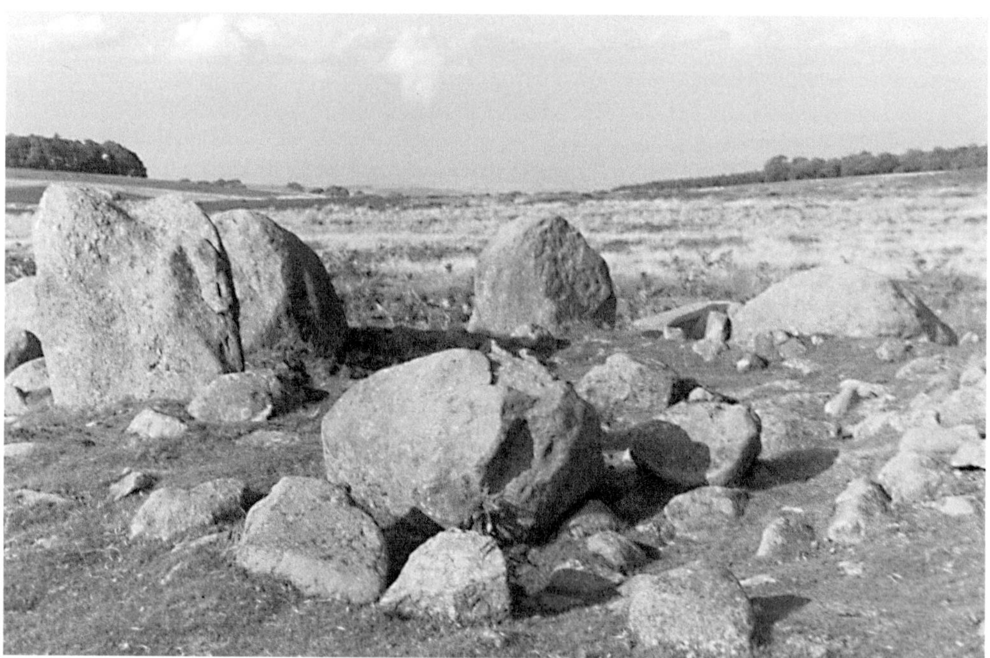

125 *The cairn, with the marking on the kerb at the back*

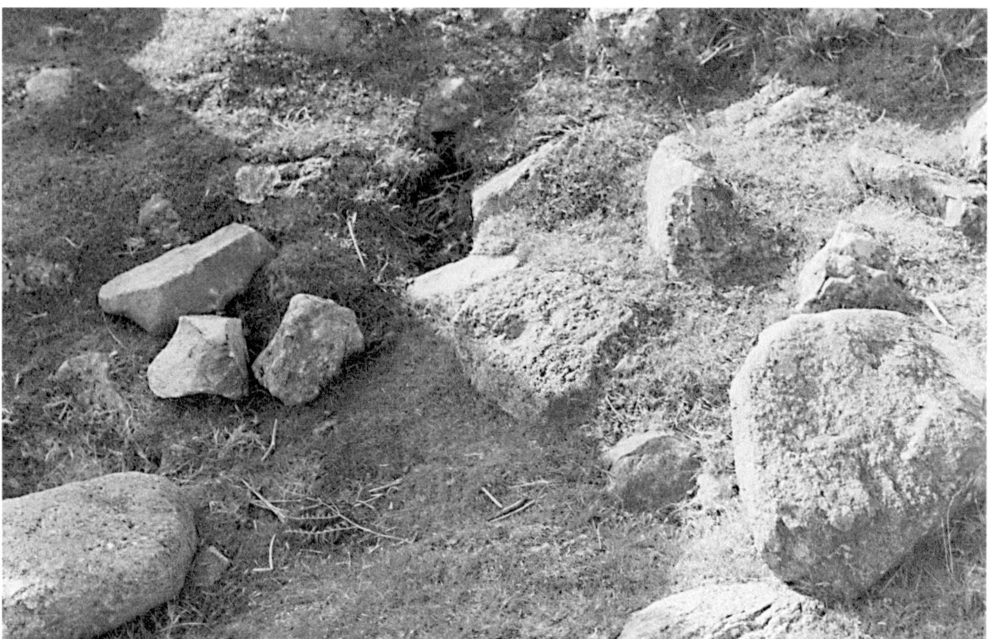

126 *A small marked cobble or slab at the centre of the mound*

Hardendale Circle Cairn (H01107 NY59651475)

Hardendale means a valley by a high enclosure. This is a double circle of boulders on a limestone ridge overlooking the Hardendale quarry to the south-west. It commands extensive views, and presumably is a structure for burial. Close by lies a bowl-shaped cairn.

It is interesting that all the stones that form the circle are volcanic except one, and this sandstone has six smooth cups on its top surface, the largest being 8-10cm (3-4in) in diameter. Whether the cups have become smooth as a result of erosion, or whether they were ground in after being pecked is not known.

The choice of sandstone was probably made because it is easier to work and stands out among the granite boulders. Cups are the most common symbols used in all British rock art.

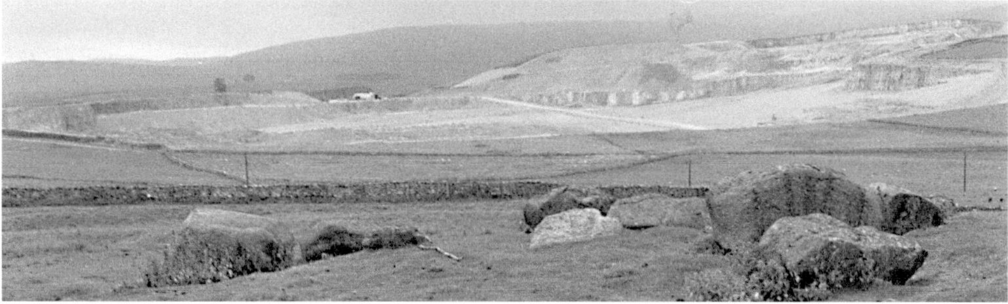

127 *The Hardendale cairn overlooking a cement works*

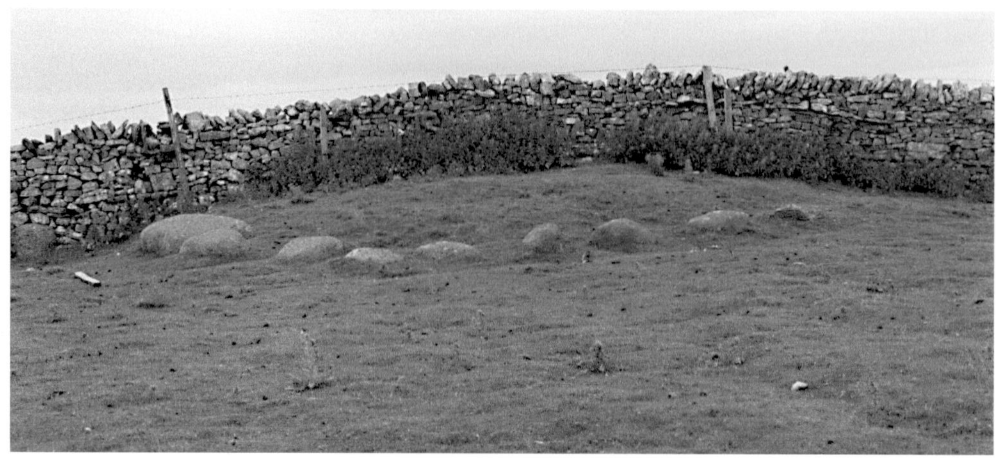

128 *The curved kerb of a nearby cairn*

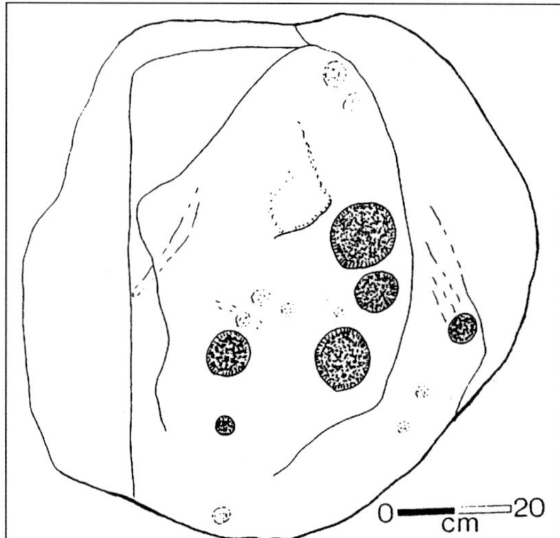

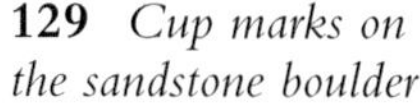

129 *Cup marks on the sandstone boulder*

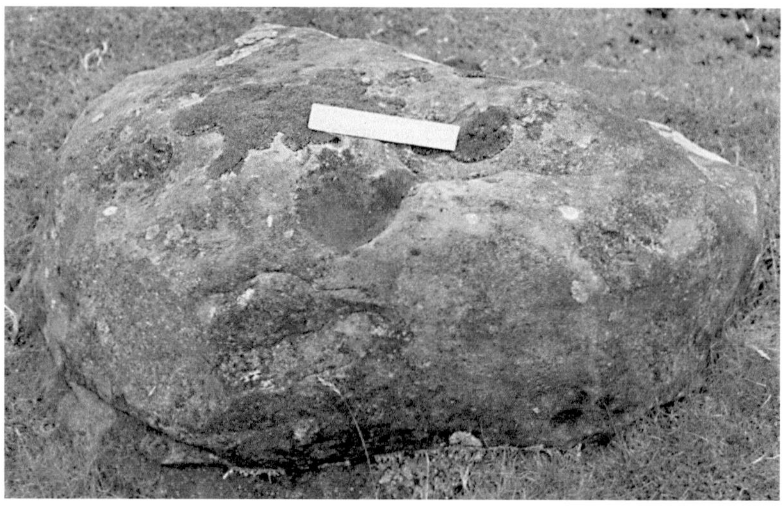

130 *Cup marks*

5 Standing stones and others in south Cumbria

The Shap Avenue

We now turn to a different and unique monument, the Shap Avenue. 'Shap' means a heap of stones ('Hepe' in 1228). The village of Shap on the A6 is the starting place for access to two standing stones on which there are markings. On the east and west side of the road through the village are important megalithic remains. Campden wrote: 'there were several huge stones standing in a row for nearly a mile'. Today a stone circle to the south of the village is partly covered with a railway embankment. There are nine other stones; five of these, aligned north-west/south-east, include the Goggleby Stone and the Asper's Field Stone. They are close together, on private land in fields that are walled in. The Thunder Stone was not dug into the ground, but lies on the original surface left by the ice, and may not thus be part of the constructed avenue.

One of the earliest accounts of the stones was given in Sir Y.R. Simpson's *Archaic Sculpturings*, printed in Edinburgh in 1867:

> Camden, in his *Britannia*, writing towards the end of the sixteenth century, describes the avenue at Shap as consisting of 'huge stones of a pyramidal form, some of them nine feet high and four thick, standing for nearly a mile at an equal distance'. In Gough's edition of Camden's *Britannia* published in the latter part of the last century, it is stated that within the memory of man this avenue, or 'double row of immense granites', extended for about a mile through the village of Shap, but has since been 'removed to clear the ground'. A few of the stones, however, of this avenue still exist. One of them is an oblong massive block, about nine feet high and five feet broad, now half fallen, and prostrated against a bank of earth in Aspers' field. On its flattish top I measured one cup six and a half inches broad, and one inch and a half deep; and a second cup nearly three inches in breadth, three-quarters of an inch deep, with a single ring nine inches in diameter, cut around it . . . A second of the Shap avenue blocks stands still erect about one hundred and fifty yards south of this marked monolith, and is known under the name of the 'Goggleby Stone'. It is a hard, round block about ten feet in height and eighteen in circumference.

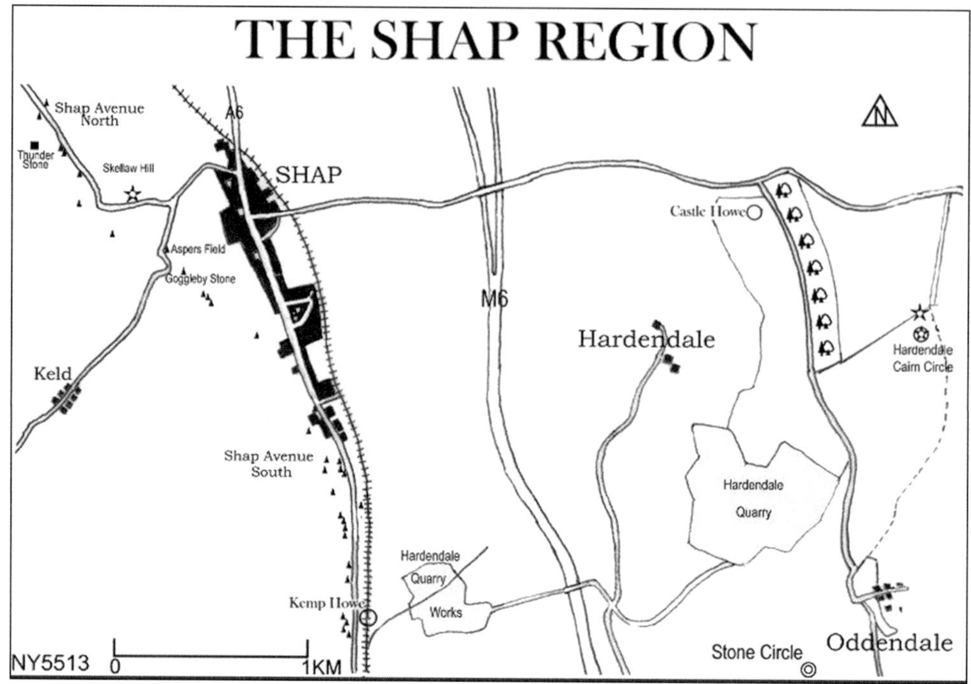

131 *The Shap Avenue*
132 *The position of the Asper's Field and Goggleby Stones*

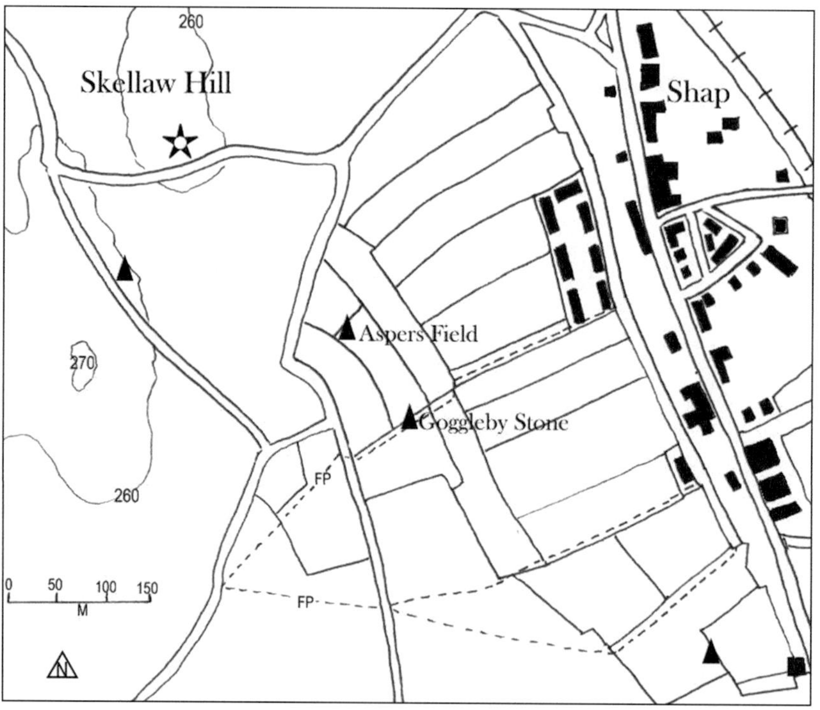

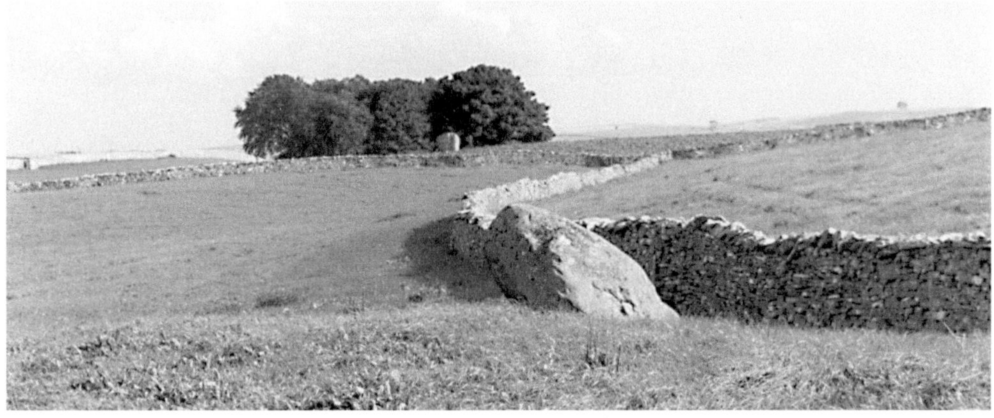

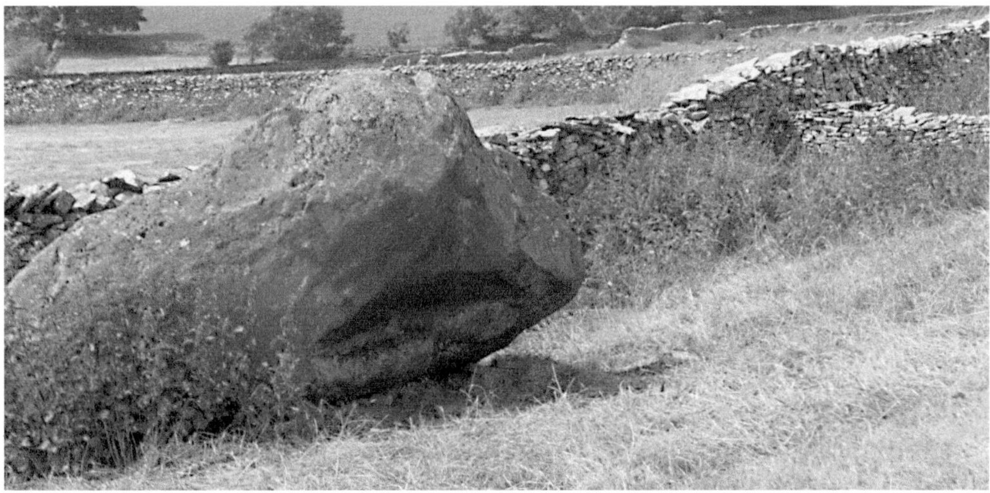

133-4 *Two views of the Shap Avenue, focused on the Asper's Field stone*

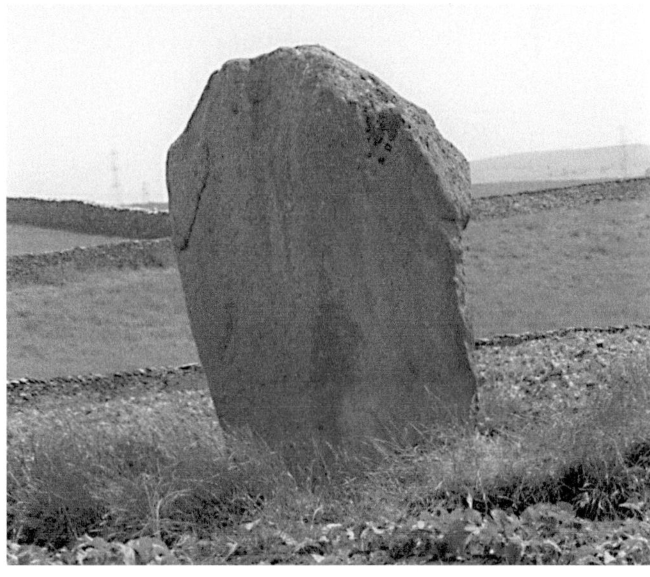

135 *The Goggleby stone*

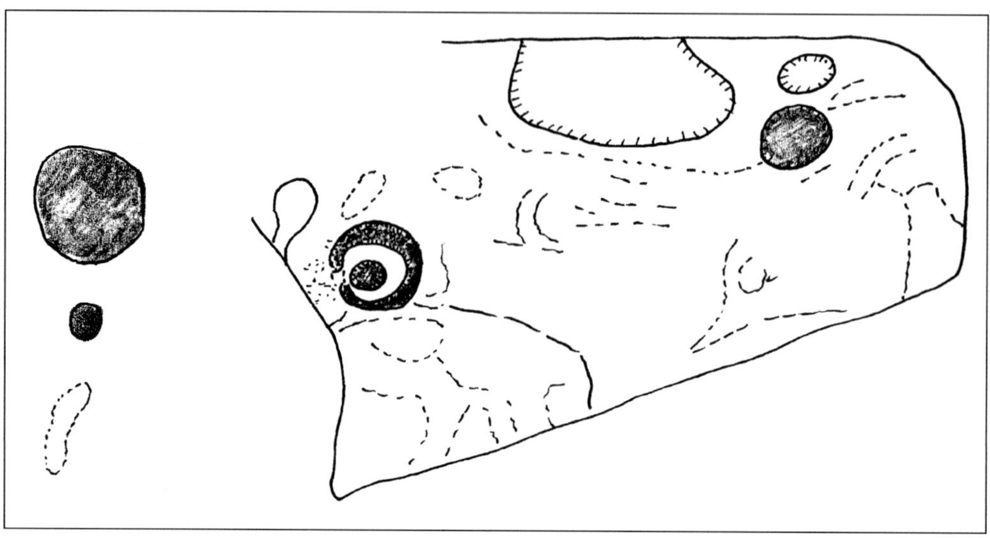

136 *The Asper's Field and Goggleby stones. The drawing of the Asper's Field stone below is from Sir J.Y. Simpson's* Archaic Sculpturings, *1867*

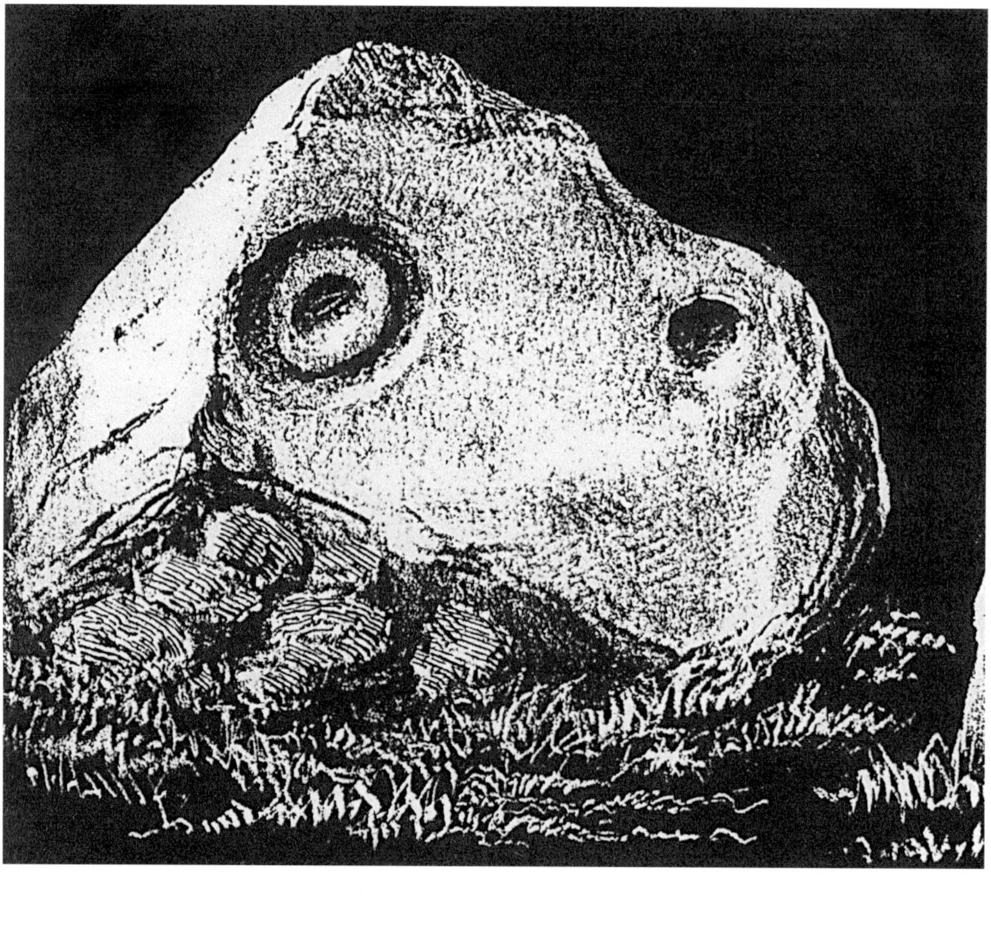

On its north side, about two and a half feet above the ground, there is carved out upon it a circular disc, five inches broad, excavated, but flat in the centre – the remains, I believe, not of a cup, but of a worn-out ring-cutting. I could not trace any evidences of artificial tooling on any of the stones of the Shap circle placed by the side of the railway, about a mile south of the village, nor on the double circle of Gunnerkeld, two or three miles northward.

I should have already stated that it was Mr Barnwell who discovered the circle-cutting in the Goggleby stone after several antiquaries had passed without noticing it, and I confess to have been one of the number.

To the east of Shap, many glacial boulders of granite lie on the limestone and are built into walls and other structures. Many are chosen for use in cairns and cairn circles. The symbols on the Goggleby stone are a shallow wide cup mark with a smaller one beneath it on the vertical face of the stone. The Asper's Field stone, leaning inwards now towards the avenue, has a cup with a single ring on top. These do not equal some of the more elaborate art that we see in this book, but the fact that the symbols are used on a very long ceremonial avenue may link them to the ritual of the avenue.

The Giant's Grave, Kirksanton (H01109   SD13608110)

Kirksanton is the site of St Sanctan's church (1185). In 1872 J. Ecclestone reported six stone circles, a 'Giant's Grave', and a huge cairn south of the Esk, and by then three circles and the cairn had already been obliterated. He writes:

> The Giant's Grave consists of two huge unhewn stones, 15ft (4.57m) apart, profusely covered with shaggy lichen. The taller one, said to be at the head of the grave, is 10ft (3.05m) in height. There is a circular cavity on one of these stones (the larger), on the inner side, about 3in (0.08m) in diameter, and 1 1/2in (0.04m) in depth . . . It appears to have been made with some blunt instrument, as a flint head or obtusely pointed drill.

The two stones lie on a coastal plain that opens up inland along the valley of the Whicham Beck (Hwita's peoples' settlement, 1125), flanked by high ground that includes a hill to the north-east above Bankfield with stone circles. When I revisited the area in October 2000, I recorded a possible cup mark on one of the stones of a depleted stone circle. I also observed that although there was abundant outcrop rock on the site that could be levered off to make large flat slabs for a circle, the favoured material was ice-scoured volcanic erratics; they must have been abundant before farming cleared them away to enable rig and furrow ploughing to take place on the hill. Perhaps the boulders had a significance to the builders that is now lost to us. To the north is the dramatic mass of Black Combe.

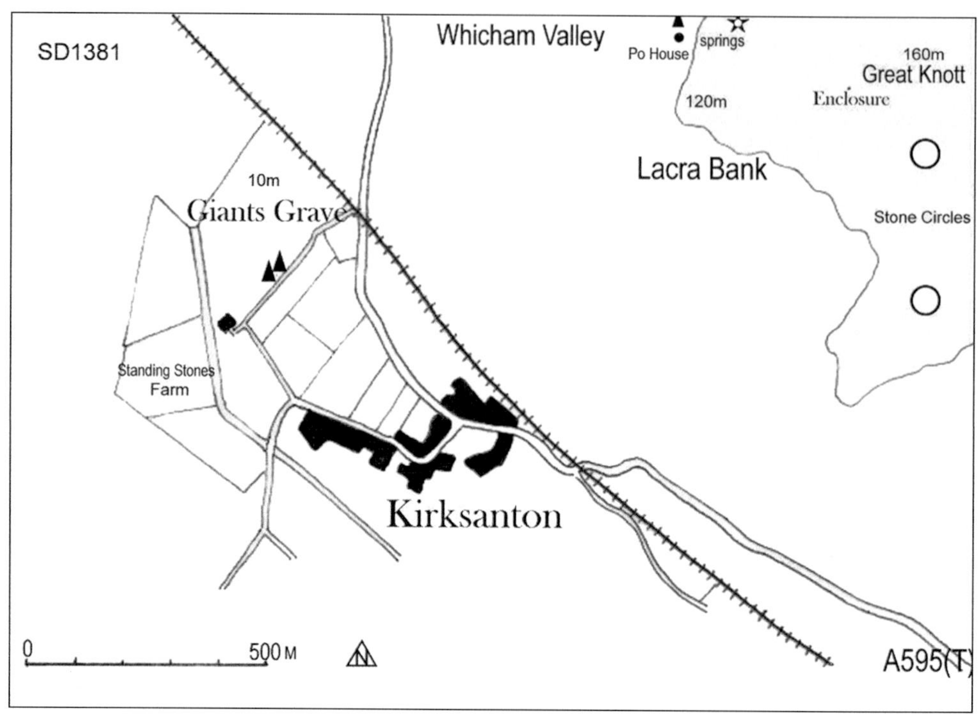

137 *The Kirksanton area*

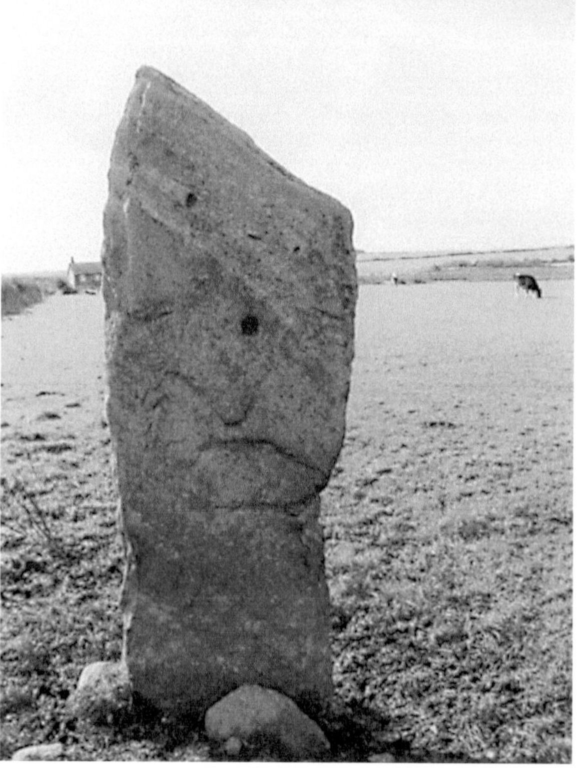

138 *The Giant's Grave: the north face of the south stone*

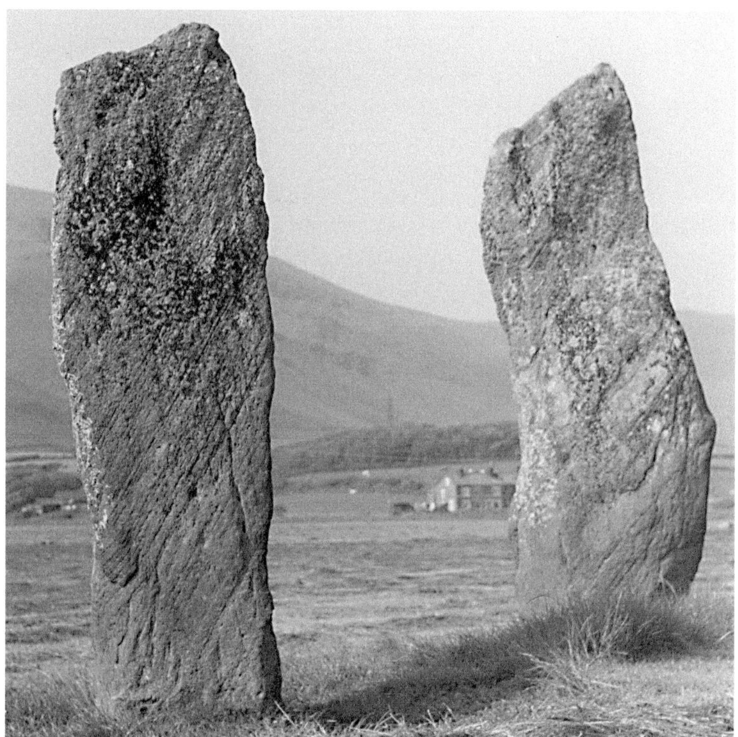

139 *The Giant's Grave*

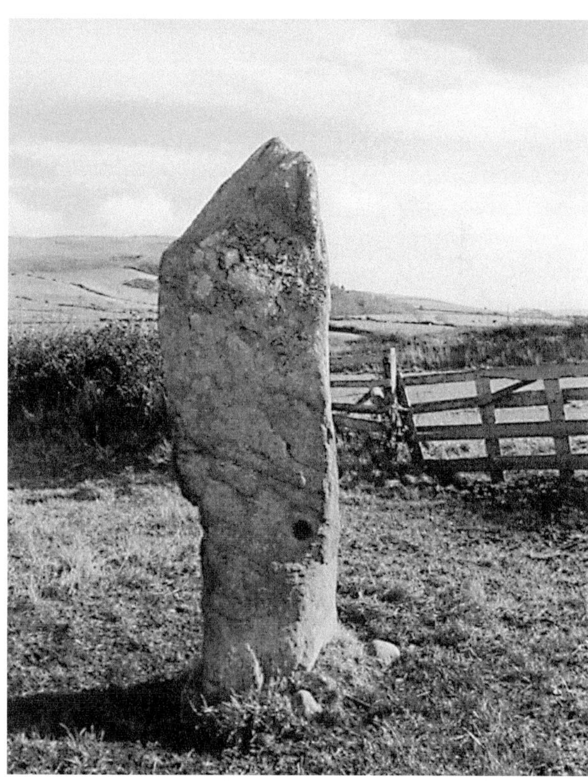

140 *The south stone*

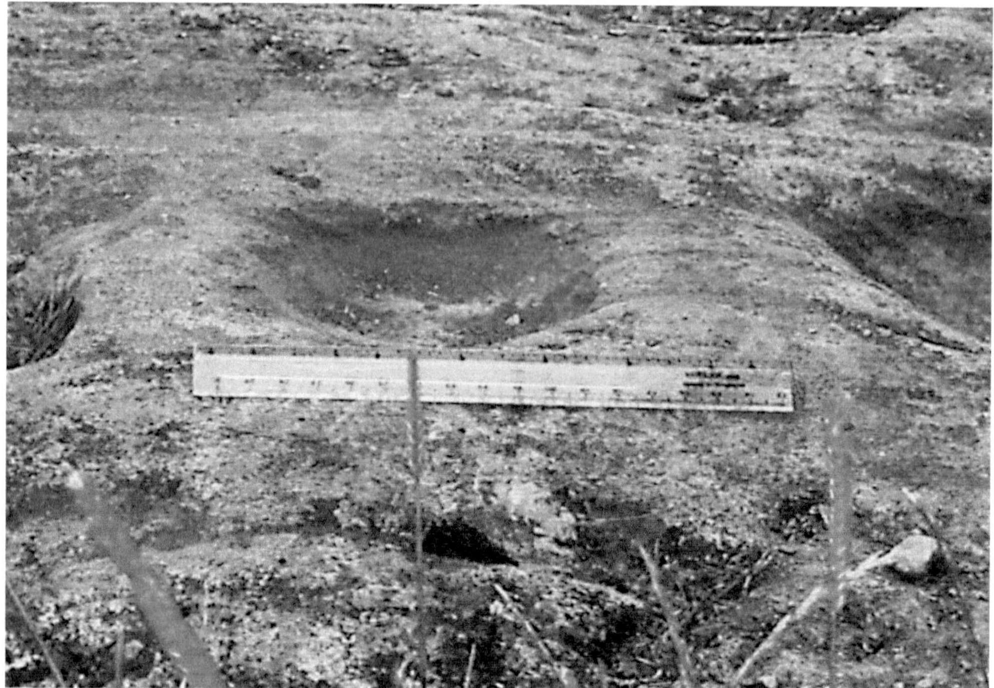

141 *Po House, Lacra: a line of large cup marks*

The site of the Giant's Grave itself is striking in the contrast that it provides between flat land and hills; the flatness accentuates the standing stones. It is impossible to say whether they are part of a larger, destroyed monument.

I have revised my previous observation on the number of cup marks on these stones: there are two small cups on the north face of the north stone and one large cup on its south face (the one noted in the 1872 report). There are two cups on the south stone, on the south and south-west faces, and two cups on its north face. The site is easily reached by public footpath from Standing Stone Farm.

Po House, Lacra (SD14636 82067 and 14668 81975)

Sharon Croft, during her research at Reading University, recently located a site in the same region as the Giant's Grave, in the mouth of the Whicham Valley. A solitary 1.5m standing stone at the foot of Lacra, near Po House, is situated some distance in front of a spring at which there is a cup-marked slab of rock. The cups, in a line, are much wider than the usual.

Po House in 1586 was *Powlehouse*, from the Welsh *pwll*, a stream.

6 Other contexts

Ash House Standing Stones (SD192873)

The site can be reached from the A5093. Two kilometres west of Broughton-in-Furness at the head of Duddon Sands, opposite a small lay-by close to Hazel Mount, a public footpath leads to Ash House, the site being on the large hill due east.

Two smooth boulders on a sloping bank are surrounded by small patches of exposed outcrop rock. One boulder has fallen. Hutchinson in 1794 referred to a 'lost' stone circle close to Swinside, which consisted of 22 stones with a diameter of 30m from which Duddon Sands are visible. An Ordnance Survey report suggests that this level platform with 2 stones 3ft high could be the 'lost' circle, the remainder of the stones having fallen into the ghyll below. Duddon Sands can be seen from these glacial boulders, but the views to the north are restricted. The circle is estimated to have been 30m in diameter, but there is little evidence that these formed part of the Hutchinson circle, despite reference to being on the mount close to Ash House.

The upper smaller boulder has on its western side a series of at least eight parallel grooves up to 25cm long, 3cm wide and 1cm deep. They have a polished appearance and are much wider than that made by a metallic tool; they have been made by

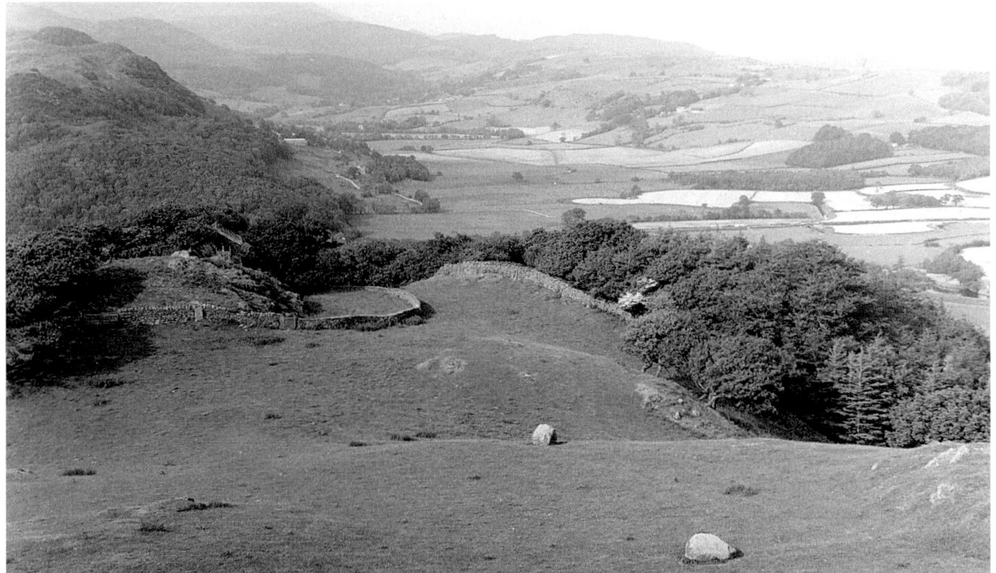

142 *The view north from Ash House*

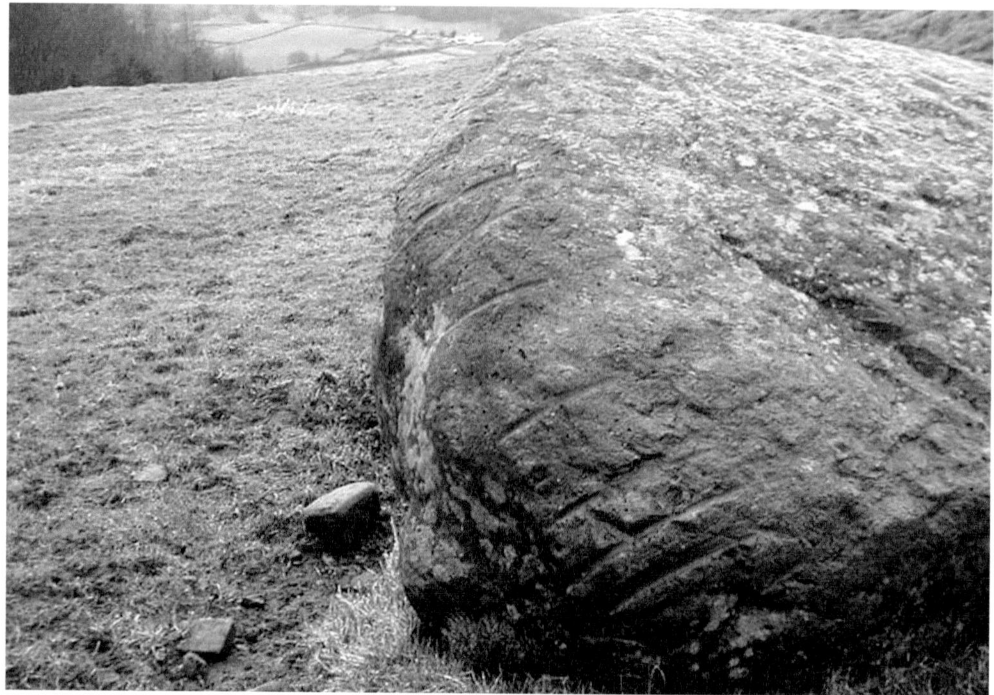

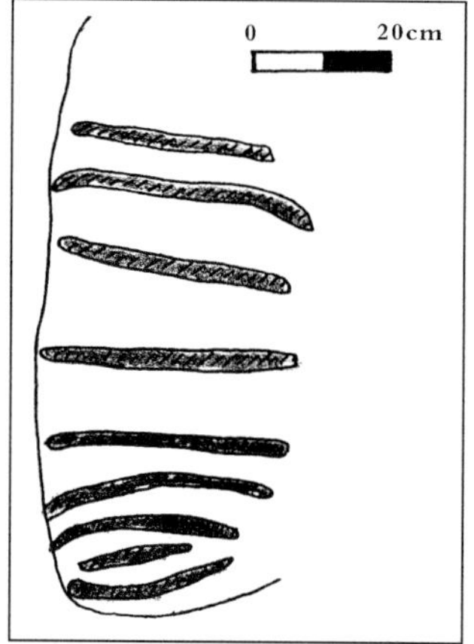

143 *Ash House boulder*

144 *Ash House grooved boulder*

an axe or Stone Age implement, and possibly used as a 'polissoir' stone to finish rough-outs of Langdale axes. These marks are not in the cup and ring tradition. There is also a possible cup-marked stone at SE19248710.

Due west of the standing stones a gate leads to a terrace. Approximately 200m from the gate, a flat earthfast slab of volcanic rock 1 x 0.8m, lying level with the surface, has what appears to be artificial marks consisting of a single cup 8cm in diameter and two shallow oval marks. The origin of the markings on this slab is uncertain. They may well be quarry marks, but of the many fine outcrop rocks and large stones nearby, none bear any similar marks and this example would be difficult to quarry. The view from this slab is panoramic across the Duddon estuary.

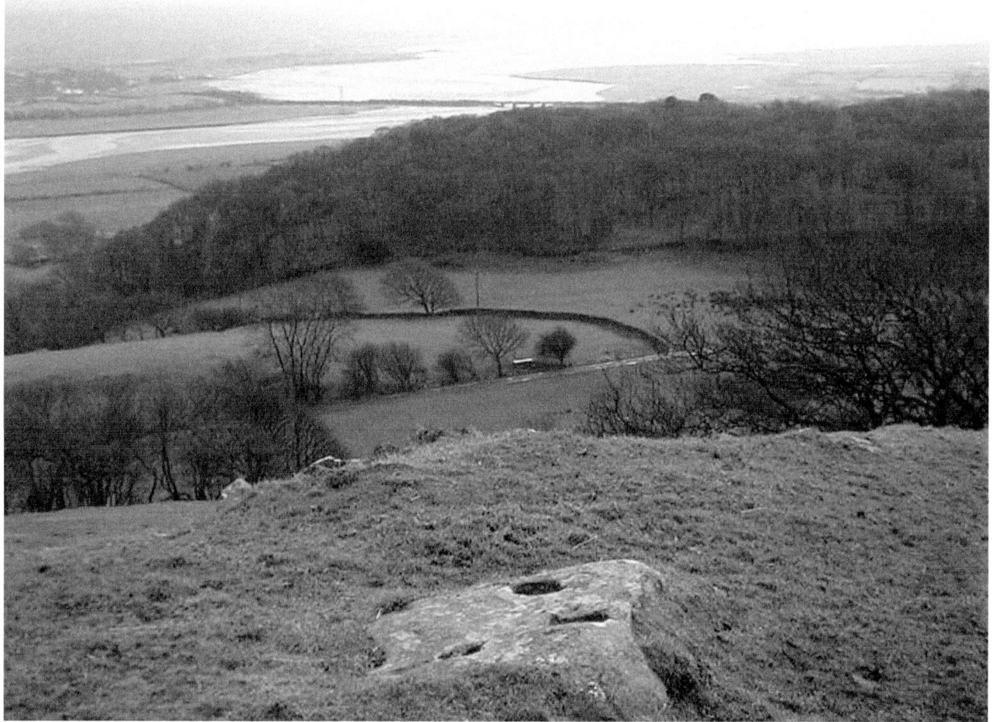

145 *View to the Duddon estuary*

Hugill (H01107   NY43730097)

The remains of a settlement, a walled enclosure containing hut circles and other features, were surveyed by C.W. Dymond in 1891, when he reported three cup-marked stones:

> I was unable to do more than note the positions of such as were observed during the progress of the survey.

The site is a very interesting one, seldom visited as far as I know, although it lies just off a public right of way. The name itself is interesting, as the first element may be from the Scandinavian *haugr*, a burial mound, and *geil* is a ravine. To the west is High Borrans, the meaning of which also connects it with high burial mounds, so there is a tradition here of ritual importance.

To the east of the site is an ideal place from which to view the settlement: a smooth-topped hill that has probably been cleared for pasture, but would make an ideal high place in the landscape for a look-out or a high-status burial cairn. The prehistoric village, used today for grazing, has its original surrounding wall that is then enclosed by a modern wall. Nearby up the hill slope is outcrop from which building stone could have been taken, and immediately to the south is a steep valley.

270
250
Hugill CP
Hugill Settlement
Gate
256
200
High Borrans
High House
Minsit
Hugill Hall
Grassgarth
Heaning
A591
Ings
Windermere
1.5Km
Kendal
7 Km
0
1km
NY4300

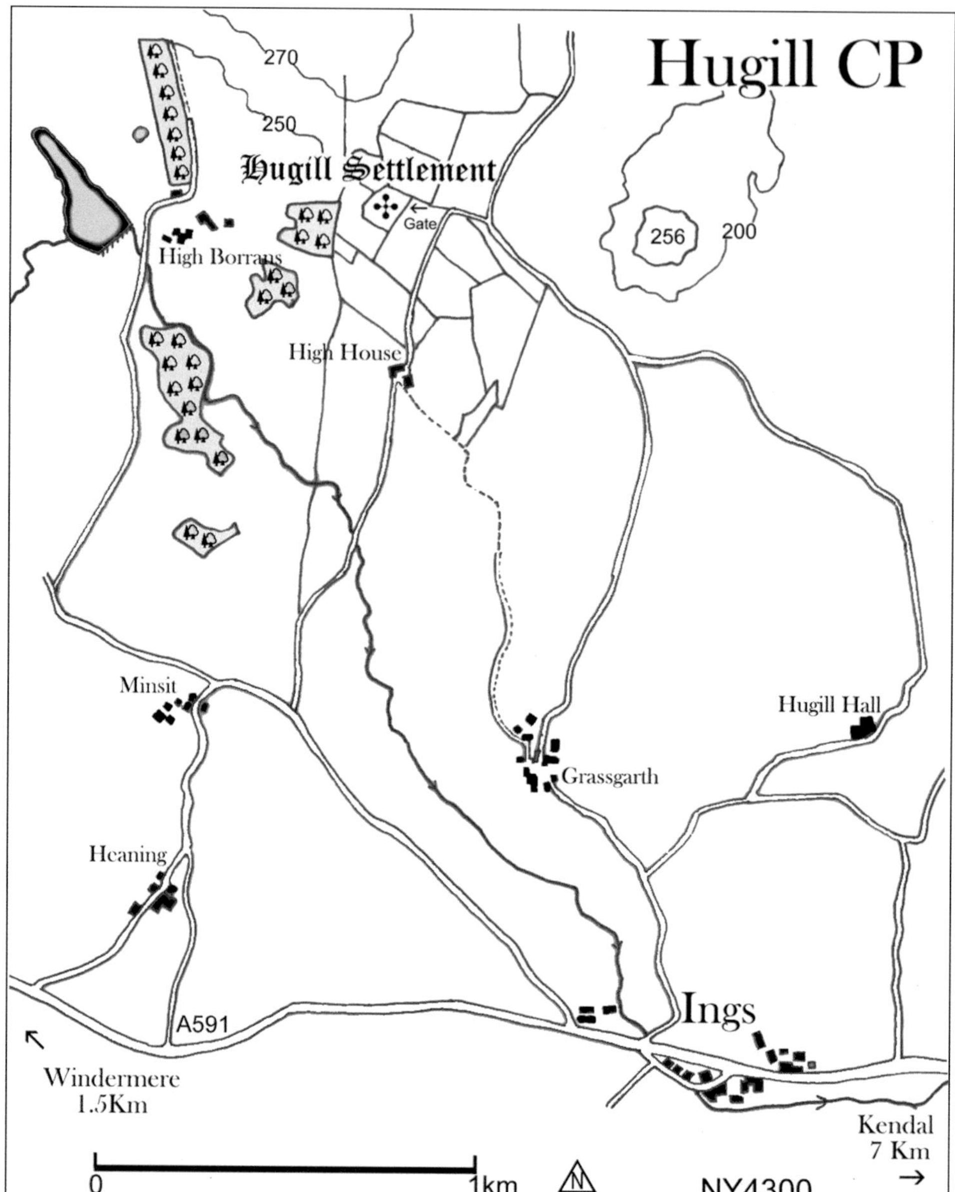

146 *Hugill*

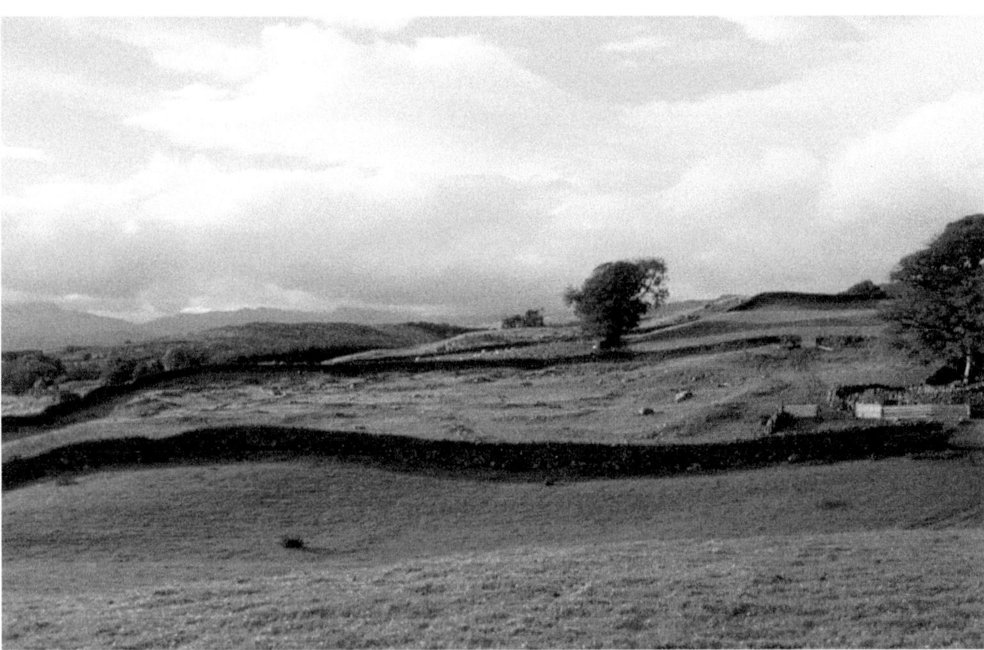

147 *Hugill from the east*

The village, consisting of a large and small roundhouse and different sizes and shapes of enclosures, is not situated for defence, as it is easily overlooked from the north. Rather, it is a farm complex concerned principally with animal husbandry. Some of the walling has been dug and put back into place.

Dymond's report includes the siting of cup marked stones within the enclosure. I have located all but one of his stones, but have found another one. It is likely that the cup marks were on outcrop that has been quarried to make the enclosure, and as such may be regarded as accidental to the building material. However, the two largest cups are placed on the inner face of the external wall facing each other at opposite points across the enclosure. They are on large, chunky slabs, the one at the north-east being erected like a standing stone.

Inside the south wall is outcrop in situ, with a cup mark on a triangular piece of it tilted towards the centre of the enclosure. Not far from this is a slab that has natural depressions that look like cup marks, but we are not convinced that they are artificial. I was unable to find another cup marked stone reported in 1891, although I have its position.

It is unwise to be categorical about the 'use' of cup marked stones in this complex, but it does seem that their significance as 'special stone' is suggested by their deliberate placing, facing inwards into the enclosure from the surrounding wall.

During a recent visit to the site, rain cleared in time to produce a wonderful low-light picture of the enclosure from the eastern hill. As a bonus there was a spectacular rainbow. One's experiences of a site go well beyond a narrow academic interest in the past!

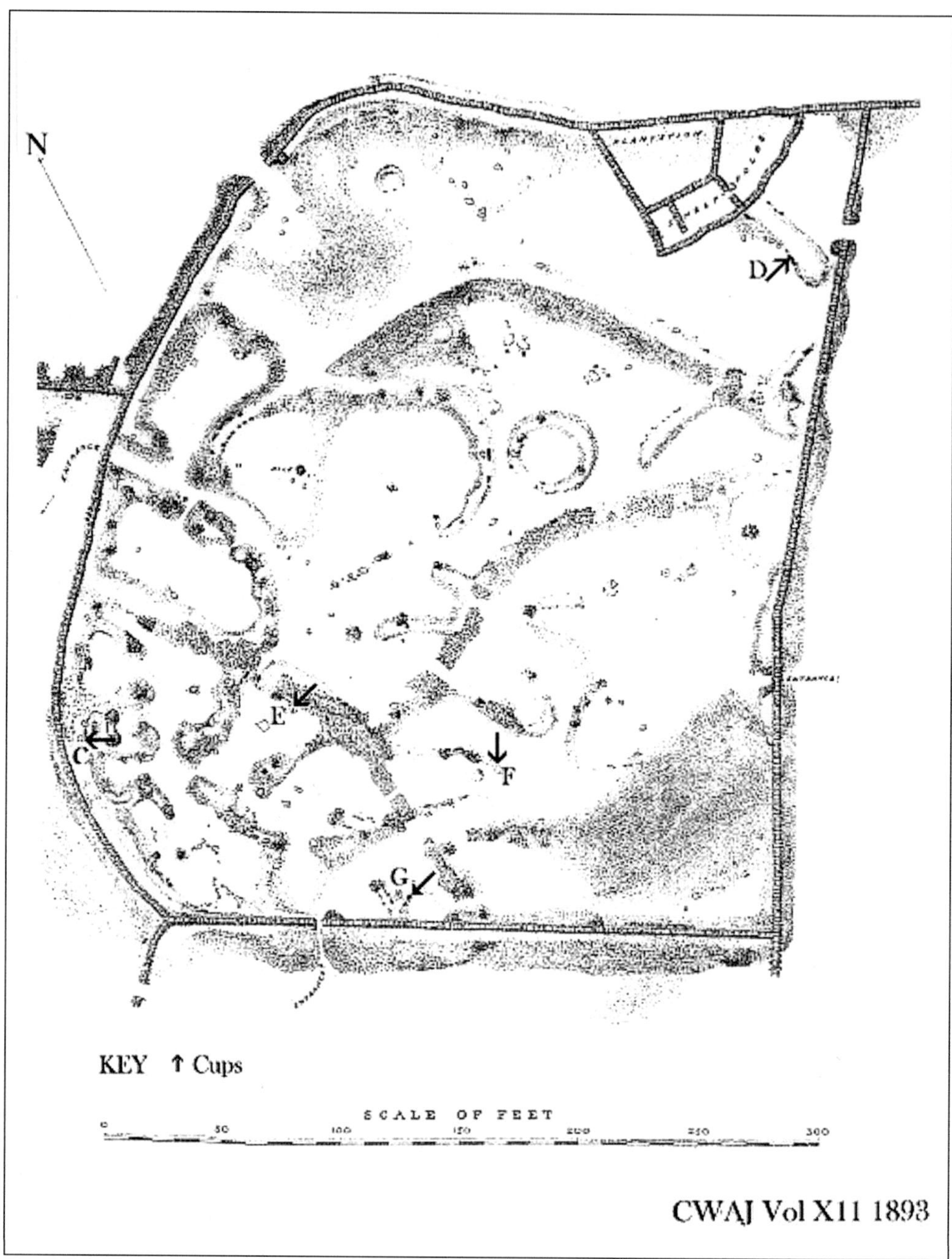

148 *Hugill site plan, 1893*

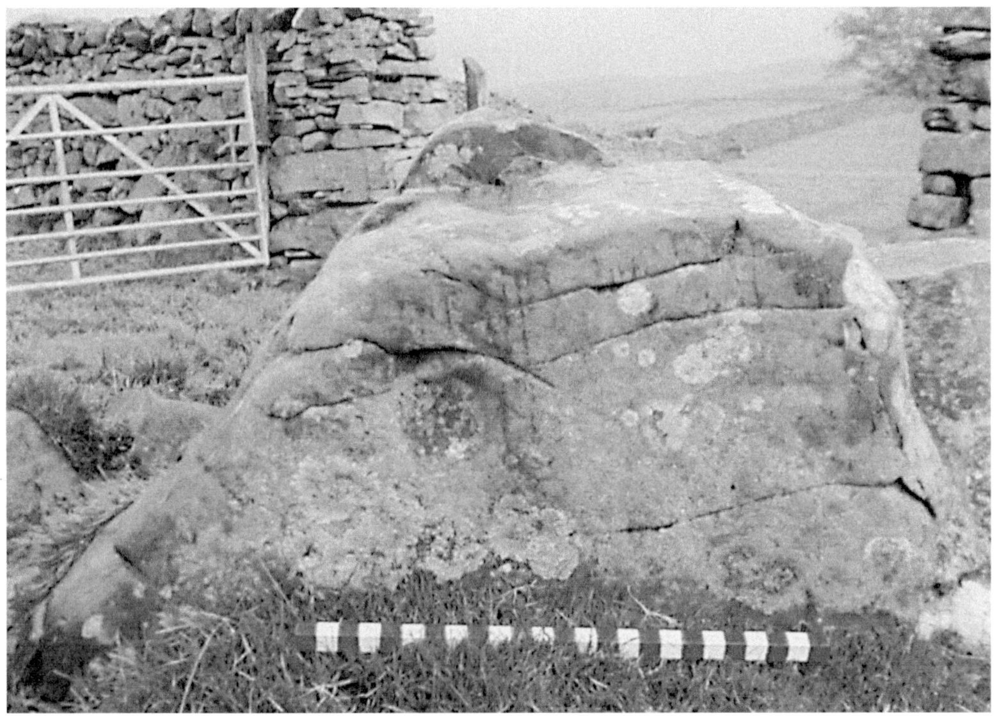

149-50 *Two prominent cup-marked rocks facing into the enclosure*

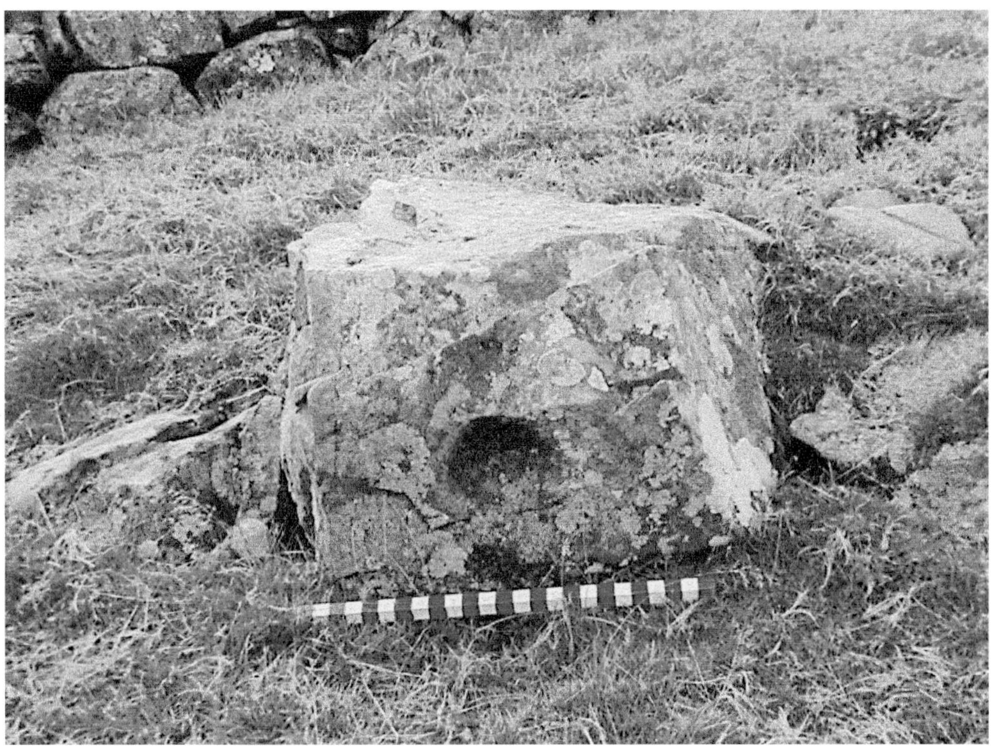

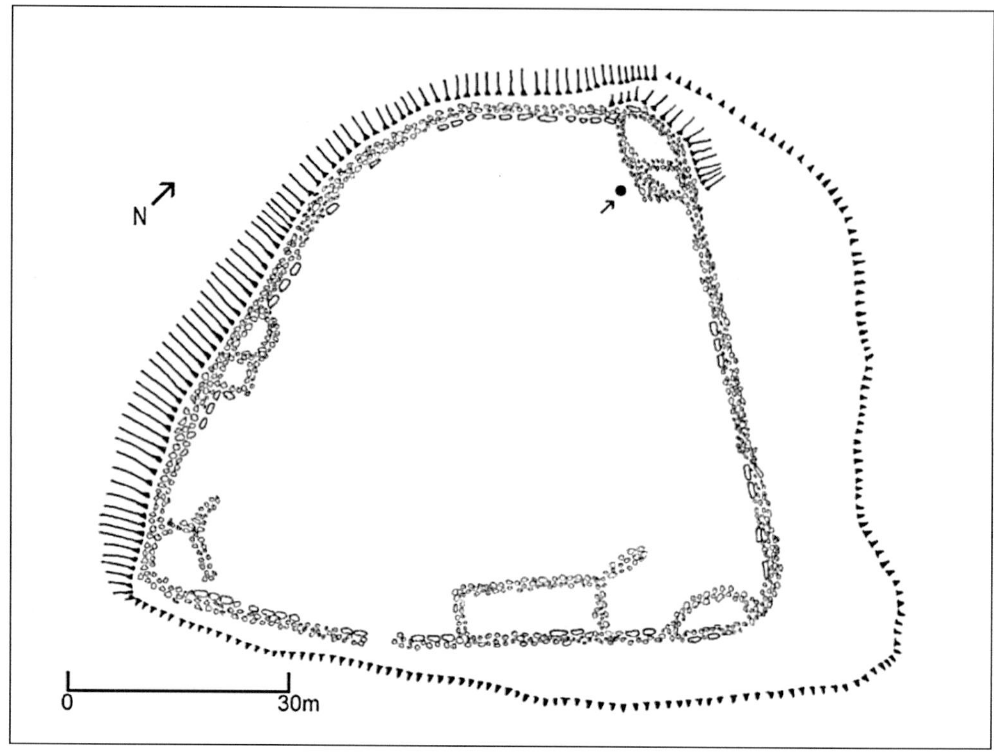

151 *Castle Folds, based on I.A. Richmond, 1933*

Castle Folds, Great Asby Scar (NY673109)

Access to the site is by public footpath. The settlement can be reached by starting at Sunbiggin Farm going north-east. Following a steep climb for 1km and passing through a stile, follow the field wall due west along the scar for 2km to the settlement, 100m north-north-east of the wall intersection.

This site is located in an area of outstanding natural beauty between the villages of Orton and Great Asby and is close to the summit of the famous limestone scar that stretches several kilometres east to west close to an Ordnance Survey triangulation station at 412m OD.

The area consists of deeply fissured limestone pavements and the site occupies a flat-topped knoll at 400m OD in an area extending 90 x 100m. The enclosure measures 0.5ha. This Iron Age/Romano-British defensive site contains the remains of at least 12 stone hut circles. The perimeter wall, constructed with large limestone blocks and fill, has a diameter of 2.4m and with the parapet giving a total height of 4m.

There is evidence of multi-occupation of the site with the remains of a medieval shieling 22 x 9m. Today the enclosure walls are reduced to rubble piles, as the limestone blocks were removed in antiquity.

A stone, 38 x 28cm with an 8cm cup-mark, was located in the north end of the enclosure. This smooth weathered sandstone cobble is in an area of predominantly

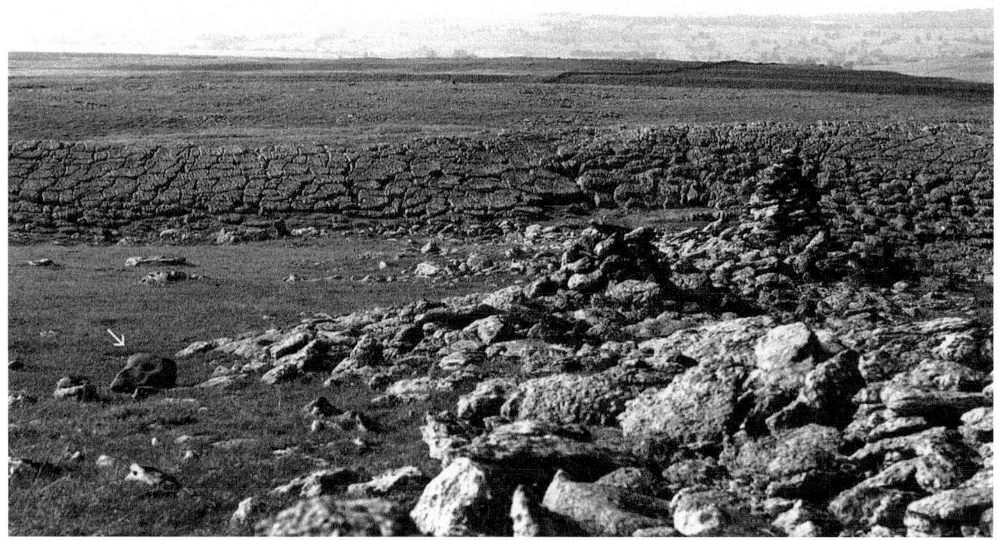

152 *The site, with an arrow indicating the position of the marked rock*

153 *The cup-marked stone*

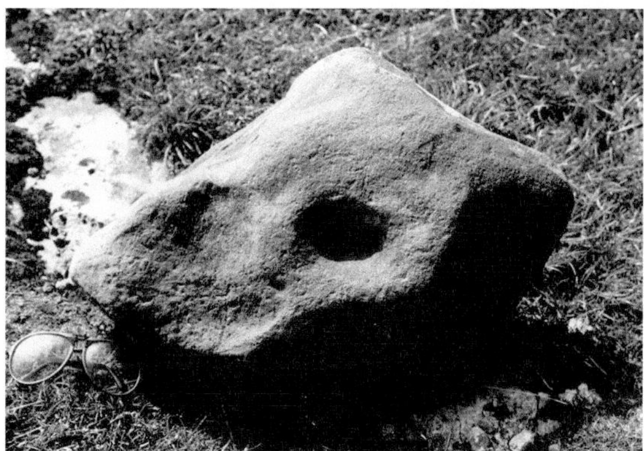

limestone, possibly deposited by glacial action. Other sandstone blocks lie within the enclosure, but none of these carry artificial markings.

It is debatable whether this cup-marked stone is contemporary with the site, or originates from a destroyed earlier period Bronze Age cairn. The surrounding area is rich in early prehistoric remains including the Neolithic long cairn at Rayseat Pike, NY683073, Gameland Stone Circle at NY640082, Hollin Stump Cairn at NY652117, and numerous cairns and barrows recorded on the nearby fells.

It may not be coincidental that cup-marked stones were incorporated within the boundaries of later settlements; the symbol of the cup may still have offered powerful ritual significance within these periods, having been reused and placed in prominent positions.

Asby means the village where ash trees grew (from Old Scandinavian). 'Castle' refers to a fortified enclosure.

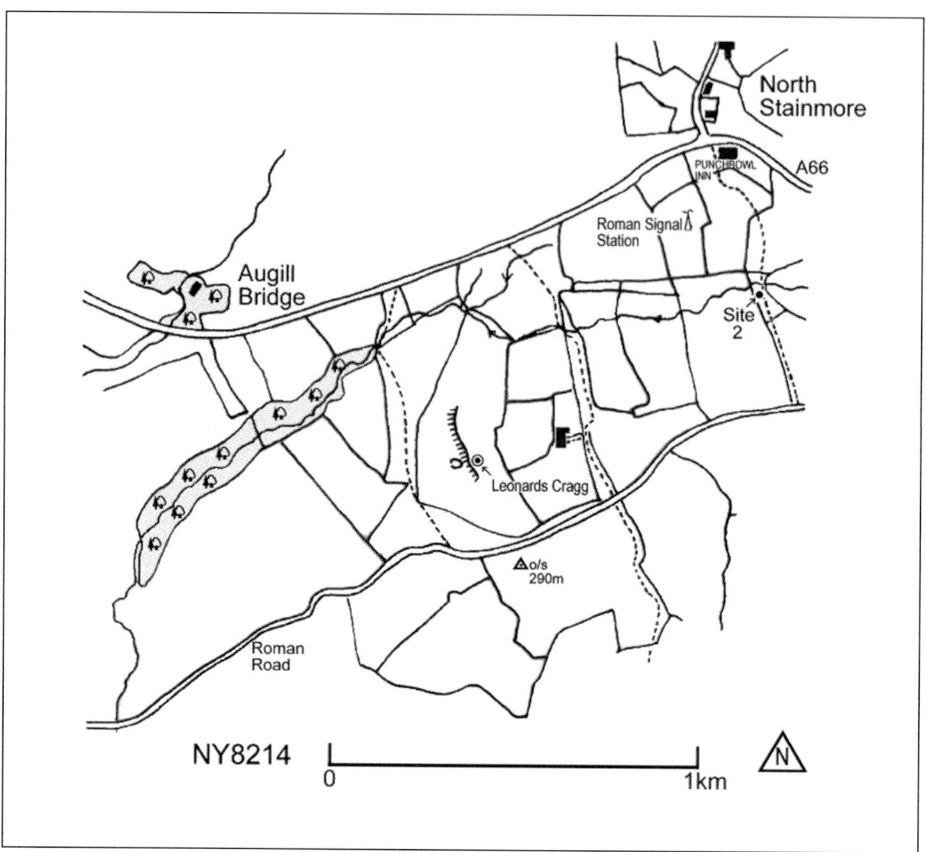

154 *North Stainmore*

North Stainmore

Access to two sites is located to the north of a Roman road that runs between Hard Hills on the A66 and Brough Sowerby off the A685.

Site 1: The main site of Leonard's Cragg is on private land, below Leonard's Cragg Farm.
Site 2: A public footpath that runs between Long Rigg and the Punchbowl Inn, North Stainmore, leads to a portable stone.

Leonard's Cragg Site 1 (NY82351423)

The main site is located at Leonard's Cragg. It is the most easterly of sites found within Cumbria, and was first reported by Dr Anthony Flood, MC.

The crags are to the north of the Roman road and can be reached through two gates. Some 150m along the crag top a large boulder marks the position of the intriguing motifs, which include three penannulars with a fourth that is incomplete surrounding a central cup and linked groove that follows the slope of the rock to its edge. An isolated single cup is spaced 1m from this motif. A further search of the crag and field walls has so far not located others.

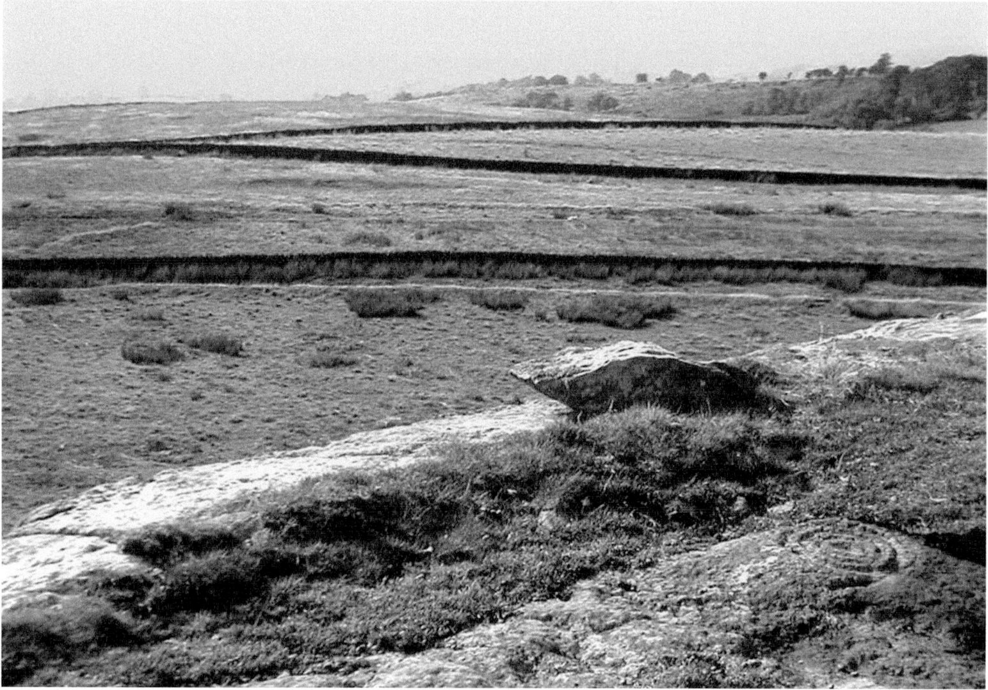

155 *Leonard's Cragg*

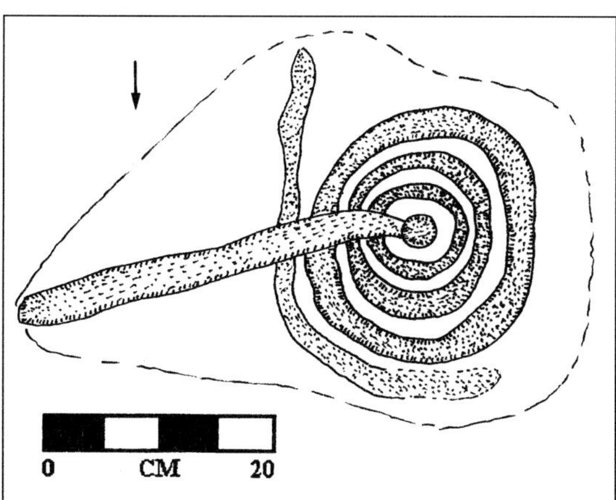
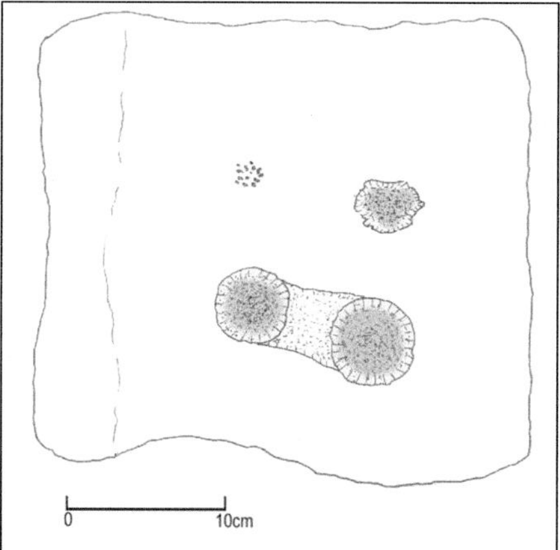

156 *The two marked stones*

Below the crag is a marshy area within a bowl depression. It possibly contained a small lake before the land was drained for pasture. The site may have offered a temporary camp for transient people passing through the valley between the Stainmore Gap and County Durham. The nearest contemporary sites are located at Baldersdale 11km to the north east, and Scargill Moor 17km to the south east, both sites within the County Durham boundary.

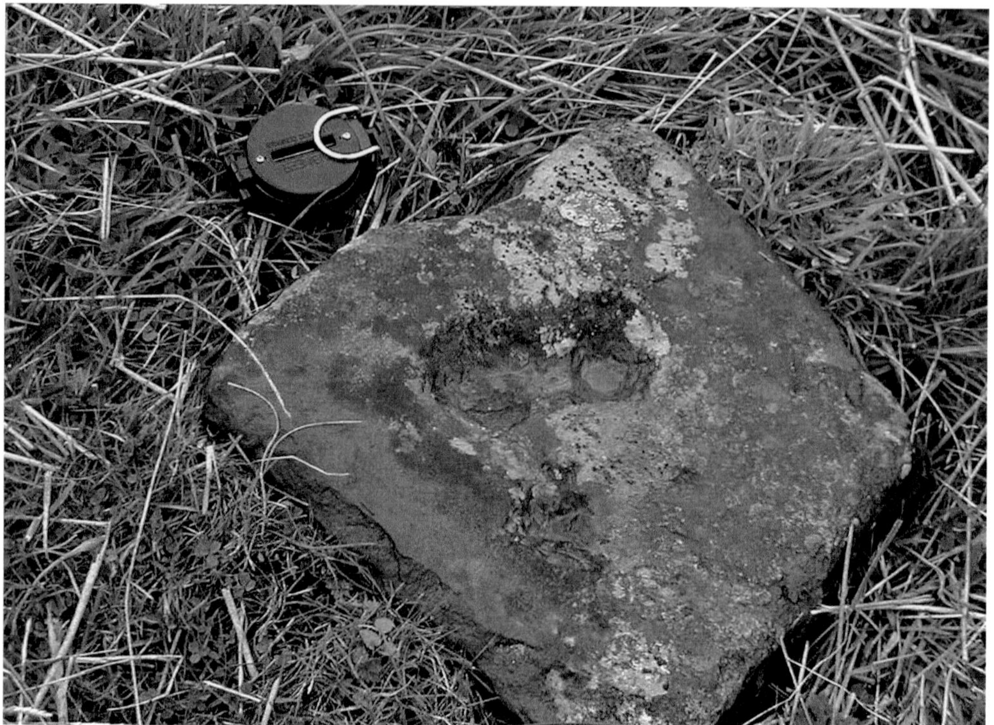

157 *Linked cups on a slab*

Today most of the land within the Stainmore area is enclosed and much of the outcrop rock and boulders have been built into field walls. A full survey of the area may reveal other sites that would provide a more accurate picture of past land use.

North Stainmore Site 2 portable (NY83161466)

This portable cup marked stone is located 1km north east of Leonard's Cragg. A public footpath lies between the Punchbowl Inn, North Stainmore and Long Rigg. The flat slab, 27 x 25cm, is embedded in a bank side close to the footpath a few metres south of a small stream, leading into Powbrand Sike. The motifs consist of two linked cups 4.5-5cm, a single 3cm cup and an area of peck marks.

The slab may have been cut from nearby outcrop to construct a wall, and it is most probable that it became dislodged and moved to its present position. It is unlikely to have been transported from any distance.

7 Portables

We now come to the final type of rock art found in Cumbria. Some stones have no known record of where they were found; some are not recorded sufficiently accurately for us to know what their purpose was; and some have been moved from known locations and contexts for their safety. In other parts of Britain they may be found in museums, in field walls, in field-clearance dumps, in rockeries, cemented into a house wall, or cemented into cobbled paving stones and a bridge foundation.

Ruckcroft (Armathwaite) (approx. NY536447)

A portable from Ruckcroft produced a surprise for me as late as the final draft of this manuscript. The River Eden passes through a deep, wooded valley south of Armathwaite, which means 'the hermit's clearing' (*Ermitethwayt* in 1232). The Croglin Water (*Crokelyn* in 1140, meaning a bending and fast-flowing stream) meets the Eden and forms the point of a triangle containing undulating land. North east of Ruckcroft (*Rucroft* in 1223, the 'rye croft') and south-east of a reservoir a hill slopes down towards the Croglin Water: it is in one of these fields that over 30 years ago a small piece of decorated sandstone was found by the farmer's wife. The lady is now dead, and we cannot be sure of the exact location of the stone. It was taken to a farmhouse and has been kept there safely by her relatives ever since. I came to know of it in December 2000, when I was invited to visit the house and record it.

The rock is a flattish triangular-shaped local sandstone cobble that is smooth on one face, where there is a groove that could have been made by a plough or harrow. The other side is irregular and must have suggested the design that was to be added to it. The smooth side may have been tempting too, as there is a depression that looks like the beginning of a cup. The scratch suggests that it was face downwards in the field, as the decorated surface is untouched.

The design is centred on a cup, nicely symmetrical and partly smoothed, with a duct running from it to the apex of the triangle. Two well-made concentric penannular grooves were added after the duct was pecked in. The slightly bulbous rise at the centre is occupied by the cup and rings, but the natural curve around the centre must have suggested a third ring, for a small arc has been added to the right-hand side of the duct to echo the natural curve opposite. Above the top ring there are some faint pick marks that may have been intended for the continuation of this third ring.

As the drawing shows, the design fits into the 34cm length of the stone. A flat base is 16cm long, but the widest part is 25cm with the cup at almost dead centre.

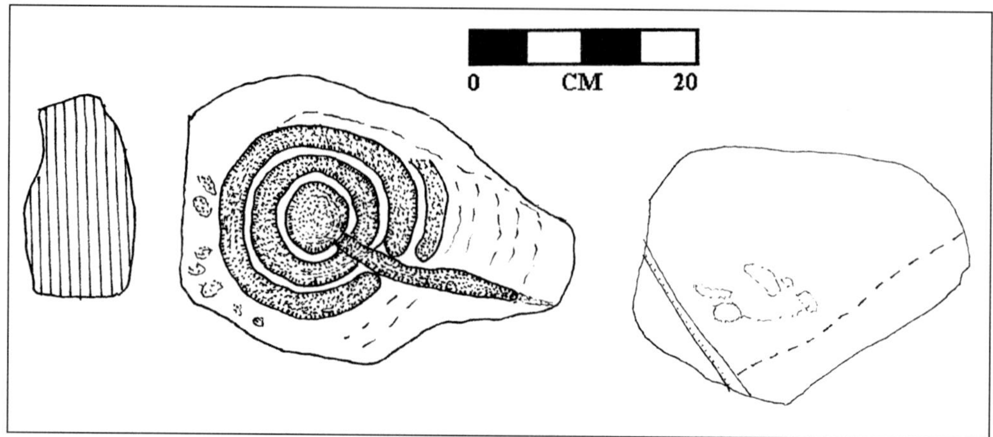

158 *Ruckcroft*

The base of the triangle is so flat that it looks as though it could have been shaped deliberately like that, but there are no signs of working. The basic shape owes more to smoothing by ice or water.

Although there are many parallels for this design in British rock art, one stands out: a triangular stone at Deershed Plantation, Fowberry, Northumberland (now in the stone store of the Museum of Antiquities, Newcastle).

Many decorated cobbles can be traced to burial cairns, and this may explain its position here. (Interestingly, the Fowberry example comes from an area where two cairns produced over 50 such decorated cobbles.) Unfortunately there has been no record made of any other scattered stone in the area that may have marked the destruction of cairns. It is certainly not reused outcrop rock; the decoration is purposely designed to fit the cobble.

It lies in the area of the major monuments that stretch from Broomrigg, where there are stone circles and a ring cairn, to Long Meg, all to the east of the river Eden, and is the type of design that is similar to those found in the Little Meg cist.

A search of all the stone heaps in the area might produce more surprises. Meanwhile, it may be of interest to note the derivation of some of the place names in the area: Ainstable (*Ainstapillith* in 1210, a bracken slope); Barugh Cottages (*berg*, Old Norse for a hill); Bramery (le *Bramrey*, 1610, possibly covered with brambles); and Bascodyke (*Bascordycke* in 1568, a village ditch).

Two portables have already been described from Little Meg; these are now in Penrith Museum. Also at the museum is:

The Stag Stone Farm stone (H01118 NY53663157)

New discoveries are always being made; this stone was found at the base of a drystone wall in 1984 during work on a gas pipeline. It is not in its original position, but the

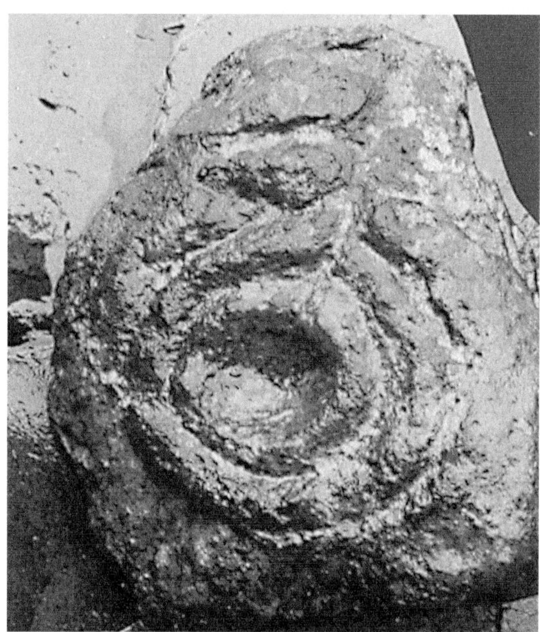

159 *Ruckcroft*

160 *A comparison: the Deershed stone from Northumberland.* Newcastle Museum

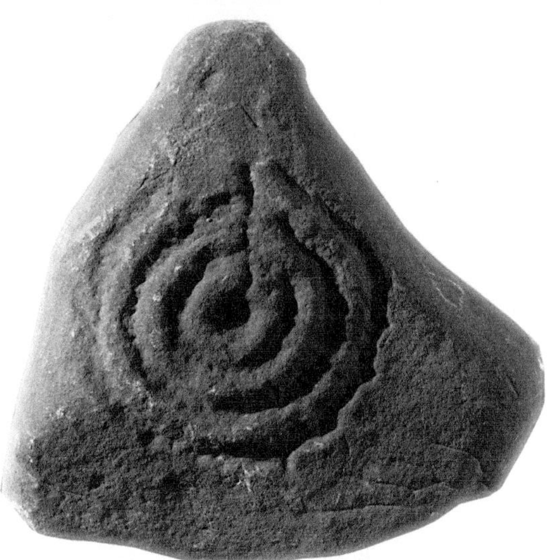

freshness of the pecking on this slab suggests that it has been covered for thousands of years; possibly it could have been used in a burial structure, forming part of a cist.

Firmly in the cup and ring tradition, it has three penannulars round a cup, with no groove coming out of the centre. Other cups, oval and groove suggesting further work were begun, but left incomplete. This is a classic example of how cups and rings were made. The slab is in such pristine condition that all the pick marks that make the design are clear, and one can see how a pointed tool was impacted on the rock, perhaps with a mallet. The pick marks produce a wavy edge where no attempt has been made to smooth the edges.

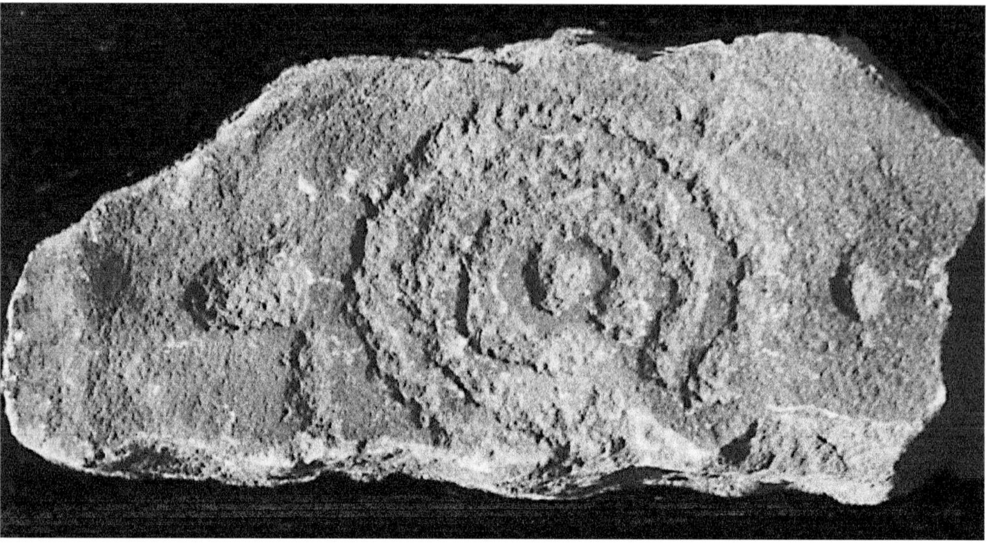

161 *Stag Stone Farm*

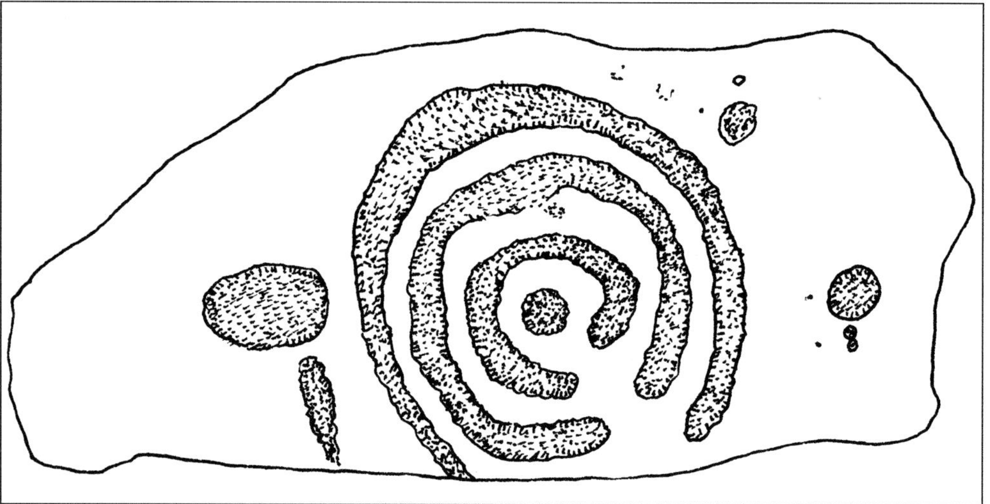

162 *Stag Stone Farm*

An unprovenanced cobble

This interesting stone has cup marks on two sides. One side has four cups and two
fainter ones; the other has eight cups, some touching. In Northumberland cobbles
of this sort are to be found especially made for the building of ritual cairns, and
are incorporated into the mound structure rather as one would bring wreaths to
a funeral.

Two standing stones from the Old Parks site, described here, are now in Tullie
House Museum, Carlisle. There is another major piece of rock art on display
alongside these two:

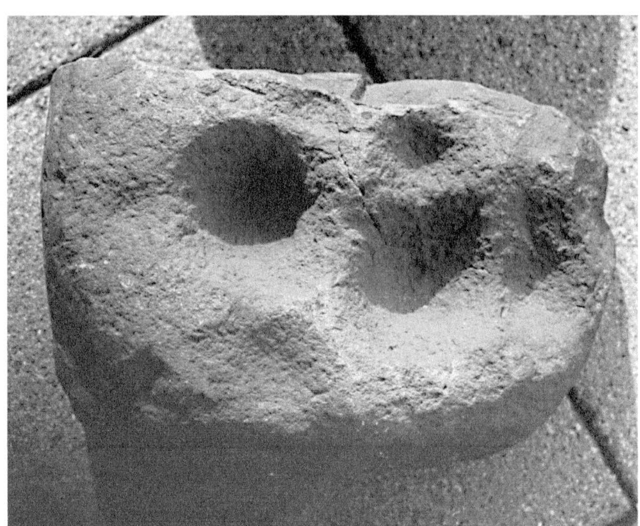

163 *An unprovenanced cobble, marked on two sides (Penrith)*

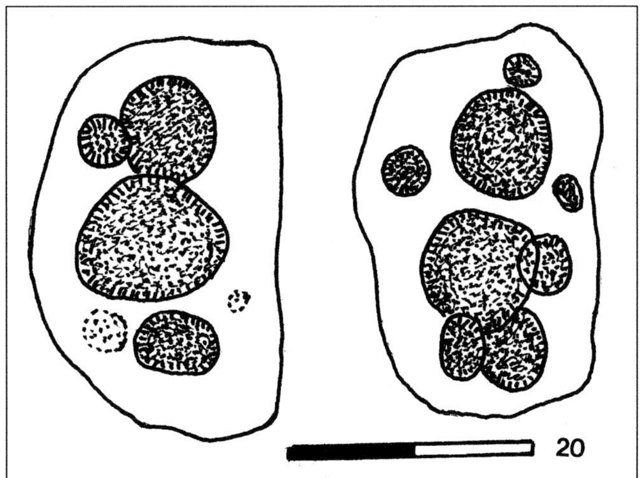

164 *Cobble*

Honey Pots Farm (H011119 NY552299)

It's sad to think that otter hunting should be responsible for the discovery of this fine stone beside the River Eamont. It was 'a large boulder stuck in the ground, upon which there seems to be rings', wrote Major Spencer Ferguson in 1910, then went on to explain its position: 'It lay on the edge of a high scar on Honeypots Farm on the Edenhall estate, above the banks of the Eamont.' It was transported by lorry to Tullie House from its position beneath a wall, and 'After lifting it we grubbed beneath its site, but found no trace of bones or other remains.' The finder thought that it might have come from an old drystone wall. The search for bone and other remains was no doubt inspired by the results of other discoveries described above.

The stone has a very good design, firmly based on the cup and ring tradition, with the use of long curvilinear grooves to enclose the various circular design elements. It

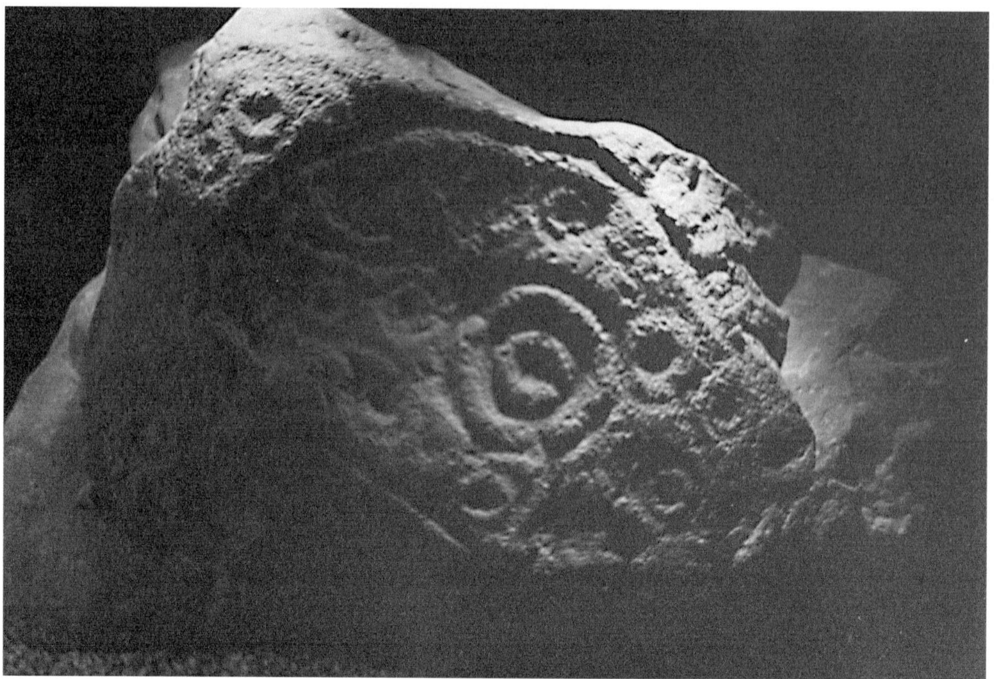

165 *Honey Pots Farm*. Tullie House Museum

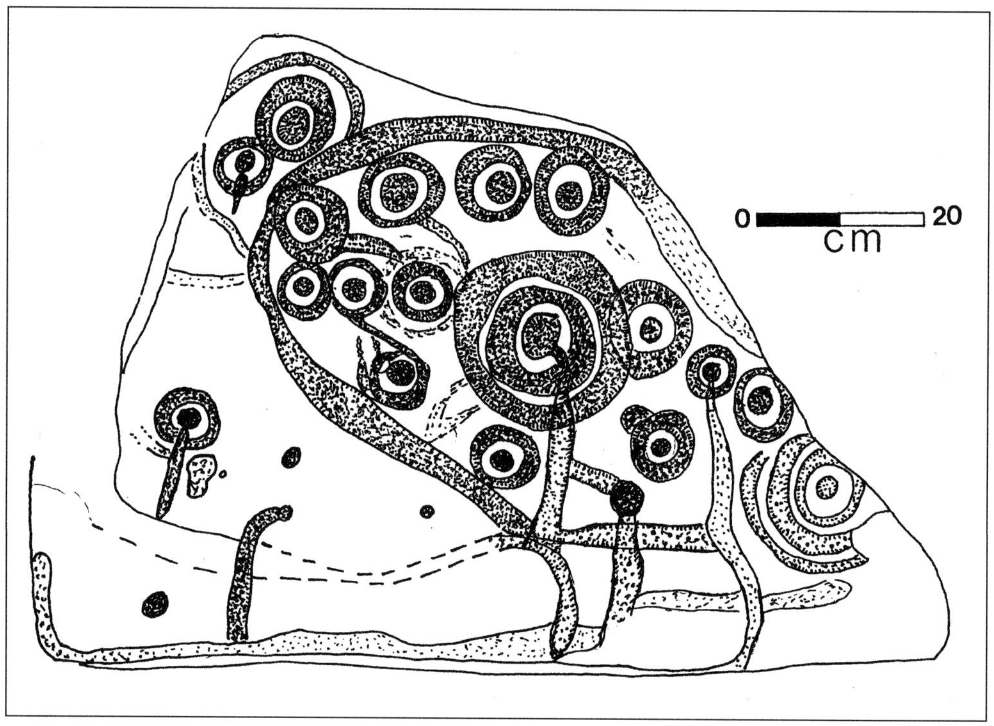

166 *Honey Pots Farm*

is quite different from anything else recorded in this book. It is whinstone, which is unusual because it is so hard to work, compared with the more commonly-favoured sedimentary rocks. The shape of the boulder determines the design, a sign of a good artist making the best of his or her material. The central figure is a cup and two concentric rings from which a groove runs, cutting the rings, linking with a large ovoid groove that encloses lots of small cups and single rings, all circling the central figure. Another long linear groove runs along the present base of the rock, linked to the figures above it with vertical grooves. Three cups stand alone on the left-hand side of the rock, and there are additional cup and ring figures, two of which are enclosed by a curved groove that is attached to the large oval groove. The overall effect is one of enclosure, containment, and of fluidity. To the modern eye it is a satisfying design.

Ewanrigg and Dean

The small cupped sandstone cobble pictured here came from an area of Bronze Age cremation burials at Ewanrigg, but it has no definite context.

The very fine stone from Dean (NY073250) was outside the church when I first saw it, and has been since moved into the church porch. It is a substantial sandstone boulder with freshly picked motifs on one surface. Central is a cup and two complete concentric rings, and a third ring that remains gapped. The outer ring has a large oval incorporated within it, which may have preceded the making of the ring. There is a cup outside the second ring and a thin groove from it towards the large central cup. Outside these motifs is a very large cup with two grooves cutting away from it. Below is another large cup. The design is strong and firmly executed.

An interesting insight into how people view the past may be seen by apparent opposition to moving a prehistoric stone into a church because it is 'pagan'. Near to Hexham in Northumberland a similar stone now stands in St John Lee church between the font and a Roman altar. If one were not allowed to have pre-Christian stones in churches, the famous Anglo-Saxon crypt at Hexham Abbey would have to be removed because it is made of recycled Roman stone, including altars.

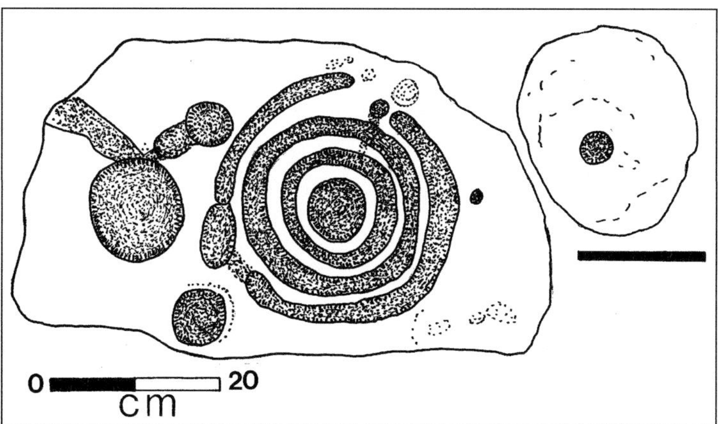

167 *Dean and Ewanrigg*

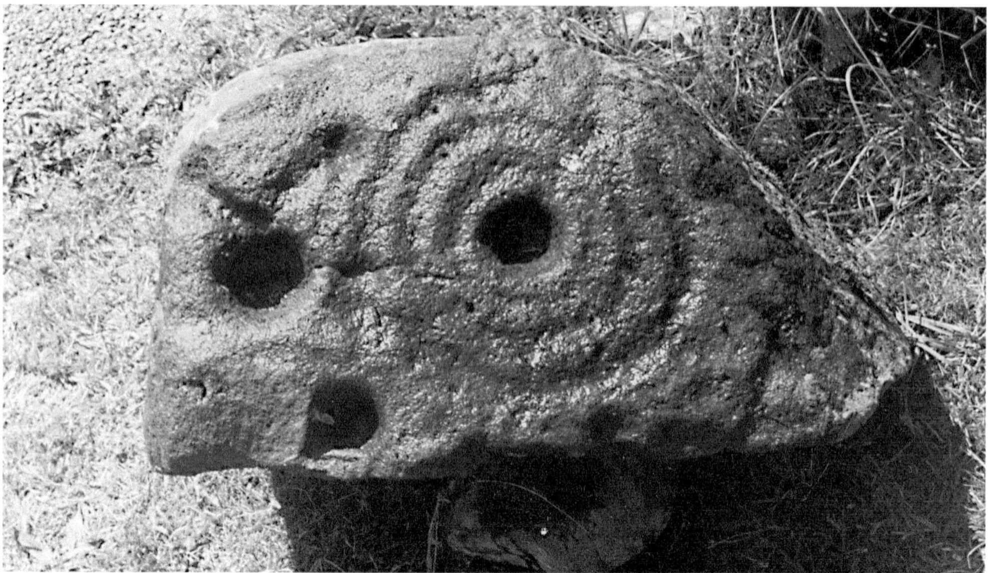

168 *Dean (in the church)*

Maryport

I was very grateful when Brian Ashmore invited me to record two decorated stones that were kept in store at Maryport as part of the Senhouse Collection.

Stone 1 is a boulder of St Bee's sandstone, roughly circular, with no signs of breakage. It has a high side that slopes towards the part where there may have been an attempt to add a penetrating groove, and tentative signs of the beginning of another ring. There are peck marks below the top surface and a cup mark.

The design at the centre of the boulder is a cup with three concentric rings, all very well picked out and fairly evenly spaced. The berms (unmarked raised areas) between these rings are rounded. We do not know anything about its history, but the compactness of boulder and design suggests that it may have been made and meant for inclusion in a cairn or other monument, not as a piece of broken-off outcrop.

Stone 2 is approximately 10cm thick, shaped like a flattened circle. Part of the surface is smooth, and elsewhere no attempt has been made to remove the slight natural ridges. The flattened edge has been broken off, possibly in modern times with a metal bar.

The design is in a different tradition from the normal cup and ring type. There are concentric ovoid grooves that do not have a cup at the centre. In this respect they can be compared with Chapel Stile and Glassonby. Two of the ovoids at the left of the drawing are joined and the edge has not been broken. All the motifs have clear pick marks with little sign of exposure; some close pecking gives a substantial groove.

The effect is of semi-ovoids with their curved edges towards the centre of the boulder. It is likely that it was taken from a monument such as a cairn.

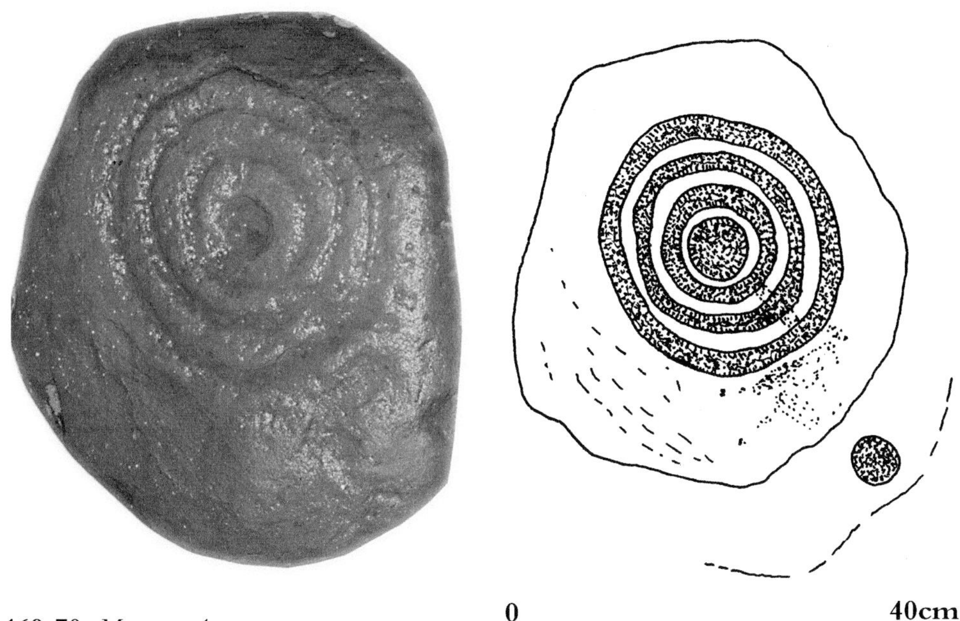

169-70 *Maryport 1*

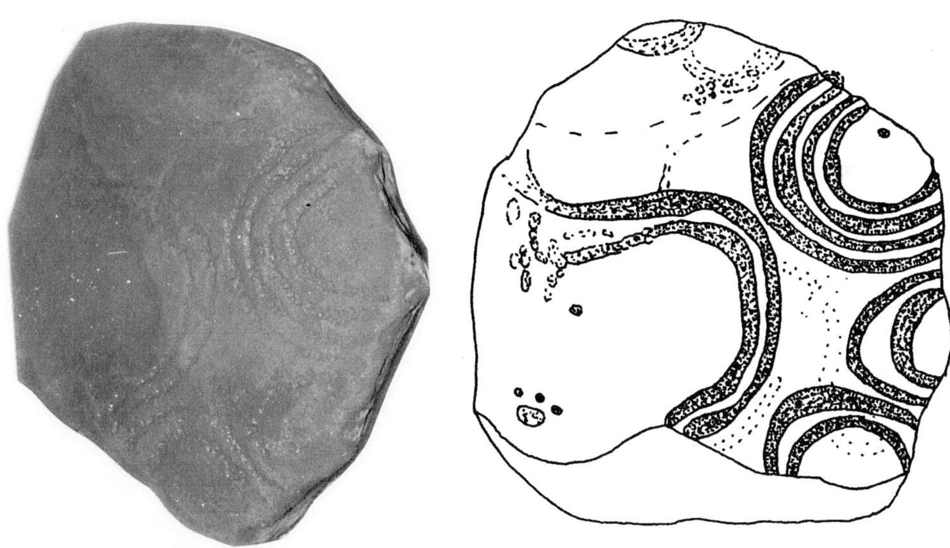

171-2 *Maryport 2*

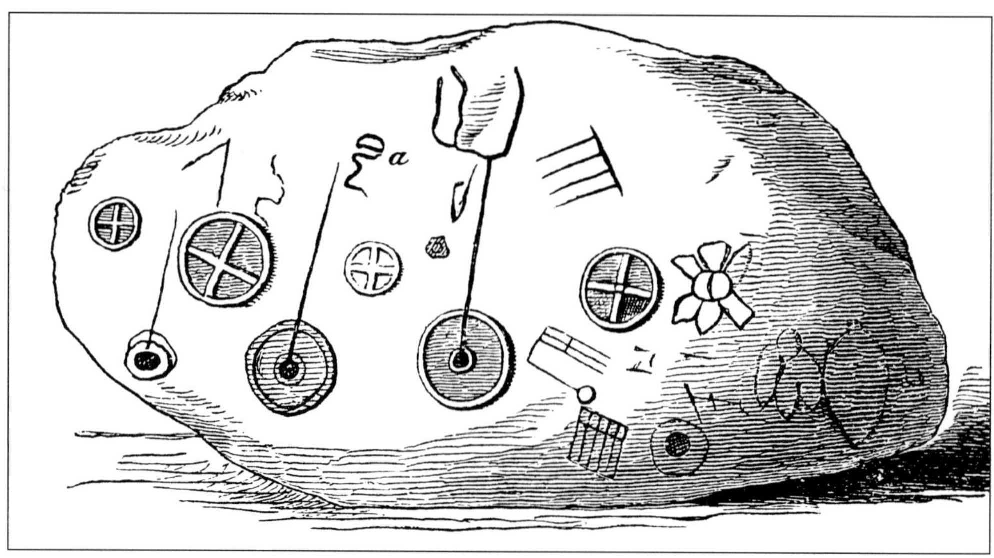

173 *Aspatria*

Aspatria

Two additional marked stones are from Aspatria (Aspatria means Patrick's ash tree). They are not in the cup and ring tradition, and were found in a burial mound as the sides of a cist that contained a skeleton and several metal weapons (NY14134185). Unfortunately everything was lost, so we do not know whether the claim that they were 'Viking' is valid, neither can we say that some of the motifs bore a close resemblance to Irish Passage Grave art, making it possible for the stones to have been reused in a later age of metal. A grid pattern and concentric circles would fit a Neolithic context. Perhaps the stones still exist, in which case it would be very interesting to see them in the light of what we now know about rock art.

8 Endpiece

Although antiquarian interest in Stonehenge began centuries ago, it was not until the mid-twentieth century that someone noticed that there were carvings of axes on some of the standing stones. This is hardly surprising as the sheer scale of the site and its thrust up to the sky can obliterate a consideration of smaller details from people's minds. In less-visited areas and even among famous monuments the discovery of markings made in the cup and ring tradition did not begin until the nineteenth century. One imagines John Charles Langlands leaving his family business of silver-smithing in Newcastle to make his home in the wilds of Northumberland. One day when he walked up Old Bewick hill, that is dominated by a double hill fort, he became aware of a multiplicity of cups, concentric circles and grooves on a large table of rock outside the fort area. There, at a splendid viewpoint, his reaction was that an idle shepherd must have made those marks, but as he looked more deeply and further afield, he came to the conclusion that they were very ancient.

Langlands had his life as a farmer, father and centre of the local community, so this interest in rock markings was peripheral to the main course of his life. Yet his discovery attracted others to look too, people who had leisure to pursue an histor-ical interest in their localities and who were connected widely to others with similar curiosity about the past. Notable among them were clergymen, especially Canon Greenwell whose interest in excavating and recording the past coincided with locations where there was good fishing. His work on British Barrows was well known among the learned and inspired others to investigate further, although his methods did provoke some contemporary criticism. Interest spread; local history societies were inspired to explore and record, they attracted speakers of note, and this interest included rock art. Leisure, money and a good formal education ensured that their findings were presented to others. High quality lithographs, photographs and drawings were part of this recording.

My own interest in British rock art owes much to these early scholars. By a fortunate coincidence, unknown to me at the time, the very rock that triggered Langland's interest triggered mine. It was not exactly a road to Damascus, but that huge block of marked rock was a turning point. I was soon to learn that we didn't know much about rock art, and I set out like these early antiquarians to find out, not as my main occupation, but as a hobby, as a small part of my life. In retirement I have had more leisure to pursue this hobby more thoroughly.

A lack of interest in rock art among professional archaeologists has probably been due to the fact that the study of rock art was not the best career move. It involves considerable exploration of the landscape on foot, with not a great deal to show for it, apart from an increase in fitness. Even when sites have been found and recorded, the bewildering questions about how the marks originated, what they mean and why they are where they are, are so open-ended and in some cases unanswerable that many have ignored it. Even now, despite the increase in world interest and the amount of research being done, many find it difficult to incorporate into a thesis on the Neolithic. There are other interesting and safer areas of research that produce more impressive results more quickly. Only recently has this changed. When the great panel of rock art at Chapel Stile was discovered, some people who visited it thought that it must have been done very recently because no one had found it before. It takes experience to assess what are natural marks, what are artificial and how artificial marks were made.

In 1867 Sir J.Y. Simpson, an eminent Scottish physician and Vice President of the Scottish Society of Antiquaries at the time wrote in his study of 'Archaic Sculpturings' about the problems of distinguishing between artificial and natural, 'for all the cup-like excavations that we meet with on megalithic circles, monoliths, &c. &c., are not by any means the work of man'. Some he attributed to weather erosion, others to softer portions of rock weathering out, or of 'the enucleation of fossilized organic remains or of imbedded nodules.' However, he says that various 'collateral circumstances', such as their limited size, regular rounded forms, smooth surfaces and shallow depths, their presence on rocks too hard to be weathered, their arrangement in artificial groups, and their co-existence with other cups and rings confirm their artificial origin.

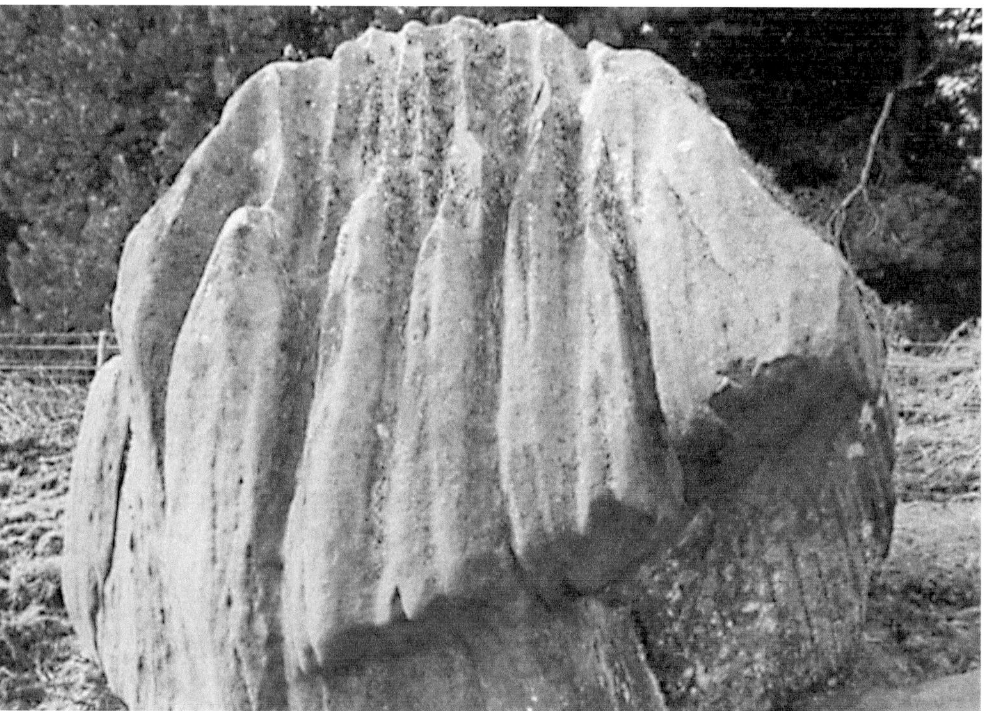

174 *Grooved stone*

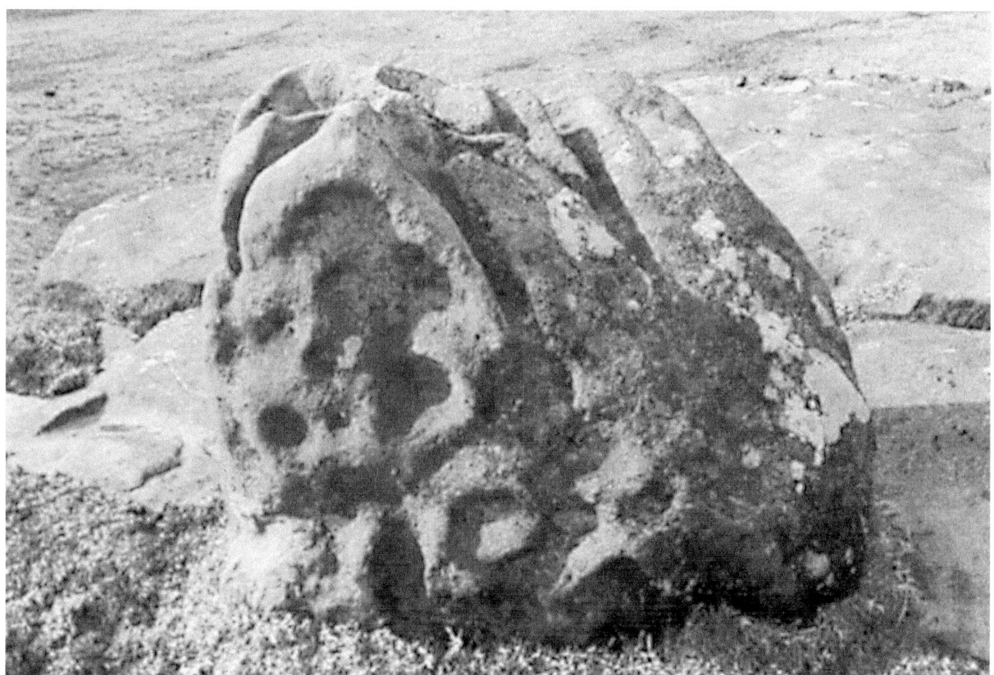

175 *Natural and artificial cups*

Those of us who have seen hundreds of cups are able to distinguish the natural from the artificial in almost all cases. Natural erosion can produce some dramatic fluting effects on sandstone when the bedding planes are up-ended and the rain acts upon the top surface for hundreds or thousands of years. Some grooves can be started by pecking cups into the top, or cups and basins can be added to the already-interesting surface irregularities. A naturally cup-marked stone can also act as the 'real' thing. Sometimes cups can be added to a naturally cupped surface. Those cups that have not been eroded show their origin in the small pick marks hammered into the rock to achieve them, and they take the form of an inverted cone. This can be demonstrated practically by trying to make one. The photograph (**176**) is of one made by Ray Mears when we did part of a programme called *An Essential Guide to Rocks* with BBC2 in Northumberland. He made it quickly by using a pointed andesite stone that we picked up in the River Glen, and used it as a hand tool on soft sandstone. The Chapel Stile and Patterdale surfaces are of hard rock that required considerably more time, persistence and skill to shape the patterns.

Cup marks are the most common marks made and can produce elaborate patterns when used in conjunction with other cups, lines and rings. The finding of a single cup mark on a rock can be of as much importance as an elaborate panel. Assuming the marks to be of deep significance to the people who used them, an artificial cup must have had a similar significance to that of multiple cups or cups and rings. To find them today requires a plan to cover an area and occasionally the help of low-angled sun. Walls and stone piles must be included in the search. Once they are

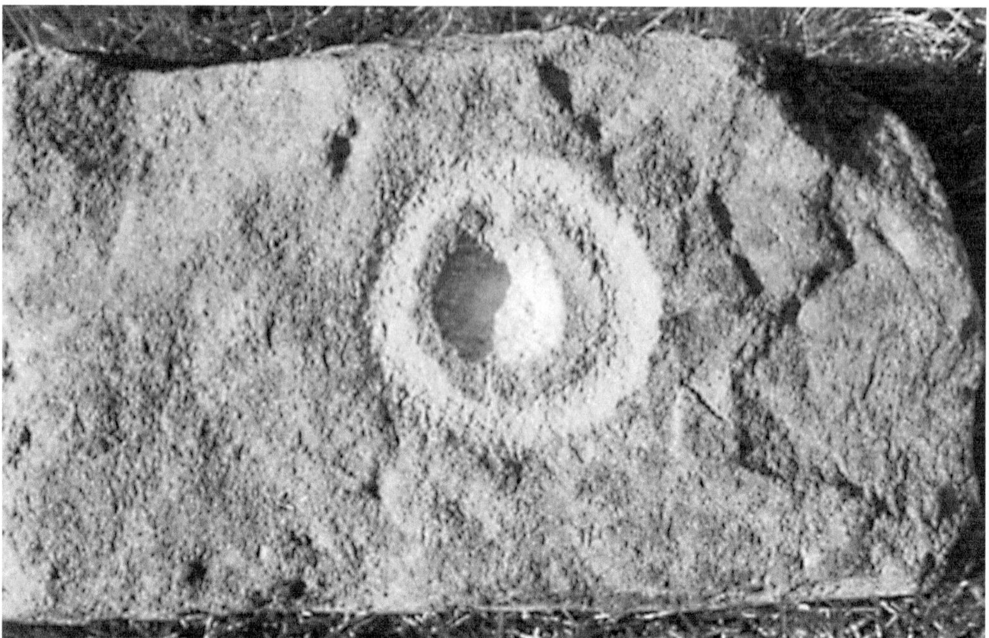

176 *Ray Mears' cup and ring stone*

plotted, it is important to relate them to natural and man-made features. I have recently found 'new' cup marked stones in an area of presumably later enclosures and cairns by walking and looking for hours. I try to see the landscape as it might have been to the people living there and using it in the past, with rock art as an essential component. These landscapes have been modified since then. At Beckstones, for example, the cups are on a large outcrop that has been quarried; we can only guess that there were far more.

It is important to find as much surviving rock art as possible, but what then? We still have the big questions. Are these marks copies of anything in the natural world? Are they pictures of real objects? In their natural world prehistoric people used natural features in the landscape to guide them through country that was considerably less changed than it is today, when obstacles to movement may have been great. Features such as hills, mountains, large pieces of rock that had broken away and rolled downhill, rivers, caves and rock overhangs may have taken on a special significance not only as directional landmarks but as places associated with events in the lives of the people. These may be seen from a distance, but markings on rock are much more low key, visible only close by, and perhaps you had to know where to find them, especially if they were in woodland. In that case they marked or commemorated something, but why do they take the form of cups, grooves and spirals? Most of the marks are circular; in so many other contexts of early prehistoric life the circle is a dominant form.

There are many circular forms in nature. The heavens at night are full of small spots, the stars. Sun and moon appear circular, and the moon's phases as arcs. A stone dropped into water produces circular ripple marks that radiate from a centre. A fallen tree or chopped branches reveal annual rings. Some mosses and lichens form circular patterns on rocks.

When I lived in Malta I was impressed by the fluidity of tendril and spiral decoration in the megalithic temples and by the curved lines of the ground plans of the buildings themselves. At one time people used to see such forms as representative of an 'Earth Mother', the source of all life, with her abundant fertile figure. It is easy to see the cup and ring designs in the same way, as representative of breasts and the womb. To carry that idea further, the grooves that run from the centre of rings or penannulars can be seen as sexual penetration. However, this is not something that can be proved. One of my earliest responses to rock art carries an emotional response that I share with you:

The Sculptured Rocks
In this design you petrified the language of your soul –
Your own symbolic logic;
Linked a little world with universe,
Arrested time with space.
You saw the cycle of your birth and death with clarity
As sun and moon spun round,
As buds burst into leaves and fell upon the nourished ground.
A rhythmic pulse beat out like water flow,
Rippled from your centre to the stars.
The living rocks bear traces of belief,
Knowing all you used to know.
The curlew cry spills out
A plaintive, bubbling message to the moors
Above the desecrated graves and broken stones
As it has always done.
Its curved beak swings down from the sun
To execute parabolas in heather-scented air,
Or sink in silence to an unresponsive earth.

The Neolithic period has a profusion of circular monuments and other circular structures. The earliest house may have been rectangular, but later plans were circular. We must not attribute the digging of circular ditches and the making of circular walls only to some sort of ritual structure, as a hilltop enclosure, for example, used such structures as a good way to defend and define territory at the same time. We must not assume that the structures remained static; they developed over centuries and changed.

A circle announces: we have marked off an area that is ours. We may exclude others from it, and allow them to come in when we choose. We can erect a barrier to hide what is going on inside. We can look out from it to the wider world. The enclosure does not have to be 'ritual', for ritual and secular may be distinctions used mainly by us, and not apply to the Neolithic. But circles do impart their own feeling of exclusiveness when necessary, or of togetherness. We see each other better when we are in a circle. We are equal in order, for no one is in front of anyone else. It is quite unlike the situation in old church arrangements where a priest conducted a service at a literally high altar with his back to everyone. All the circles of wooden posts, ditches (continuous or causewayed), walls and standing or recumbent stones are alike in their choice of form, if not of use.

Is there a definite link between the choice of a circle for an important communal meeting place, like a stone circle or henge, and the use of the circle to make marks on outcrop or earthfast rock and for its incorporation on slabs and cobbles in ritual cairns and on cist slabs? Very few British rock art panels use anything but circular marks, although lines are incorporated. A few rare rectangles and squares exist, usually with rounded corners. There are a few feet and hand pictures, a tiny minority. This leaves us with non-pictorial marks. If we look at Galician art, which shares so many of our cup and ring motifs, the main difference is the inclusion of pictures of deer. Sweden has boats. Animals are widespread, including in such areas as the Sahara desert or the Alps. Human figures direct ploughs pulled by oxen. Figures with human characteristics at least let us know what was going on in the world of their creators: farming, honey-gathering, people taking to water in long ships, hunting and herding animals. Some human figures share characteristics with animals, may be dressed in strange clothes, and be involved in rituals the meaning of which is difficult to decipher, but at least we know roughly what is going on. The same cannot be said for the British rock art tradition. That is why we call the markings symbols and motifs: we feel they stand for something even if we don't know what that something is.

One of our leading researchers into world rock art is Christopher Chippindale, of Cambridge University Museum of Archaeology and Anthropology. He is not happy with the term 'abstract' to describe the markings. In his supportive assessment of my recent *Prehistoric Rock Art of Northumberland* in *Antiquity* he says this:

> All that we can actually say is that we do not recognise what natural things they are images of . . . They may be abstract or they may be naturalistic images of which we have simply failed to recognise the subject depicted (stones, sticks, the marks made in water when stones and sticks are dropped in pools?).

He does not like the terms 'symbols' and 'motifs':

> Why choose to call them symbols when we do not know whether they *are* symbols, and if they are abstract as he says, then surely they are *not* symbols!

As the rest of the review of 'this first-rate book' deals with the depth of research into Northumberland, I find this disagreement stimulating, especially as there are so many issues on which I find it impossible to be categorical. It shows that we cannot yet agree on terms that we use as our main points of reference. I invited Gordon Highmoor, a professional artist who has produced the splendid covers of my books in this series for his views, and the result is a fascinating essay at the end of this section.

Once we say that the marks are symbolic/representative of *something* (like a cross to a Christian) we invite others to speculate on that something. In which case we have to cope with some very strange ideas that come from people's associations, like an inkblot test. We may not be able to say how the marks originate or what they mean, but those people who think they know have to give evidence. It is quite depressing to find someone with the status of Professor Anati, who has done such fine work for world rock art studies, writing this in 1993 about a rock 'engraving' in Ireland at Derrynablaha:

> The anthropomorphic face is above the ideogram of circle-and-dot which are likely to symbolise 'fertility'. Below the ideograms a male sexual organ is depicted. Further below there is a line, probably representing the standard pole of the spirit. Around the being there are several ideograms meaning 'intercourse' or 'penetration'.

I suppose that we all from time to time think that we may have an answer, but to state anything so categorically with no proof whatsoever is quite unconvincing. The 'meaning' of marks not only may change from country to country, but from region to region, and from time to time.

I will not go through Ronald Morris' famous 104 explanations of what rock art 'means' again, but they do reveal some of the absurdities that have been produced. Believe what you want to believe, but don't tell me that it is true without proof.

One of the most intriguing aspects is the use to which the symbols are put. Despite the simplicity of the basic marks there is an impressive ingenuity about the way in which people arranged them on rocks, with so much variation. If you like, they had the same vocabulary, but some were more articulate than others. The results of such creative individual expression can be very pleasing to us today. I cannot detach the place from the image; looking at pictures in books is not enough, for it is their place within the whole landscape that is so impressive and that brings me closer to the people who made them.

Because cups, cups and grooves and spirals have such a wide currency in the world, one must wonder what the link is. Given the range of distances, cultures and time, there must be something in people that responds to such shapes inherently. I do not attribute similarities in some of the patterns produced in British rock art *solely* to the movement of one group of people to another region, carrying their ideas with them. It is possible for people to come up with the same ideas independently, or to produce something unique like the motifs at Chapel Stile or the Morwick spirals in Northumberland. If the human form or animals are involved, their occurrence all over the world is more understandable because the life forms were there to observe and make use of.

In Britain prominent viewpoints are chosen from which to make the marks. The problem of what can be seen from them depends upon the vegetation cover, and insufficient scientific work has been done on this. Other places include spring and other water sources, vital to pastoral nomadic activities. In Northumberland rock shelters are a focus for marking and burial. Caves and holes in the ground are universally seen as 'special', perhaps as an entry to a spirit world. There is a link between routes and markings, which the sites at Patterdale and Chapel Stile attest. The importance of mobility, guidance through the landscape and marking special places are key factors.

It is their use in a few monuments that is particularly striking, and this is nowhere better illustrated than in Cumbria. Stone circles and burial mounds carry their special signs. In burials the images are buried, which marks a big change in function from the open-air panels. Nearby Northumberland and Durham have good examples, some well excavated. Thoughts of death and what follows, fear of the unknown, the wish not to be dealt a blow by forces beyond their control, and the need to propitiate these forces may be the bases of ritual. But there is also love of those who have died, the need to feel part of the past, a sense of ancestors and rights to the land that bring people together in a common cause. The henges and great stone circles provide such foci; they are not just for ritual but for practical gatherings; trade, exchange of children in marriage, a place to catch up with the news, or to meet friends whose farms and grazing areas may be remotely scattered in a vast landscape. That some stones in such complexes should be marked may give to that part an extra special significance. Long Meg is certainly dominant physically. It may also be older-established than the circle to which it leads. Yet only a few of the hundreds of British stone circles are marked in this way, just as only a few burials contain marked slabs and cobbles, so we are looking at something exceptional and not commonplace. The Redhills slab had cup and ring marks face-down on the cist cover looking into the grave. In County Durham the late Neolithic cist cover at Fulforth Farm was decorated on both sides, with the more elaborate cups and rings facing down into the cist. Little Meg may be multi-period. Old Parks looks as though a Neolithic long barrow marked the beginning of its life, after which it attracted so many later deposits of pottery and cremation. The same happened at Glassonby; sites go on being used.

My thoughts about those prehistoric people who lie buried under their mounds find their way into a poem:

Cairns

Stamped with lichen, bound by bracken root,
Sunk in acid soil,
Each heap of stone affects disguise.
Death's ritual leaves slight signs.
Slanting sunlight, morning, evening,
Shadows each circumference. Betrays.
Many gouged by curiosity and greed.

First in rank and ostentation – first to fall;
The unpretentious huddle humbly in the soil, survive.
They are the scanty evidence of another life.
A smear upon the soil,
Burnt bone, a piece of flint, a pot, a bead,
Sealed once, but not invulnerable.
We focus on these tiny scraps of time
With force that hurls jet fighters overhead
And simulates the power of sun.
We are our Age, we bring technology
To bear upon a past where writing played no part,
But symbolism loomed large.

Gods lived and were placated;
Man and woman not enough.
Force drove through grass blades, crackled in the skies,
Hurled rainbows, hid the face of moon and sun.
Awesome. Kept us in our place.
We are the piece of broken bone, the pile of dust.
A piece of flint is our technology,
A bead or two our power or vanity.

We are the hands that placed the pot inside the grave,
Love that mourns a while.
The cairn above our heads cuts out the sky
As we move on.

Cumbria has recently revealed more complexities of enclosures. Long Meg has an extraordinary pattern of them, revealed in special conditions from the air. Some much later enclosures, of possible Iron Age date or later, incorporate cup marked slabs in their structure or marked cobbles, but we cannot be sure whether we are looking here at the mere reuse of such slabs as convenient building material.

Building monuments is a way of ordering the universe. It gives us some control by providing places where we can assemble to reaffirm what we believe. Just as a 'cool web of language' can lessen the fear that we are born with, the presence of monuments as sanctuaries is reassuring. Castlerigg lifts the spirits; it is like being at the centre of a circular universe formed by mountains, and we are encircled by them and by a circle of our own creation. 'I live not in myself, but become portion of that around me.' When a stone is planted upright in the ground it takes on a new life. When combined with others that vary much in shape and texture, they can be awe-inspiring.

I tried to capture some of this feeling about a small, beautiful stone circle at Duddo in Northumberland.

Solstice
On such a night the hills dissolved
And re-assembled in a shifting mist,
Numb with moonlight's touch.
We learnt that silence was not hostile,
Took upon ourselves its deepest strength
Waiting for dawn's layered sun.
A moon that paced
As crow's shout cracked the sky
Fled from the triggered bird-song
Hesitant, then loud.
Before our eyes, a second birth,
A new-created universe,
Green and blue and gold.
Fluted stones whose shapes had shifted
With emitted heat
From bearded barley heads,
Buried to the hips,
Reclaimed their circle and identity,
Introspective, Janus-headed,
Guarding and inviting
As the sun's diurnal course
Played a slow game
With shadow shapes
Time and time and time again.

I may not commit myself to theories about what people did or did not think in the past, or how the cup and ring symbolism originated or was used. I save my feelings for my poetry. That is where they properly belong, for feeling for places and hunches about people in the past is a different kind of truth. It may be fiction, but it is not paraded as fact. I wish that more people would do the same.

I welcome this contribution from Gordon Highmoor:

Towards a more precise definition of 'rock art' Gordon Highmoor

As a professional artist/teacher and amateur archaeologist, I have found myself constantly irritated by the sometimes glib use of the term 'rock art' to define those marks which have been pecked into the rocks of our landscape. Although some archaeologists, especially those with the integrity and enthusiasm of Stan Beckensall and Richard Bradley, are slowly piecing together evidence to support the existence and creation of so-called rock art, by examining and recording geographical and geological locations, distribution and frequency, types and groupings of marks, we are still no nearer to deciphering what the marks actually mean or why they were made. So, since we clearly don't know what these marks are, why do we choose to call them 'art' when there seems to be no evidence to support any such hypothesis?

The term 'art' is an exceedingly emotive one and our understanding of it depends very much on a personal viewpoint which can be often obscured by subjectivity. If we believe John Ruskin, for example, who suggested that man is humbled before great art and that the whole function of the artist is to be a seeing and feeling creature, then we may concur that art should not only transcend mere representation, but also serve as a function in which it can be seen to be uplifting, contemplative, challenging, even controversial. If we consider the major themes that have been universally employed in the making of art from religion, history, allegory, to landscape, genre, portrait and still life, then it can also be seen to be reverential, informative, mysterious, narrative or socio-documentary. But even if so-called rock art can be made to fit any of these descriptions, the marks do not seem to follow any of the known sequential patterns that have established the development of ideas, ethos or style. Indeed, it may seem to run contrary to them. Perhaps I am being naive in assuming that, with the preponderance of what some might be regarded as bizarre theories such as maps, or mother earth symbolism, or even space-ship landing sites, archaeologists have seized on a logical, sensible, and above all safe solution. We also have to be careful that our perception of the kind of landscape in which cup and ring marks exist is not coloured by our preoccupation with atmosphere or myth or our susceptibility to the romantic notion of what that particular landscape represents to us. Anyone who visits such sites, however, either as painter or archaeologist, must become aware, as Paul Nash was, that that they are *special places* which may appear to be charged with powerful forces above the purely visual. Nash's resultant paintings, although empty of human figures, seem nevertheless to be saturated with human presence and meaning. The danger here, of course, is that the work becomes a private language to which only the artist's experience can contribute, and to which, correspondingly, only he has access.

The position is exacerbated by the apparent 'abstract' nature of the 'art' and the common usage of such terms as 'symbol' and 'motif' to describe certain configurations of 'marks', and some clarification of the nomenclature is essential. Although frequently used as a relative term, we generally understand abstract art to be that which does not imitate or directly represent external reality (I have used the term 'figurative' in this context). In modern art history, pure abstract art has originated from the developments of Paul Cezanne and twentieth-century cubism through to the neo-plasticism of Piet Mondrian which, on the face of it, may seem to be nothing more than a reworking of such geometric forms as the square, the cube, the sphere. In truth, however, these shapes are more often derived from landscape and still-life forms which have undergone a deliberate process of analysis and simplification. One of the reasons why this came about was that it was made at a time when artists had begun to challenge the limited fixed viewpoint of the camera. Many artists, such as Pablo Picasso, went back to such primitive art forms as ancient Iberian sculpture or African masks and carvings for their inspiration.

A second type of abstraction, less geometric and formalised, springs from the notion that, while colour and form alone can seem to move the spectator emotionally, like music they have no representational purpose. Put simply, it derived first from the so-called *improvisations* of the Russian artist Wassily Kandinsky from about 1910 and later from a manifesto written by André Breton in 1924 in which he described an art of pure automatism. Freud's psychoanalysis and the discovery (or rediscovery) of the subconscious in the early twentieth century led art to examine those paradoxes and relativities which are to be discovered in the domain of the psyche, and the surrealists sought in their art to mingle reason with unreason, using dreams, chance effects, with the resultant *automatism* uncontrolled by aesthetic or moral considerations. The inspiration for these 'unconscious' marks was often the result of controlled experiments in which the artists were given hallucinatory drugs such as mescaline, LSD or benzedrine, something that became quite commonplace after the publication of Aldous Huxley's *The Doors of Perception* in 1954. These influences can be seen in the late work of the British painter Bryan Winter and the American abstract expressionists Willem de Kooning and, particularly, Jackson Pollock, whose 'drip' paintings emphasise a spontaneity of expression that seems completely random. This may support those theories that propose that cup and ring, spiral, serpentine and chevron marks are the kinds of marks often associated with the loss of conscious control. Whilst these marks are neither chance-made nor formless, the makers of them may have been induced by agencies such as drugs or 'sweat boxes' in the form of chambered tombs to perceive such images during shamanic trance.

Some archaeologists seem particularly unhappy with the words *symbol* and *motif* when used to describe the various configurations of marks made in rock art. Symbolism, as applied to art, offers a synthesis of many aspects of reality, aimed at evoking ideas by means of ambiguous and powerful symbols; in other words, with the emphasis on suggesting rather than depicting. By the symbolic representation of an event, whether it be the desire for progeny, the death of an enemy, survival after death, or the exorcism or propitiation of an evil spirit, primitive man perhaps believed that he could secure the actual occurrence of that event. It is also probable that Neolithic man possessed a higher degree of that sensual faculty that our 'civilised' instincts have tended to erode or destroy. Symbols, by their nature, imply something vague, unknown, or hidden from us. Many Cretan monuments, for example, are marked with the design of the double adze, an object that we know but, in this instance, not its symbolic implications. The ambiguity also occurs in Pictish cross slabs and symbol stones where common objects such as mirrors, combs, crescents and V rods are used in a symbolic context to which we have no cipher. In many societies, representations of the sun have come to express man's indefinable religious experience (the circle without beginning or end is the sign of God or Eternity), but in other contexts it can just as easily depict planets, the eye, the season Spring, the Roman Sunday (*dies soles*), light or even nothingness. To add to the confusion, a symbol, when depicting an object or an action, is usually known as a *pictograph*, whilst a motif is a distinct or separable element in composition of a painting, a graphic design of a sculpture or, sometimes, the subject of a work of art itself.

What seems clear to us is that Neolithic and early Bronze Age people added their marks to the landscape as a conscious creative act and these cup and ring, spiral and chevron marks were an integral and significant force within that essentially pastoral society. Much of the drawn or sculpted imagery produced by what we, perhaps mistakenly, describe as pre-literate man, were realised before spoken and written language developed into the sophisticated means of communication we know today, and it is easy to assume that this use of pictorial (whether figurative or abstract) association should be thought of as crude or illogical. On the contrary, they may be the clearest and most economical of all language forms, and a perfect synthesis of the subtleties of human thought and experience.

I am not conducting an enquiry, still less attempting to prove a theory, but my experience and reading of art has shown that man's primitive instinct to make marks and, through them, to assert himself over what he thus makes, is still strong today. Such signs and marks can be simulated on the working surface of canvas or paper, as in the work of Alan Davie or Antoni Tapies, or made by the act of manipulating the earth itself as in the so-called 'land art' of the American Robert Smithson or the British Richard Long and Hamish Fulton. Often the signs they make are so basic (lines, spirals, circles) that their aim cannot be simply to leave a message. Moreover, if, as is commonly assumed, they are meant to encourage contemplation, then it must raise their art to the level of poetry and philosophy.

These proponents of the notion that Neolithic 'symbols' are some form of art can take heart from the knowledge that a creative and aesthetic sense was inherent in most primitive people irrespective of any intellectual standing. This is shown clearly in those examples of the art of the Palaeolithic or Old Stone Age from about 30,000 to 10,000 BC, and more recently in the art of the bushmen of south-west Africa. Those drawings which have survived on the cave walls of Altimira in northern Spain or at Lascaux or Trois Freres in southern France were executed in charcoal, chalk and some of the basic mineral or earth colours, and represent usually side views of animals such as mammoth, bull, wild horse, wild boar and reindeer. The images all have certain features in common, the most important of which is that there appears to be an abandonment of detail and a distortion of natural form in order to express the prime significance of the animal (such as its strength, speed, power) rather than its physiological or genetic characteristics. Images of humans, by comparison, appear infrequently and are only depicted in simplistic pictographic form. Interestingly, among the thousands of images drawn on the walls and ceilings of these prehistoric galleries, there are none that show any scenes of fighting or warfare, which is in great contrast to the art of most civilisations. Furthermore, there is a complete absence of either formal composition or pictorial organisation, nor is there any attempt at perspective, although more recent discoveries at Charvet in France clearly show animals overlapping, which may or may not be a perspectival device. If the positive can ever be proved then it anticipates the discovery of linear perspective by Italian Renaissance artists such as Alberti, Paolo Uccello or Piero della Francesca. Whatever the origin of these drawings, it seems unlikely that the artist's primary concern was the creation of beautiful images. It is much more probable that they served some pragmatic function, whether religious, magical or totemistic.

If the figurative art of the Palaeolithic is mysterious and perhaps inscrutable, then the abstract marks on the cave walls is an enigma wrapped in mystery. First, if we are to judge them by the frequency with which they occur, they seem to have been as important as the figurative works which they outnumber. An integral feature of this abstract art is the curved and straight lines shown singly or in a complex arrangement of grids, dots and groups of dots. These symbols appear on their own or in groups far away from the animal figures; in other instances they can appear between the figures. Sometimes they have been painted on top of the animals. Theories, of course, abound; for many they are not seen as abstracts at all but represent things in the real world, such as hoof prints, hunting nets and dwellings, for example. Some anthropologists such as Andre Leroi-Gourhan claim that these abstractions are, like the animals, part of a whole male/female cultural code, a theory in which all animals were symbolic of either the male or female principle. This demonstrates that the world at large was perhaps perceived in a binary way, reflecting the social roles of man the hunter and woman the gatherer. Similarly, certain male/female attributes have been applied to rock art, with the figures interpreted as fertility or procreative images. It is over simplistic to assume that all Palaeolithic cave art served the same purpose. The problem with all-embracing theories is that they cannot hope to encompass human creativity over such long periods when the intentions of each artist and the cultural codes that he or she sought to express varied so much from place to place and epoch to epoch.

However much I would like to believe that these notions might be applied to the cup and ring phenomenon, there remains the problem of historical context and contrasting environment. In general, the Neolithic was a fast-growing and wide-spread culture that experienced increasing stability and domestication of both animals and humans, and it may be that artistic creativity was being channelled elsewhere. Where hunting man had visualised everything in terms of his immediate physical needs, the more settled herder-farmer projected himself beyond the everyday and came to see the world both as physical and spiritual. Certainly animal figuration had been replaced by a more utilitarian art with formal and rhythmic 'designs' based upon geometric forms used merely as decorative elements on pottery or jewellery. That much of this decoration uses similar basic forms such as circles, spirals, lines and chevrons is not to suggest that rock art is anything as mundane as mere pattern-making, nor that it had a purely aesthetic purpose. Its very time-consuming, labour-intensive nature and its siting out of doors in the landscape would seem to rule that out.

There is so much we don't know and a great tendency to hypothesise and theorise, to fill in the blanks. Who made these marks? Was it a shaman drawing on his trance-induced subconscious, or simply an artisan sculptor working to a set of rules? Was it the older, perhaps more sagacious members of the community, or those too weak to hunt and build? Because of the similarity of many of the configurations they could possibly have been made by itinerant carvers, employed on the basis of later 'court painters' to widespread groups. Unlike painting, however, there are no clues to be found in the individual brushmarks or the colour schemes that identify

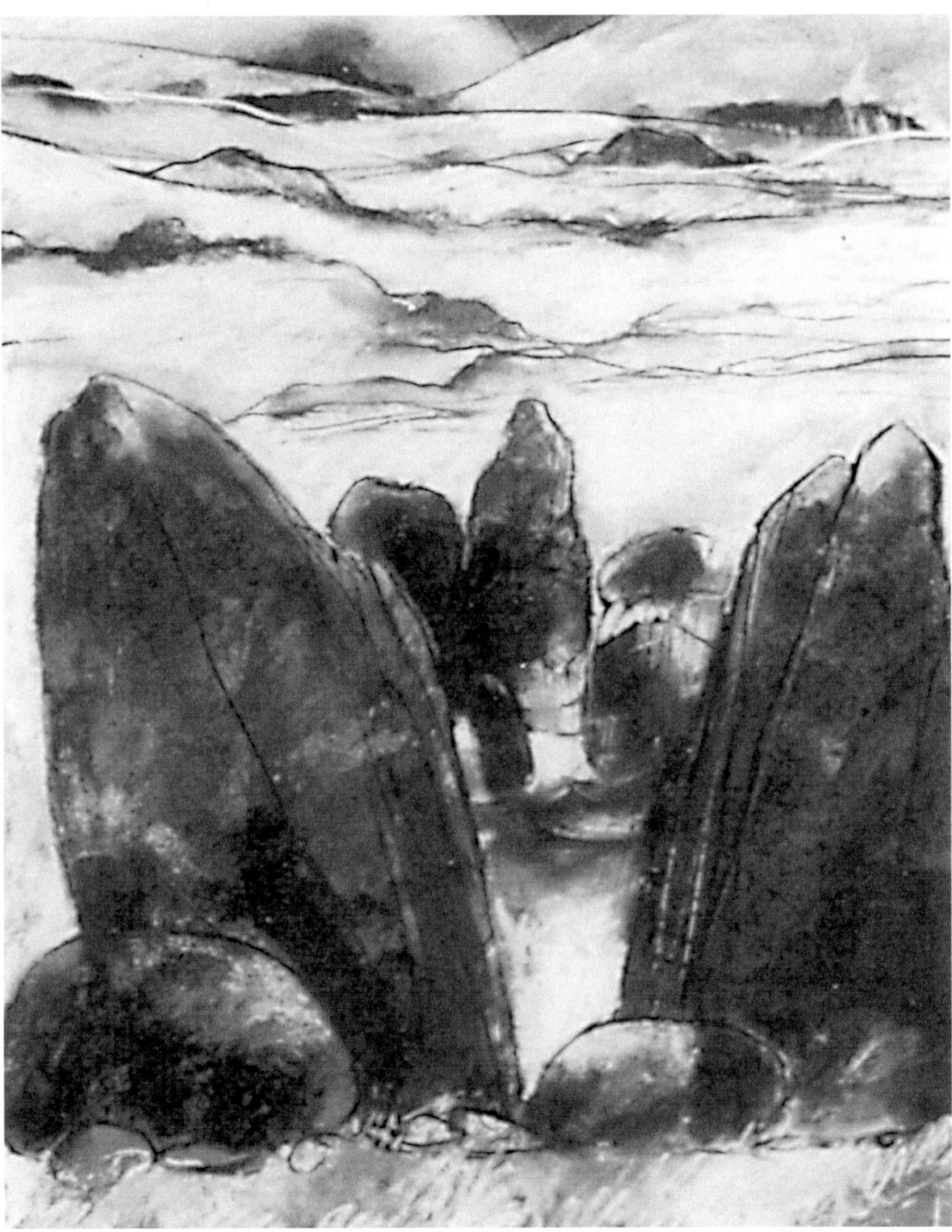

177 *Landscape.* Gordon Highmoor

individual or school of artists, so we would need to be able to examine peck marks scientifically to establish a common hand. Given the time span, it seems unlikely that the marks were made at the same time and some surfaces even suggest that there was overworking, even enhancement of established symbols. Given the erosive nature of much of the rock, it is impossible to tell.

Much as I would prefer it to be otherwise, the most rational explanation seems to favour a more pragmatic form of visual communication – if not a language, then a sign system concerning locations of people or animals in the landscape, or the movement of sun, moon or planets. When we consider the knowledge of mathematics required to set out stone circles, it would seem logical that they must have had a spoken, if not a written, language.

The alphabet forms we use today, for example, were developed by Greeks and Romans out of ancient sign systems, which were essentially abstract marks or symbols to represent goods to be traded. Eventually, as a more practical and speedy system was demanded, *cuneiform*, named from the wedge-shaped stylus they used to impress the marks into clay, came into being. What is interesting is that the Sumerians were able to develop a written language out of a relatively small range of symbols at roughly the same historical time as those who carved cup and ring configurations. Like the Mediterranean scribes, Neolithic man has also managed to produce a wide number of variations out of the limited themes available to him, and we must marvel at his invention, but to suggest that those configurations of cups and rings which are to be found on sometimes vertical, but predominantly on horizontal, outcrop rock, are merely a form of language or accounting system is to ignore the religious or ritual significance of those examples that often appear in association with burials, either in cists or on the walls of such chambered tombs as Newgrange or Gavrinis. This is not just a carved symbol system confined to Europe, for examples are found in places such as Spain, Switzerland, Russia and even in the Sahara. This is an indication, perhaps, of the deep-rooted need man has to make his mark, as a medium, with an implement and on a surface.

I began this essay by confessing my irritation at the use of the term rock art, but the more I explore the landscape as a painter and sense the atmosphere of mountains, fells, valleys and moors, the more I feel that this is how Neolithic people saw it. My long-standing interest in, and subsequently realised experience of, archaeology has heightened my knowledge and perceptions, yet, in a curious way, has deepened the mystery. Instinctively I feel and sincerely hope that it is some form of 'art', but in truth unless someone discovers a Neolithic version of the Rosetta stone, it is unlikely we shall ever know.

What about the future?

In this country we have not solved the problem of how to look after our rock art. Only a few have thought of its preservation as a priority. A mound like Old Parks was removed for road metal by the council. There is evidence all over the country of sites being quarried away and blown up. The Aspatria stone just disappeared; no one followed it up. Some of our most famous and important sites are abysmally displayed and maintained.

In my *Prehistoric Rock Art in Northumberland* (2001) I set out my stall on what I think ought to be done about our rock art heritage. A step in the right direction has been made by English Heritage with its Rock Art Pilot Project of 1999, but this will only mean something when its recommendations are put into practice. Producing a report is important, but so many public bodies seem to think that a report will solve a problem. It doesn't. It's only a start.

We need to know what threats there are to rock surfaces, not just from being plough-scratched, trampled by animals or people, but what growths are bad for them. Does lichen growth (and of which kind) protect a surface or destroy it? Does it protect it from further erosion?

The immediate environment of rock art has been little studied. A programme is needed in which we can more carefully look for clues about what the immediate landscape was like at the time when art was pecked on the rocks. There are some important questions that we pose, and palaeobotanists may be able to answer. We need to know what was growing around the marked outcrops at certain times so that we can begin to understand what could have been seen from them thousands of years ago, otherwise our assumptions about their being at viewpoints remains conjectural. If we could go even further and determine whether there were woodland clearings and paths we would further be able to understand how the marked rocks were used to focus on some particularly significant places. Of course, there may not be any material there today to give us such information, and we must be prepared not to know very much. That some material is present is indicated by the uneroded rock surfaces that sometimes emerge; if they have been covered for so long since they were made, perhaps the surrounding soil may also be relatively undisturbed.

Another issue to be addressed is that of access. Whose rock art is it? Should people be excluded from it? There are sites that cannot, for good reasons, be open to all. I would resent it if one happened to be in my garden and the public came crashing in to see it. It is the responsibility of all landlords, tenants and County authorities to agree on a programme of access and display of rock art sites. Some sites are fragile and should be covered over if that is the best way to protect them. Others are more robust and have been open for centuries without much harm. If we have money to spend on our past, one way forward might be to get landowners to set aside patches of ground and access to them, and to co-operate with them in its management and access. Once a spread of rocks to which the public has access is agreed, and others covered over, the next issue is how they should be displayed. An example of intelligent and sensitive practice is to be found in the Kilmartin area of Argyll; there the largest panel of rock art in Britain has been cleared of trees and scrub, and surrounded by a fence that has a wooden walkway in parts, and provides the visitor with information panels that blend well into the site. We may not like the idea of metal fences, but it is one way forward. One only has to visit the Cow and Calf rocks on Ilkley Moor to see the results of terrible vandalism on open sites. We may not be able to control it fully, but we can make it clear to the public why these sites are important by giving them concise and interesting information, and by appealing for their help to preserve them.

Excavation

The discovery of rock art at Chapel Stile has prompted me to use this site as an example of the way forward in research. A database of sites is only a start, a means of recording what is here; what we want to know now are the answers to some important questions that excavation may help to solve. To make marks on this rock, two things were done: (a) a stone of sufficient hardness had to be found to make the marks, and (b) some means of impacting the tool against the rock had to be made. Experiments should be extended to include many rock surfaces in Britain to find how this could be done. At Chapel Stile we have the opportunity to excavate the base of the marked surface to recover fragments of rock chipped away to make the

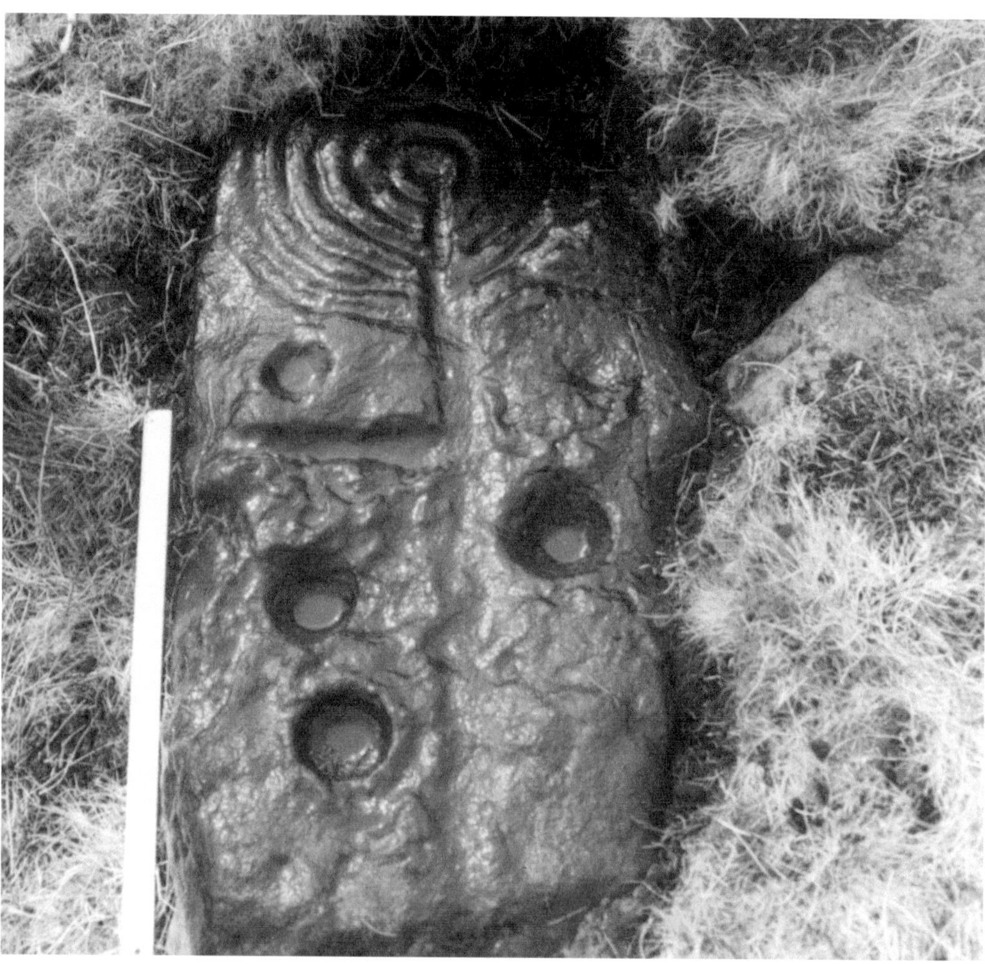

marks, and possibly to find evidence of the type of rock used in the tool. Depending on the depth of the soil, there may be pollen grains and carbon that will yield information about ancient vegetation.

At Kilmartin, Argyll, experiments have already begun. If a stone harder than the rock surface to be marked is found, how was it mounted to achieve the impact needed to make a mark? Was it held in the hand and hit with a mallet, or was it fixed into a haft?

In County Durham there are possible burial cairns recently recorded that incorporate marked stones, and a programme of excavation might relate the structures and their use to rock art.

In Northumberland I have recently discovered a rectangular slab of sandstone within a low stone-dump walled enclosure that has very high quality motifs, shown in the photograph here. This is unlikely to be outcrop, but a slab that may cover a burial. It appears to be joined by other flat slabs (to the right). If this is a burial, then it is in a rare context, for the area around it and the oval enclosure may be relatively undisturbed, and provide material for pollen analysis. It is a rare opportunity for a highly specialised excavation. Northumberland has an admirable system for recording sites and monuments; an excavation would add considerably more significant information.

I asked Deborah Long, of the Kilmartin Trust, who has read this work, to add her own thoughts about the importance of rock art:

> Stan's book has illustrated one of the most celebrated landscapes of the UK. It does not offer the answer to what rock art means, as indeed it cannot. What it does offer us is the chance to 'see' rock art: to see it in the landscape, to see what it could have meant to those who made and used it and to see what it means to us. We can still appreciate its significance and value even without having all our questions answered. Today we can only understand these images as ancient art through their appeal to our sense of wonder; we have lost the symbolic meaning, if there ever was one. They may have had some sacred meaning; perhaps the act of pecking images onto the rocks was as important as the resulting image.
>
> Rock art occurs across the world and in many cases the motifs are the same and include cup marks, rings, spirals and lines. These symbols may have had the same meanings from place to place or they may not. Our rock art is mostly non-figurative; we do not have the stags of Galicia or the boats of Sweden, for example, and our images are much harder for us to understand. Perversely, this is what, in a way, makes it more accessible to everyone.
>
> We are beholden to look after what has been made and used by our distant ancestors and left to us. Although 'carved in stone', rock art is not as permanent as we generally take this phrase to mean. These images are not indestructible and are continually subject to the weather and human interference. Many of the sites in this book are not protected by law, but

our actions today will help to ensure that they remain for future generations. This art is for everyone and we all need to protect it.

I end this book as I did my last one, with this statement of belief:

People enjoy rock art. Pieces of pottery and flint implements may be some of the things that help us to understand the past, but people like being in a vast, beautiful landscape, able to stand at a place with great views, look at art on the rocks, and to continue to wonder what it's all about. People love places. People love a mystery. Give them the chance and they will be the best preservers of our rock art heritage. Try to exclude them physically, intellectually and spiritually, and they will resent you, for rock art is not exclusive to a favoured group. It is the earliest means of 'communication' that we have in symbols with people from the deep past. It will continue to intrigue us, worry us, and we want to remain linked to it.

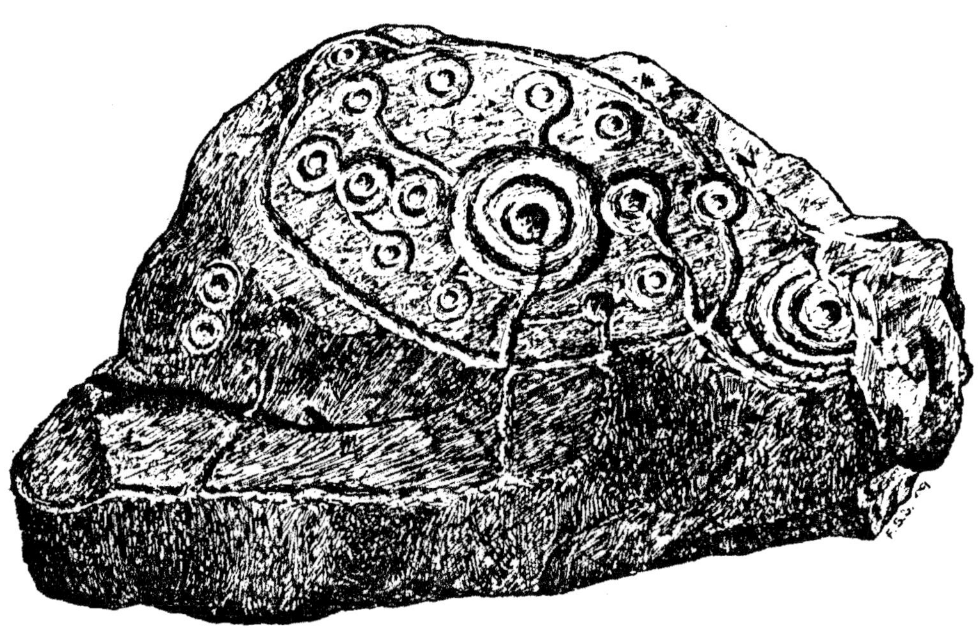

Bibliography

General

The following books include extensive bibliographies for British rock art sites:

Beckensall, S. 1999. *British Prehistoric Rock Art*. Tempus
Beckensall, S. & Laurie, T. 1998. *Prehistoric Rock Art of County Durham, Swaledale and Wensleydale*. County Durham Books (Durham County Council)
Beckensall, S. 2001. *Prehistoric Rock Art in Northumberland*. Tempus
Beckensall, S, 2004. *The Prehistoric Rock Art of Kilmartin, Argyll* (Kilmartin Trust)
Bradley, R. 1993. *Altering the Earth*. Edinburgh
Bradley, R. 1997. *Rock Art and the Prehistory of Atlantic Europe*. Routledge
Bradley, R. 1998. *The Significance of Monuments*. Routledge
Bradley, R. 2000. *The Archaeology of Natural Places*. Routledge
Nash, G. & Chippindale, C. 2001. *European Landscapes of Rock Art*. Routledge

On stone circles:

Burl, A. 1999. *The Stone Circles of the British Isles*. Yale
Burl, A. 2000. *The Stone Circles of Britain, Ireland and Brittany*. Yale

Local references

One major source referred to in the text is *Transactions of the Cumberland and Westmorland Antiquarian and Archaeological Society. (TCWAAS)*

Bailey, J.B. 1988. 'Notes on Cup and Ring-marked stones found near Maryport', *TCWAAS* 1 (9), 300-2
Bewley, R. 1986. 'Ewanrigg – A Bronze Age Cremation Cemetery', *Popular Archaeology* 7 (2), 36-42
Brown, P. & B. 1999. 'Previously unrecorded prehistoric rock carvings at Copt Howe, Chapel Stile, Great Langdale, Cumbria', *Archaeology North* No.16
Clare, T. 1978. 'Shap Avenue', *TCWAAS* 78 (5)
Collingwood, W.G. 1902. 'Tumulus at Grayson-lands, Glassonby, Cumberland', *TCWAAS* 2 (1), 295-9
Cook, T. 1999. 'Rock carvings in Patterdale – A Neolithic Puzzle', *Matterdale Historical and Archaeological Society Year Book 1999* and *Transactions* 6, 38-42
CWASS Prehistory Record Cards. *Stone Circle and Tumulus at Chapel Flat, Dalston Parish*
Dymond, C.W. 1893. 'An Ancient Village in Hugill', *TCWAAS* 2 (12), 6-14

Ferguson, S.C. 1910. 'A Cup-and Ring-marked Stone from Honey Pots Farm, near Edenhall', *TWAAS* 2 (10), 507–8

Frodsham, P.N.K. 1989. 'Two Newly Discovered Cup and Ring Marked Stones from Penrith and Hallbankgates, with a Gazetteer of all known Megalithic Carvings in Cumbria', *TCWAAS* 2 (89), 1–19

Hallam, A.M. 1990. 'The Bronze Age Pottery of North West England and its Social Context', unpublished dissertation, University of Liverpool

Hodgson, K.S. 1952. 'Further Excavations at Broomrigg, near Ainstable', *TCWAAS* 2 (52), 1–8

Mason, J.R. 1923. 'Antiquities at Dean', *TCWAAS* 2 (23), 34–5

Richardson, C. 1992. 'Excavations on a Cup-and-Ring Marked boulder on Tortie Hill, Midgeholm Parish (NT5895781) and a Newly Discovered decorated rock in the vicinity (NY588578)', *TCWAAS* 2 (92)

Simpson, J.Y. 1867. *Archaic Sculpturings of Cups, Circles, &.* Edinburgh

Soffe, G. & Clare, T. 1988. 'New evidence of ritual monuments at Long Meg and her Daughters, Cumbria', *Ant.* 62 (236), 552–7 and plate 4

Taylor, M.W. 1883. 'On a Cup-marked Stone found at Redhills, near Penrith', *TCWAAS* 1 (6), 110–18

Thornley, C. 1902. 'Ring-marked Stones at Glassonby and Maughanby', *TCWAAS* 2 (2), 380–3

Victoria County History (Cumberland) 1968. 'Cup, Ring and Groove markings', Vol. 1, 241–3

Waterhouse, J. 1985. *Stone Circles of Cumbria.* Phillimore. 153

Whellan, W. 1860. *History of Cumberland and Westmorland.* 161

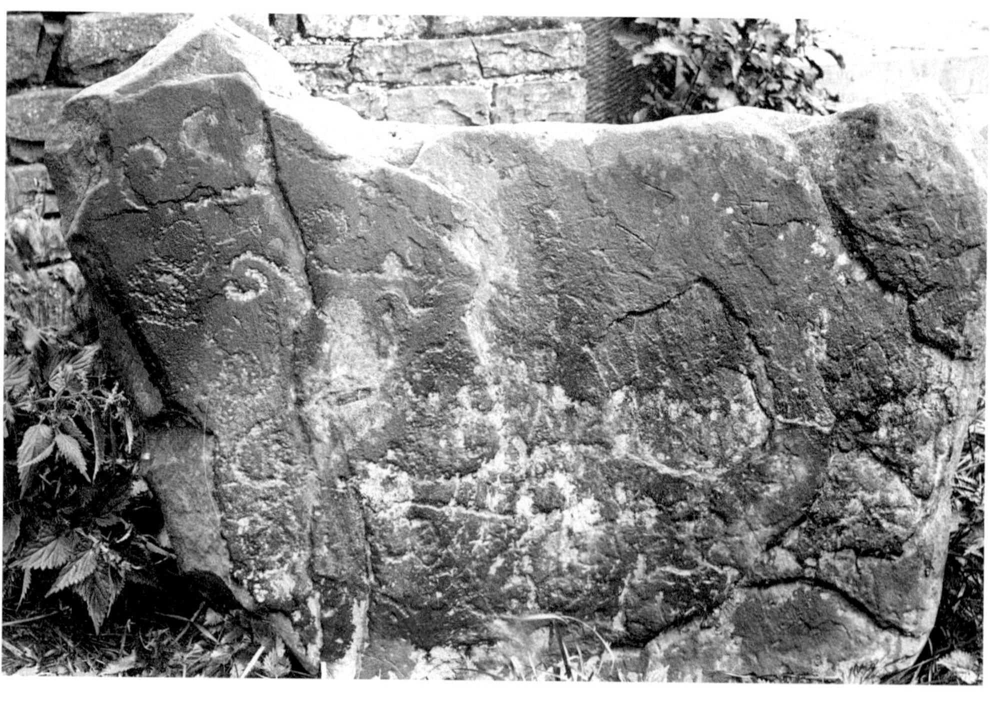

Acknowledgements

To all those who have made new discoveries, especially to Jan and Tony Ambler, Mary Bell, Tim and Patricia Cook, Neil Stevenson, Nick Best, Steven Hood, Sharon Croft, Dave Hankin, Ray Bird and Mrs Joyce Nicholson.

I particularly thank Paul and Barbara Brown of Darlington for their detailed survey work and discovery of sites and marked rocks at Copt Howe, Great Langdale, Beckstones, Castlerigg Stone Circle, Stainmore and Castle Folds. I thank Paul for his detailed maps that are included in this book, for his photographs (that have not been acknowledged separately from my own), and for Barbara's suggestions for making the text accessible to everyone.

Brian Jenkins read the text with great detachment and accuracy, and I thank him for his incorporated suggestions.

To Stephen Hope, for once again helping with his computer skills.

Some of the sites discovered earlier have national data base numbers given in Iain Hewitt's 'Helics' system.

My thanks to all landowners and tenants, and to the National Trust and National Park authorities, on which the sites lie, and to the museums that house some of the rock art.

I thank Deborah Long and the Kilmartin Trust for their work of attracting so many people to look appreciatively at the past, and for Deborah's contribution to this book. Their centre in Argyll is a model for other regions to follow.

Finally, I thank Gordon Highmoor not only for his outstanding illustrations to this and my other books in the Tempus series, but also for his valuable reflections on rock art.

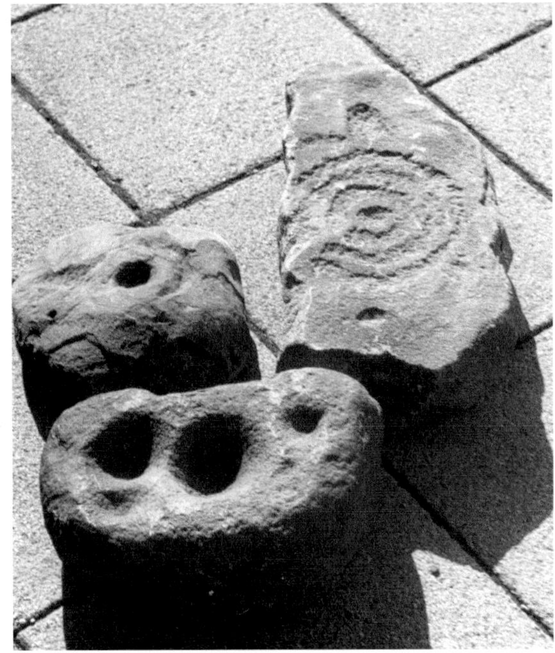

Index